THE POCKET-SIZE GOD

Dear Fr. Joe,

We offer this book in gratitude
for your ministry at Our Lady
of the Lake, and as a
companion we hope you
find useful for your future
mission.

With gratitude,

Brad and Paola

Portrait of Notre Dame Glee Club Chaplain Rev. Robert Griffin, 1975.
Photo by Chris Smith. Courtesy of University of Notre Dame Archives

ROBERT F. GRIFFIN, C.S.C.

EDITED BY

J. Robert Baker and Dennis Wm. Moran

THE
POCKET-SIZE
GOD

ESSAYS FROM

Notre Dame Magazine

University of Notre Dame Press

Notre Dame, Indiana

Manufactured in the United States of America

Library of Congress Cataloging-in-Publication Data

Names: Griffin, Robert, 1925– author.
Baker, J. Robert, 1954– editor.
Title: The pocket-size God : essays from Notre Dame Magazine /
Robert F. Griffin, C.S.C. ; edited by J. Robert Baker and Dennis Wm. Moran.
Description: Notre Dame : University of Notre Dame Press, 2016.
Identifiers: LCCN 2015047534
ISBN 9780268029906 (pbk. : alk. paper)
ISBN 0268029903 (pbk. : alk. paper)
Subjects: LCSH: Christian life—Catholic authors. | Spiritual life—
Catholic Church. | Spirituality—Catholic Church.
Classification: LCC BX2350.3.G7535 2016 | DDC 282/.73—dc23
LC record available at http://lccn.loc.gov/2015047534

∞This paper meets the requirements of ANSI/NISO Z39.48-1992
(Permanence of Paper).

CONTENTS

ACKNOWLEDGMENTS

We gratefully acknowledge the permission of Father Arthur J. Colgan, the Provincial Superior of the Congregation of Holy Cross, Eastern Province, which holds the rights to Father Griffin's writings, to collect and republish the essays gathered here; the work of Kerry Temple, editor of *Notre Dame Magazine*, in providing copies of the magazine issues in which these essays were published; the encouragement of Harv Humphrey and Stephen Little of the University of Notre Dame Press in the preparation of this book; and the meticulous editorial assistance of Rebecca DeBoer in improving the manuscript. The help and support of these people were generous and vital.

We have provided the text of Father Griffin's essays as they appeared over the years in *Notre Dame Magazine*, with very minor changes for accuracy, consistency, and clarity, following the *Chicago Manual of Style* in most questions of capitalization and numbers. Although we have added the serial comma, otherwise we have tried to retain the original punctuation because Griffin was an aural writer, who put in commas where he heard a pause in his sentences.

INTRODUCTION

The Pocket-Size God is a collection of essays by Reverend Robert F. Griffin, C.S.C., that were published in *Notre Dame Magazine* between 1972 and 1994. The forty-nine essays selected here, written over the course of twenty-three years, provide an incandescent look both at Father Griffin's developing spirituality and at a remarkable period in the life of the Catholic Church. These essays take up Griffin's vocation at the University of Notre Dame, his pastoral work at parishes in New York, the pain suffered by his family, his attempt to parent children not his own, the church's efforts to evolve, and more. Griffin was doing what the Council fathers had asked faithful Catholics to do when they closed the Second Vatican Council; he was reading the signs of the times and trying to respond with the generosity and love of Christ, although he was sometimes bewildered by these times—as he was when Notre Dame theology professor William G. Storey, whom Griffin refers to as Wystan in "A Bridge Too Far," confronted him about his understanding of gay people.

Griffin's reflections trace his deepening awareness of the face of Christ in every human person. They remind readers of the struggles that the American church experienced as it adjusted to the reforms of Vatican II and the upheavals in American life in the late twentieth century. Through them he also tells the story of some of the changes on the Notre Dame campus, such as Gerry Faust's tenure as head football coach and Father Theodore Hesburgh's retirement as president. Griffin also ruminates on larger social issues with which he struggled, including sexuality, declining attendance at Mass, poverty, and intolerance. Through all of his writings, his own priesthood is a theme so deeply laid that it informs and animates every aspect of his ministry and his life. The essay "*Alter Christus*" hints at the archetype that priesthood became for his life. These essays remain luminously alive long after his death, for Griffin's spirituality remains focused on the ways in which God participates in our humanity and we in his divinity. Griffin consistently touches on the brotherhood of all humanity and resists the squabbling and animus that can divide people as they approach spiritual questions. It is a spirituality that we still need today.

Griffin's writings were part of his ministry at Notre Dame, a ministry that had deep roots. He converted to Catholicism in 1944, after reading the stories of writer John O'Brien, and arrived as a student at Notre Dame the following year. He graduated from Notre Dame in 1949 with an English degree and went on to seminary; he took his first vows in 1950 and, four years later, was ordained a priest in the Eastern Province of the Holy Cross. He taught at Father Baker High School in Lackawanna, New York, for two years before taking a master's degree in English from Notre Dame in 1957 and going on to further graduate studies at Boston University. For seven years he taught at Stonehill College, but he was not very successful as a faculty member, according to Father James T. Burtchaell, C.S.C., who reckoned that Griffin's antipathy for academic discipline made those seven years a wilderness for him. A nervous breakdown returned him to Notre Dame and Holy Cross House. He taught at the high school seminary on St. Mary's Lake for a year before taking up residence in Keenan Hall in 1967 as assistant rector, becoming its rector two years later. In moving him out of that position, the university made him its official chaplain. Griffin's departure from Keenan was bitter for him, but he took his new role of university chaplain seriously. Despite his efforts to work with the office of Campus Ministry, his affinity and true ministry were for the marginal and the defenseless. After thirty years of service, he went once more to Holy Cross House, this time closer in age to the other priests who were in residence there. He died on October 20, 1999, after a life of struggle and goodness.

The obituary for Griffin in the *South Bend Tribune* described him as "one of Notre Dame's most affectionate and affectionately regarded characters." Trailing after or leading his dog, Darby O'Gill, Griffin was a campus familiar, one whom everyone knew. In fact, it was hard to miss Darby O'Gill and Griffin. Dogs were a rarity on campus, and Griffin's weight made him instantly recognizable. (He once remarked that he and Father George Wiskirchen shared the friendship of overweight men living among youthful, thin students.) Darby and Griffin were highly approachable, too. The few students who were afraid or too bashful to speak directly with Griffin found an approach through Darby, who seemed not to mind the attention and, in fact, generally took it as his natural due. Griffin referred to Darby in such human terms and with such affection that most of us forgot the little beast was not quite a person. By his presence, Darby made Notre Dame more human; he was a reminder of the homes that students had left and sometimes longed for. It was easy to find the dog endearing. Griffin humanized the place as well; it was easy to find him lovable. One signal of the affectionate response came from the Glee Club, which made Griffin its chaplain and took him on their tours here and abroad. Another was the regularity with which students and alumni asked Griffin to preside at their marriages.

Griffin was, however, more than a character whose eccentricities inspired the affection of the campus. He was a serious minister of the Gospel, who took his priesthood as a vocation so deep and vital that it animated everything he did. He was constantly trying to find ways to minster to those who, like himself, were insignificant in the world's eyes and, sometimes, in Notre Dame's eyes. Though he loved both the world and Notre Dame, he knew the worth and dignity of those human persons whom the powerful treated, often unthinkingly, as inconsequential. He sought in every pastoral situation to temper the wind, as he puts it in these essays, to the shorn lamb.

Griffin regularly presided at the late Saturday afternoon Mass in Sacred Heart Church on campus. The church had not yet become a minor basilica, and its interior had been radically simplified in the wake of the liturgical reforms of the Second Vatican Council. Griffin invited the children in attendance to come up to the altar for the Eucharistic Prayer. There, amid the children seated and standing, he said the words of the canon with an intensity that resonated through the church. For the acclamation, he led the children and the rest of the congregation in "Jesus Loves Me, This I Know." The Baptist hymn melded his childhood with the children's, and it sounded, in Griffin's vernacular, as much a part of the Roman liturgy as the invocation to the Holy Spirit to bless the offerings. Sunday mornings found Griffin in the chapel between Stanford and Keenan Halls, presiding at what he called the Urchin's Mass. Stripped of its pews in those days, the front part of the chapel, nearest the altar, was reserved for children. On some Sundays the chapel seemed chaotic, with children getting up and walking around; on most Sundays, it was crowded with children, parents, and students; and every Sunday, Griffin broke open the Gospel in terms that young children could comprehend and that simultaneously took hold of the hearts of the adults in the chapel.

Late Sunday afternoons found Griffin back in the chapel to preside at a different urchin's Mass, this one for Notre Dame students. The chapel was usually packed; students sat with their knees in each other's backs, so close together that no one could stand for the Gospel reading. In the crowded chapel, there was no hope of a communion line, so the patens were passed from person to person at the offertory, and the assembly held the hosts in their hands until Communion; the consecrated wine Griffin sent around in small glass cups mounted on a brass tray. These tiny communion glasses may have been another link to his Protestant background; they certainly earned him a reprimand from officialdom, which judged them unorthodox, at least for the distribution of Catholic communion. Something of Griffin's unadulterated piety and his awe at the mysteries at which he was presiding were palpable and even contagious among the students there, and they passed those patens and glasses from one to another with tender, reverential care. Three liturgies in a single weekend must have been taxing, but Griffin kept at them for years.

In the spring of 1975, he began saying Mass in the second-floor ballroom of LaFortune Hall during Lent. On Ash Wednesday, at a table draped with fresh linens, he had a student read from the prophet Joel, and then he preached on the meaning of Lent for Catholics and for the world. It was as if he were blowing the trumpet and proclaiming a fast for the campus. He had Barbara Budde sing "Let All Mortal Flesh Keep

Silence," as the students moved forward to be anointed with ashes. Those noon-time Masses, like so many of his others, were crowded. Later, he would regularly preside at the Saturday afternoon Mass at St. Patrick's parish in South Bend. In the late 1980s and early 1990s, he was criticized for his liturgical style, particularly by graduate students in the liturgy program. Perhaps he had gotten tired with age or found the routine of saying Mass dulling, but his critics had brief historical memories and no grasp of his longer tenure of reaching out time and again to children, students, and others, of finding places and ways to bring the disenchanted, the lonesome, the angry, and the forlorn to the Lord's table.

As part of his reaching out, Griffin started "The Children's Hour" on WSND-FM in 1973 and spoke to his audience, both the children who were his intended audience and the adults who eavesdropped, with respect for their intelligence and understanding. He worked seriously to prepare for these weekly shows. Once, in the mid-1980s, he asked me to drive him to Chicago so that he could look for records he was interested in playing on the show. After he had found some of the records he was after, he spent time browsing through the children's section of the music stores we visited. He was so intent on looking for material that would suit the show that he said hardly a word to me until we stopped for lunch. Then, he seemed wearied by his searching but pleased by what he had found. When he left South Bend for vacations, he was particular about who substituted for him, and when he was too ill to continue hosting "The Children's Hour," he was anxious that Carole Walton take over the show, for he knew that her attention to the intelligence and imaginations of children matched his own.

Also in the 1970s, Griffin created Darby's Place in the basement of LaFortune. There was not much to it—tables, chairs, and coffee and donuts. Open until the wee hours of the morning, it was a place for students or anyone else to come, a place to study, a place to find companionship, a place to talk. Griffin made the rounds with Darby when he arrived and then settled into a large armchair near the stairs that led up under the main entrance to LaFortune. There he presided, talking with students, reading, and keeping a watchful eye over the place. He imagined it to be one of Hemingway's "clean, well-lighted places," where people, especially those who felt they had no other place to go, could find refuge. It was also a place for Griffin to minister quietly and indirectly. In time, people played the piano or guitars, and Darby's Place was more than a refuge; it was another home, a place where night after night anyone could go and be received with easy informality. When the last student had left Darby's Place, Griffin walked slowly back to Keenan. With the dog sniffing ahead of him, Griffin was usually energized after his night watch and steadily in love with Notre Dame.

Darby's Place was an extension of the hospitality that Griffin had offered for years during his rectorship in Keenan. When he was in, his door was open in the evenings, and students of every temperament stopped by. Some were in need; some were in high spirits. Some were silly, lightheartedly looking for the affection and mirroring of an adult; others were earnest, wanting to be taken into the camp of adults. Griffin welcomed them all without fanfare, and he took them seriously. The men of Keenan repaid him with a double bed when they learned his size made sleeping on the standard twin bed problematic. The double bed cramped his small room, but he was embarrassed, amused, and grateful for it. The senior class in 1973 repaid his availability, his concern, and his ministry by naming him their Fellow. Griffin was the first person at Notre Dame to receive this honor, which usually went to someone of national prominence. Griffin was pleased, but in "A Letter to the Class of '73: Darby and I Never Said We Didn't Love You," he dared that class—and all his readers—to become better people than they knew they could be. There was prophetic challenge as well as hospitality and healing in his ministry.

Over the summers and the Christmas recesses in the 1970s and early 1980s, Griffin went first to St. Joseph's Church and then to Holy Cross Church and St. Malachy's in New York City, where he helped with parochial duties and ministered to street people, some of whom he writes about in these pages. He was available to the people of Greenwich Village as easily as he was to the Domers on campus. For several summers in the mid-1980s, when there was a change of pastors at St. Joseph's, Griffin served in a parish in London. It was a different venue but the same work of reaching out to the disenfranchised and the disenchanted, tempering the wind. He spent at least part of the money he earned while there to help Sister Dolorilda Walton, C.S.C., join him in London for a vacation. She had helped him when he was ill, and he wanted to repay her with a holiday in London. She was then in her eighties, and he in his sixties, but the two of them rode busses all over London to see the sights.

For all of his hospitality and generosity, Robert Griffin was an intensely shy man. His room was open to students, but that took more effort than many recognized. When I became his editor at the Notre Dame student newspaper, *The Observer*, he sent me a note in which he diffidently asked me to stop by his room because he had a small gift for me. That gift turned out to be a bottle of bourbon; it was clearly Griffin's reticent and hesitant effort to establish a friendship. When Father Burtchaell invited Griffin to join him for a reading vacation, Griffin was pleased to be admitted to the circle of a man whose intellect he admired, but he worried right up to his departure about how the holiday would turn out. In fact, he enjoyed himself, but even the gregariousness of a quiet vacation of reading with people whom he had known for a long time cost him an effort. It seemed that he was at ease only with people whom he had known a very long time and who had been with him through some of the difficulties of his life. With Sister Dolorilda at the University Club and the Olive Garden, he would recite large swaths of Wordsworth, Longfellow, Whittier, and other poets whose work they had committed to memory during their school days. Alcohol and smoking helped him in social situations. He liked the University Club's executive Manhattan—no different from an ordinary Manhattan, except it was half again as large. He thought of smoking, particularly with friends, as the eighth sacrament.

Writing, too, was a kind of sacrament for Griffin, a way through word and symbol to bring God's presence to his readers. He had written pieces for Ave Maria Press publications, and he began writing regularly for *The Observer*. (Several of these were reprinted by *Notre Dame Magazine* and are included in this collection.) His column was a staple of the Friday edition of *The Observer* and, for a long time, was widely read on campus. Later, he became a regular columnist for the *Notre Dame Magazine* and for *Our Sunday Visitor;* writing became the center of Griffin's ministry. The title of Griffin's weekly column for *The Observer*, "Letters to a Lonely God," suggests that he looked upon his writing as an extension of his pastoral work. His metaphor of the loneliness of God was also a metaphor for the campus and the world. It may also have been a habit of his own heart, but it allowed him to offer a quiet, unobtrusive hospitality to the questions, difficulties, and hurts that he observed in students and in contemporary culture. The original logo for the column—a silhouette of Griffin seated with Darby—underscores the solitariness of Griffin. He and Darby appear as watchers, contemplating the passing scene, apart from but deeply and resolutely concerned about it. Griffin may have been one of the solitaries whom Thomas Merton describes, one who "realizes that he is one with [all persons] in the peril and anguish of their common solitude: not the solitude of the individual only, but the radical and essential *solitude of man*—a solitude which was assumed by Christ and which, in Christ, becomes mysteriously identified with the solitude of God." Certainly, the following depiction by Merton of the solitary man was true of Griffin: "There is in this lonely one a gentleness, a deep sympathy, though he may be apparently unsocial. There is a great purity of love, though he may hesitate to manifest his love in any way, or to commit himself openly to it."[1]

In his columns, Griffin wrote with a quiet courage that sometimes was mistaken for meekness or doggedness or even sentimentality. He was not afraid to take up, ponder, and comment on the dilemmas that were gripping Catholics in particular and the world in general. He wrote about the struggles of ordinary Catholics with *Humanae Vitae*, with premarital sex, with divorce, and with gay people. He knew the rules about each of these, but he also understood the importance of sheltering human individuals suffering under those rules. Griffin patiently and steadily tried to temper the winds of change, sin, and age as he wrote about others and about his own ministry and life. In the process, his thinking about many of these issues, particularly on homosexuality, changed. Whereas early in the column "Letters to a Lonely God" he had described gay people as having broken wings, later he came to see that the church had much to do in its theology about, and its care of, gay men and women. He encouraged hospitality toward gay people long before it was fashionable to do so at Notre Dame and long before gay people became visible in the media.

1. Thomas Merton, "The Philosophy of Solitude," in *Disputed Questions* (New York: Farrar, Straus and Cudahy, 1960), 188, 189.

Griffin was a chronicler of the pains of human life, knowing them well from his own family. In a December 1975 essay written for the student magazine *Scholastic*, he alluded to the fragility of his relationship with his Baptist father, who neither shared nor understood Griffin's religious curiosity. He was disappointed to the point of hostile silence when Griffin entered the Catholic Church in 1944. Griffin wrote about the pain this caused his father. He had his own pain, for the breach in his relationship with his father over his conversion turned out to be irreconcilable in this life. His father died during his first semester in college. Griffin also knew well the anguish of his brother George, defeated by life, and the agony of his mother, grief-stricken by losses and demented by age. The sorrows of his family attuned Griffin to the anguish of the world. In pain, Griffin saw the workings of grace without sentimentalizing the suffering.

Griffin often closed his *Observer* columns with what became one of his hallmarks—"Darby and I never said we didn't love you." It was a reminder to students and all his readers that they were loved. Still, he was not above delivering a mild chastisement when it was called for. He reminded one young man in love that he was not the first to feel protective toward his beloved; Griffin's reminder was so gentle that it was easy to miss, but obliqueness might have been the only approach he found possible to the inflation that the young feel when they are in love. The callowness of students and the fecklessness of his fellow clerics who were led into the temptations of fame and power all received their due attention. And Griffin treated these failings with a kindly acceptance, as if they were understandable, even to be expected, and as if they diminished not by an iota the love that Darby and he bore the world.

Griffin's writing was informed by his reading, and his reading was voracious. The sitting room of his apartment in Keenan was strewn with books—stacks of them on the floor and on the side tables by his chair and sofa. Some were topped by the ubiquitous ashtray and often by ashes. He was not easy on books; many had jackets that were creased or torn, and the spines of some were broken from where he had put them face down. Part of his day, when he was flush, involved a walk to the old bookstore on campus and a look at the books. He read widely, sometimes delving deeply into a topic or an author. In the 1980s he read four or five biographies of W. H. Auden, one after the other. He was interested in contemporary fiction by John Irving and others. He read theology, avidly taking up books by Notre Dame theologians John Dunne and Richard McBrien. In fact, he read new works by Notre Dame faculty as if the university were truly his parish, and he had to keep up with its goings on.

Griffin's first love, however, was for the literary modernists Ernest Hemingway and F. Scott Fitzgerald, whose novels and stories he had studied and to which he returned again and again. His essays are studded with references to them. Hemingway's clean well-lighted place became Griffin's ideal for Darby's Place, just as Hemingway's sense of 3 a.m. as the most lonesome hour of the day illuminated Griffin's penchant for late-night pastoral work. He worried about the descendants of Fitzgerald's beautiful and damned, whom he saw at Notre Dame, in Greenwich Village, in the church, and in the world. Like the high modernists, Griffin was deeply attuned to the question of how one is to live in a day when the old certainties had given way and were not likely to be restored. The literary modernists were trying to make sense of the world and to create art in the aftermath of World War I, which destroyed four empires and left a generation of young men shattered physically and emotionally. Griffin was trying to understand, for himself and for others, the world in the wake of the Vatican Council's reforms, reforms which left many taken aback and uncertain, and in the aftermath of the 1960s, a decade of war and unrest that upended many cultural assumptions. He admired Hemingway for developing a code to replace the old verities and Fitzgerald for discerning the tragedy of the glamorous, but his own eye was always on the question of salvation in a world of distress. He was always looking for the grace available in the situations he encountered. Like Fitzgerald's unerring instinct for the spoilation of the dream, Griffin's sense of the suffering of the world was infallible. Though few of us who read his writings as undergraduates could have guessed it, Griffin's writing was hierophantic; it was one of the ways in which he ministered to the tormented and miserable, to all of us, really. It was a sacrament, protecting us when we were shorn of protection, recalling us to the grace of God's love, and raising up our loneliness to the divine lonesomeness.

J. Robert Baker
Fairmont State University

LATE HAVE I LOVED THEE,
O ANCIENT OF DAYS

Before the headlines were written large upon the page with news of Rockne's victories . . . before the generation of builders that gilded the Dome and painted frescoes on walls whose bricks had been tempered in resurrection fire . . . in the years before the events in a grotto of Massabielle, when a figure gowned in light murmured of her identity with immaculate beginnings . . . in those times when the campus was little more than a lake where the sycamores were dreaming in shadows on the water, and birds of over two hundred varieties nested in the elms . . . in those days before there were computers and science labs and nearly a million books on the library shelves . . . in that ago so distant in time, there existed a Notre Dame community of priests, brothers, and sisters of Holy Cross, which still flourishes.

Notre Dame, for me, is Alma Mater; it is also the birthright of my religious family. There is something here, in this earth of Notre Dame, which is mine to bequeath to heirs: the breath of faith, the duty of commitment, the gift of unearned love.

There the breath of God had exhaled upon the Indiana wilderness to give life to a tradition of service in a priesthood which I received from venerable fathers, to be passed on to sons and brothers who will, hopefully, commemorate crucifixion and rebirth in liturgies that will survive as long as the world shall live.

Mine is a community of saints and scholars, but most of its members participate fully in the fragile humanity of the rest of the race. Take Sorin, for example, that Frenchman who built Notre Dame on his own sins of disobedience. On one stormy occasion, he was ordered by an official visitor representing French Basil Moreau, of the French mother-house, to accompany the visitor back to LeMans. At first, Sorin resisted the instructions of the visitor to pack, and kept him virtually a prisoner under house arrest. But after a few days, Sorin, in the company of the visitor, started the slow trip on horseback to the embarkation point in New York. Only a few miles out of South Bend, Sorin was arrested by a couple of sheriffs. It was not until the visitor had returned to France and reported the sad news of Sorin's criminality that the Founder learned the truth; the putative sheriffs were really a couple of priests in mufti, suborned to deliver Sorin from Moreau's interference. Edward Sorin, shaggy as a patriarch, had the soul of a rogue when roguery was demanded as the price of survival of his beloved Notre Dame.

There was Father Joseph Muckenthaler, with whom I prefected as a young priest in Dillon. He died very suddenly one morning after Mass, at the age of fifty-six, and for the second time in my life, I felt that death had robbed me of a father. There was Father Thomas Steiner, the old provincial, who would roar out bearlike protests at the speed of the cross-bearer leading processions in Sacred Heart Church. Steiner would sit, of a spring evening, on the porch of Corby Hall, surrounded by cronies; and every now and again he would bellow with the wrath of the thunder god: "There's a boy walking on the goddamned grass." His idiom was salty, like that of the engineer he was, but he was always gracious to me as a young priest, and his instincts were those of a builder.

Somewhere in the cemetery sleeps the brother whose features were memorialized in the Stations of the Cross at Sacred Heart. Having aroused the ire of the artist who was then painting the Stations, the brother's face appeared among the ranks of the Pharisees in the crowds surrounding Christ. When Sorin protested the outrage, the artist concealed his mischief by painting a Sorinesque beard on the Pharisaic face, and those whiskers became part of the art history of Notre Dame.

Memories, trivial in themselves, but they are part of the thousands of legends through which a religious family remembers its past. These men, their contemporaries, and their descendants have given, and are giving, grace and charm, direction and style, to the growth of this Christian institution; and the brightest young grad student and the most brilliant professor build upon foundations that could never have existed if the Community of Holy Cross had not begun and carried forward a labor of love which bears the name Notre Dame du lac.

But I would never think of mentioning the matter if insensitive words were not being spoken about the sisters and the alienation of their property at Saint Mary's. The Holy Cross nuns too have their community of the living and the dead; their life was incredibly harder than that of the priests and brothers; Notre Dame itself could not have survived without their sacrifice. Notre Dame and Saint Mary's College are, today, something more than the patrimony of a family of superannuated religious. As these schools are absorbed more and more into the life of the secular city, a notice should be posted for all passersby to see: please be gentle with memories of the Catholic past; please be sensitive in your judgments of the men and women of Holy Cross who are totally committed to the well-being of Notre Dame yesterday, today, and forever.

SOMEWHERE, A SUMMER OF '42

Once in a summer when you were sixteen, you walked with a girl through patches of daisies and wild strawberries in a meadow close to the sea. Her feet were bare, and you wanted to love them because they were innocent and beautiful and full of wonder at the feel of warming, loving earth. Under the New England sky of late July, in a field that stretched to the edge of the continent, you watched her dance as though light were her lover, and she had been stroked with sunbeams. In the glory of the noonday, her head was like a golden chrysanthemum skirmishing with the wind. Bluebirds and butterflies seemed her playmates as you watched, aching with love and desire. Later, at evening, you wept with helplessness, because you were only sixteen and could not own the beauty of a girl with feet stained in strawberry who danced among daisies.

Nearly thirty years later, you remember that day, or like to think you do—but you can't recall if the sea were green or blue, nor whether dimples played hide-and-seek in that face, nor whether her eyes were brown like the wings of a wood thrush. Not knowing makes you skeptical. You think to yourself: It is a fantasy, full of trite images and stale dreams from a sleep, filled with sex play, half remembered from the awakening years of adolescence.

But in your heart, you know there was a summer of '42 when a girl walked with you in the meadows that lead to the sea. Never mind if it were a dream, for dreams are the reality by which we sometimes need to live. Faith sometimes seems like a fantasy of love—a half-dream tucked in memory of the years when the Son of God walked from the kingdoms of light, over the path of the rainbow, into our darkness. Touching water, he turned it into wine; touching pain, he turned it into grace; touching death, he turned it into an affair of glory—only we can't believe the dream, because we have no experience of miracles. Instead, we have the fact of the Cross (all of us have experienced crosses) upon which the Son of Man is crucified. God the Father, stern and despotic like a dean of discipline, looks down upon the Cross and sees that his lad is dying. Painfully and punitively, he is dying, with his flesh screwed into agony by the nails and wood. God leans low to look into the face of his Son and to study the suffering, and he sees the lifeblood of his child staining the green of the tree. The bent God hears the words of Jesus, punished like a slave who must be tortured on nails. The gentle absolutions of the Outlaw are like hammers beating on God's heart, pounding away the anger. Hidden in the dark shadows over the Cross, God the Father is redeemed to mercy through the love of his Son, who revealed us men and our suffering to an Omnipotence who didn't know what it is to be human.

In our dreams of God, as in our dreams of golden maidens, we must distinguish fact from fantasy; otherwise we have a theology of wishful thinking, with dogmas from Mother Goose. Is there evidence that God loves me? Does he always scar his lovers with the fire of suffering? Is suffering a proof that there is a loving Providence that guards the victims of the cancer ward, the ghetto, the firebombed jungle, the battlefield, the abortion clinic, the street accident, the psycho ward, the children's wing of Memorial Hospital? Scripture notes that the Deity watches with interest as the sparrow falls, but so do well-trained ornithologists. Is there compassion in the curious glance of the cosmic bird watcher, and does he sometimes lift the dead feathers on his fingertips and send them beating like oars against a sea of light until they have again found the wind currents to the sun?

Faith, writes St. Paul, is the substance of things hoped for, the evidence of things unseen. Of Cardinal Newman, it is written that as a child he hoped that the Arabian Nights might be true; and that as a man, he found magic even more moving than the tales of Scheherazade in the myth of the eternal priesthood.

As a priest who serves as chaplain to this university, I often create fantasies about God, writing of him, for example, as a Lonely God who lives by himself in an empty mansion, with only hired servants to keep him company. It is easier to love a God who is as moody with loneliness as a widowed grandfather than it is to have to forgive him for being blissfully happy when he should he brooding over the broken bones of babies. Fantasies are what you indulge in, sometimes, if you are a priest, witnessing to the truth of things unseen, like the love that lies hidden in the mystery of suffering.

In the end, like Newman, I am a minister of the eternal priesthood. I am part of the myth that proclaims the wonders of Incarnation and Redemption, and Sacraments that reveal Christ under the gestures and words of ritual. I must proclaim the Good News of the Lord without dependency on miracle or magic or fantasy. I must teach the disciplines of love to a generation that often confuses love with romance, which is only love's foreshadowing. Love sometimes walks in a meadow and is holy, as sixteen-year-olds can tell you; but in its profoundest implications, it is an affair of sacrifice and crucifixion, and only faith can say with certainty whether God is watching the struggle against the nails.

I must teach the doctrine of the forgiveness of sins, without sentimentalizing either the sin or the sinner. The whole bloody crowd of us are murderers, adulterers, abortionists, sodomists, liars, thieves, and other ugly types. The Gospel images of prodigal sons and lost sheep do not apply if used by sentimentalists—so I am warned by my critics. Often, I do not understand God, and I really hesitate to like him; but I trust the experience of Christ, who gave him his whole being until the ultimate surrender in death. There was such a trust of the Father in Jesus as he hung on the Cross that I can really believe that God is as compassionate as that wonderful old man in the parable who watched the roads till his youngest boy came home in shabbiness from the harlot's house, when his dad ran to greet him with the embraces of love.

Here, then, is the faith—in God and Christ and the Holy Spirit— with its complexities and ambiguities, with its lights and shadows, that I am trying to share with this campus. The wonder of it to me is not that I witness to it badly, through imperfect liturgies and a theology of the imagination, but why I try to witness to it at all.

At my age, my pores are too brittle to sport in the meadow with Elvira Madigan. But as long as the heart can sing and the mind can wonder, then faith is always like a young girl gathering sunlight: elusive, pertinacious, saucy, beautiful, and full of love. At its best, my faith reflects the qualities—doubt, fear, passion, intensity, trust, courage, hope, grief—that are preoccupying the students, children, colleagues, and friends of the Notre Dame community. For, as a Christian, I am here at this university not only to witness the faith, but also to find it incarnate in heartbeats that dance to the rhythms of grace.

THE POCKET-SIZE GOD

On Communion calls to the apartments on the avenues of Broadway in Manhattan, a priest becomes, in a most literal way, the Christ-bearer, bringing God to the crossroads of inner-city life. Among the crowds waiting for the light at the corner of Eighth Avenue and 42nd Street, the priest alone is aware of the immensity of the gift he carries from the supper table of the immortal feast. He alone knows of the presence of the Lord hidden in the fragile trappings of a sacrament, borne as casually as coins in the shelter of an inner coat pocket. He alone is conscious of the snowflake of wheat, placed close to the beating of his own heart, where the immaculate Son of Man lives in the heart of bread; an anonymous wafer carried like a smuggler's booty along the sad avenue of lost innocence; the ultimate mystery of the hidden and lonely God.

This was the need of at least one priest this summer as he hustled up and down the dark stairways of buildings on the West Side of midtown Manhattan, doubtlessly deficient in doctrine and filled with a faith not quite stylish enough for the Christians who really swing. At times in these squalid apartments, where ailing and aged people live like prisoners in confined abandonment, one needed the doctrines that smack of priest-magic, as well as of the romances in which Christ comes, disguised like Cinderella's prince, to visit the char-girl who lives in the ash heap. At such times, the alternative need to fantasy (if it were fantasy) was a resentment colored with atheism.

I think of the wake of an old-time show girl I attended this summer. I was the only living soul who came to visit the body at the funeral parlor; the only prayers said for her that night was my recitation of the rosary. There was not a single flower, a single candle, a single Mass card in that room; there was only a cheap, unadorned casket, mounted on trestles, in which rested a tiny little woman who had retreated from a life that totally snubbed her. I left after a half hour, sick at heart for the funeral without mourners, so financially broke I couldn't afford to buy a solitary rose as a tribute to the dead. I couldn't even leave her my rosary, because it was borrowed for the evening from the housekeeper at the rectory. On the way out, I asked the undertaker to lay a crucifix on the casket so that the dead woman would have some identification with the aloneness in death of the Lord.

It was such people as my lonely show girl that I visited like a stage-door Johnny this summer, bringing with me the sacrament of love. In the heat of a New York morning, I would walk the littered sidewalks, past the massage parlors, the brothels, the gay bars, and ride the elevator to the seventh floor of a sleazy hotel, where widows waited, or wives sat at the bedside of their crippled husbands, with candles burning and linen napkins spread, as though sacristans had been setting up altars in flophouse cathedrals.

One morning, two derelicts stopped me as I was leaving a cold-water tenement house on 47th Street. Rather ungently, they demanded to know what a son-of-a-bitch like me was doing in the neighborhood, and then they asked me for money. I wasn't frightened, even though I had been mugged on a nearby street earlier in the summer, but I was puzzled to know what I would do if they searched me and found the Communion hosts inside my coat. It is a lesson taught by every nun in the grade schools that a Catholic should be cheerfully willing to die to defend the host from sacrilege. I knew I would be greatly admired if I shed my blood right there in the doorway, and might even be canonized, with my T-shirt distributed as relics, if I should become a martyr of the Eucharist, dying on those tiles that stank of urine. The question was, did I believe the Eucharist was precious enough to die for if it were stolen from me at the point of a knife? Was death what God wanted from me to protect the host from a couple of winos, and from their ignorance which could have known little of sacraments and their immortal value?

I did not die a martyr's death that morning. All those old guys really wanted was money, and they didn't even try to steal it off me. I gave them a dollar apiece, and then they went off on a spending spree. The whole episode was over before my faith (or prudence) could be tested very severely, and I still can't tell you the conditions under which I would expose myself to stabbing as a duty imposed on me by my ordination.

But I do know this: there is a strength and beauty in the Eucharist that brings comfort and peace to the aging guys and dolls in the apartments above the streets of Manhattan. Some of them would rather have Communion than their welfare checks, and welfare is all they have to keep them alive.

It is their faith, as well as my own, that makes me happy enough to dance on Broadway when I walk up 52nd Street in the company of my pocket-size God.

EMPTY SPACES, LONELY PLACES

It doesn't help, these days, to be fortified with strong Manhattans and beef simmered in wine; when the announcement comes that a colleague is checking out of the active priesthood, the news is as chilling as ice storms in the Arctic; there is a frost on the heart as though it had suddenly been buried in snowdrifts.

On three occasions lately, priests whom I love have announced their plans for leaving; twice the news came at dinner. The first time was in a posh restaurant in New York City. It is awkward to be caught by the waiter wiping one's eyes over the Chateaubriand which, if it were a painting done in oils, could have been hung in the Louvre. The maître d', alerted to my distraction from the meal, could not have been more offended if I had retched over the menu.

On the second occasion, the priest, though dear to me, did not happen to be an old college chum; we had not encouraged each other's seminary survival through the dark days of a winter in the novitiate. Nevertheless, when he introduced me to the girl he said was his roommate, soon to become his wife, it was difficult to smile across the table, set in beauty with candlelight and roses, and murmur the platitudes wishing them nuptial bliss.

Once upon a time, I met a woman for whom I developed a deep attachment. A local ingenue, then a senior at St. Mary's, met the woman, observed the friendship, and began making assumptions considerably in advance of the circumstances. She went out of her way to tell me that if this woman and I decided to marry, it was quite all right.

"Everyone," she said, "will understand."

Her words, intended as a kindness, hurt me very much. Did she think so little of my priesthood, I wondered, that she (and those others who would understand) would feel no loss to the church if I no longer celebrated Mass, or distributed the Eucharist, or preached the Word of God, or witnessed the failures and the victories of grace, to the aliveness of the Lord whose love touches us in the sharing of bread, the blessing of wine? My point is this: it is no compliment to my fellow priests, when they decide to leave, for me to smile like the matchmaker at the wedding feast of Cana, as though rectories would not afterwards be lonelier places, and as though there would not be empty spaces at the altars of the church.

I think that a priest can understand—and respect—better than anyone else the reasons why his comrades leave. But it is still almost like a death in the family to see one's contemporaries go; it is still frightening, if you are middle-aged, when the young men, to whom the future belongs, depart. That is why, from time to time, I declare my own personal days of mourning; that is why I prefer that upsetting announcements not be made over the Chateaubriand.

A question that is often asked today—a question that a priest often asks himself—is: "Father, why do *you* stay?" Or often a departing priest will leave letters, explaining his decision to his superiors and his community. I try to understand these letters, as I hope my own letter might be understood if I should decide to leave also. But these present words are written almost as a defense to explain why I am not leaving—at least, I am not leaving at any foreseeable time, not until God gives me fresher insights and different graces for other forms of service from the ones I presently have.

Let me say immediately, I have no special strength that protects me against loneliness, discouragement, or despair. There are circumstances where, without a strong sense of being loved, I could not survive, either as a priest or as a human being. From recent, firsthand experience I know the working conditions in places that leave the priest feeling tragically unfulfilled: the cold, half-empty churches where the distance between the pews and the altar is as endless as the spaces between the stars, and Sunday Mass is a lonely dialogue between the celebrant and the God of celebrations. The only real sign of life among the congregation is when they shuffle in and out of the benches as they enter or leave the church. (But here, I wonder, is not the fault my own? Lord, can these dry bones live again?) I know the confessionals where the charades of grace are played: absolutions exchanged for sins which seem like the reflex actions of concupiscence; penances imposed for shabby little acts that must bore God more than they offend him.

In a world where there are bishops too political to chide the war crimes of the President, and living fetuses by the truckload are aborted for their burial, and there are rats walking across the faces of children in Harlem, and kids get their kicks from cocaine, and the pushers are stalking the playgrounds of Brooklyn and Chicago, and the mental hospitals are crowded with patients whose illness began in infancy when nobody bothered to love them . . . in such a world torn apart by its own moral crises, I cannot as a confessor feel that I have lifted souls onto the back of Christ by absolving an octogenarian dying of anemia for missing Mass on a holy day when the snowdrifts reached the chimney tops. The confessionals are mobbed with octogenarians these days, and the priest must be content with absolving octogenarians, because if it were not for the octogenarians, or sinners that sound that ancient, the priest would have no souls to absolve at all.

Can these dry bones live again? I mean the dry bones of the sacrament of rehabilitation wherein God's pity is revealed as mercy, and the miracle of Lazarus, renewed in life, makes a fool of the triumphs of the grave. According to Pauline formulas, sin is an affair of flesh and blood and bones conspiring against the mind and spirit, or it is the heart and mind in revolt against themselves. We priests should have been trained as therapists working with the ointments of redemption; instead, we were made the tally clerks of a legal system based on moral ethics. A biblical metaphor for the kingdom is that of a vineyard where we are the branches and Christ is the vine. How many priests today, trained in the ancient casuistry, think of themselves as the Lord's vinedressers, especially when we have trained our people so carefully to consider us as their judges. (A sacrament that is dead wood in the hands of a judge can mean healing in the hands of a physician.)

Consider this typical confession: "I missed Mass twice. I read a dirty book. I cursed about a hundred times. I spoke uncharitably about my neighbor, and I always forget my night prayers."

For this list of self-indictments, a sentence is imposed (five Our Fathers, five Hail Marys), the chains of sin are unshackled with an absolution, and citizenship in the kingdom is restored. The soul, assumed to be spiritually dead because of the missed Masses and the dirty book (if he took pleasure in it), is now in a state of grace, and he can take Communion at the Supper of the Lord

Was it for this list of sins, the priest ponders—so impersonal and detached, so protective of the soul's darker moods, so indifferent to its leases on glory—was it for this catalogue of weaknesses that Christ entrusted to his church the ministry of the forgiveness of sins? Is this kind of joyless dialogue celebrated by the angels in heaven as the occasion when the lost sheep is found?

If so, why does the priest, in hearing parish confessions, feel that he is working in the dry valley where the dead bones still bleach in the sun? Lord, can these dry bones live again? Only, Lord, if you can give your church, its priests and its people, a new sense of what it means to be fully alive in Christ who sometimes uses sacraments for the fires of Pentecost.

For over three weeks at Christmas, I lived with a priest on 42nd Street in Manhattan, who was constantly preaching of the nearness of winos and prostitutes to the kingdom of God. His homilies didn't convince anybody in the crowd who really knew much about 42nd Street, certainly not the whisky widows and the spinster ladies whose intact virtue has a grim defensiveness about it as from the next of kin of Maria Goretti. Winos and harlots are not widely admired in the neighborhood to which their panhandling and sexual solicitations have given such a bad name. So the righteous folk of Holy Cross parish sat smoldering with rage as their pastor assured them that the trashy types and the moral derelicts are more precious to God than the merely mean-in-heart, and that the best thrones in heaven are reserved for the painted women and their pimps, as though eternal life were just a celestial settlement house for the scum of Eighth Avenue. The story of Mary Magdalene, though drawn from impeccable sources, is not at all inspiring to the little Catholic ladies of 42nd Street, whose own best hope of heaven is attached to the making of the Nine First Fridays. They know it is only in novels that the harlots are holy; it is only in movies that all of them have hearts of gold.

Another priest in the same parish was on a preaching crusade in support of brotherhood. Brotherhood is a beautiful word unless you happen to be from the class of Irish and Italian working people who fear every black and Puerto Rican in New York as muggers, rapists, and dope fiends. On New Year's Eve, this same priest was thrown out of an Italian home in the parish for bringing one of his black friends along on a visit. The black man was an insult, the Italian papa said, to the virtue of the Italian mamma and their daughters, whom the black man was doubtlessly planning to rape. Even among the outcasts of Hell's Kitchen, brotherhood is not a household word. I know of white prostitutes, male and female, who would rather become virtuous than to accept the money or attentions of a black man.

Almost equally strong is a hatred of the Jews, not only among the New York working class or the social lepers, but even among the clergy. I remember a priest in attendance at an interfaith meeting. He listened to a rabbi who complained of being abused in his childhood as a Christ-killer; then he went on to complain of how condescending it seemed for Vatican II to absolve the Jews of guilt for complicity in the death of Christ. Then the priest, bitterly anti-Semitic, made his reply.

"Really, Rabbi," he said, "it wasn't the Vatican Council who absolved the Jews. It was the kikes who write editorials for the *New York Times.*"

Needless to say, interfaith observances are not one of the liturgical highlights in the parish where this priest is pastor.

The point is this: often in the churches these days, a priest cannot, without difficulties to himself, preach the full dimensions of the Gospel message except in parishes where the problems he inveighs against do not exist. Little static would be expected, for example, from preaching against birth control in an old people's home. But the indissolubility of marriage might not be a popular theme at Masses to which Catholics would invite their unchurched friends in those suburbs of Connecticut which are so fashionable, Peter DeVries tells us, that divorce has been made a sacrament. One seldom hears of curates in Westchester preaching of how like getting a camel through the eye of a needle it is for a stockbroker to go home to Jesus. Nobody at St. Patrick's Cathedral is telling it like it is about the Vietnam War. When the cardinal becomes part of the Establishment as vicar of the military ordinariate, then the cathedral priests are not apt to snipe at him for his failure to become the war's critic, and Daniel Berrigan need not apply for permission to borrow the pulpit.

It is frustration from this kind of thing that causes some priests to leave. The priest is ordained, we are told in contemporary idiom, to be a prophet like Isaiah, who waggled a bony finger of rebuke in the face of his king. Today the prophetic office of the priest is often reduced to supporting the safe causes, like the lettuce boycott, provided the greengrocer is not a parish benefactor or the pastor isn't a vegetarian. If priests were free to practice and promote all the revolutionary doctrines hidden at the heart of the Gospel, there might not be a hundred priests in the country who would have the courage to risk the martyrdom their militancy might invite. But those priests who were truly prophets would not be dying of boredom as the victims of parish routine. Their riskiest decision would not be whether to distribute Communion in the hands at a Mass for the Holy Name.

I have spoken of some of the frustrations I have felt as a priest. Now I want to speak of my reasons for remaining in the priesthood. This is a highly personal and incomplete statement, and I want to acknowledge that other priests may have better reasons for leaving than I have for staying. But this is the way I feel, and my motives, which are never entirely clear even to me, are the only lights I have to follow in a thoroughly messed-up age.

Beyond the form that sacraments take, clear and free from the pretensions of hierarchy, and independent of the claims of papal power, God exists, and his Son is the Lord of life. Years before I became a Catholic, I believed in Bethlehem and Calvary, and the raising of Lazarus at Bethany, and the miracle of the wine at Cana, and storms calmed on the Galilean Lake, and the empty tomb at Easter. If the pope were to turn atheist tomorrow, and the Vatican Gardens turned into a Pizza Hut, I would still believe that God's eye is on the sparrow, and I know he watches me.

In addition to faith, I also want my life to be involved with people. Much love has been given me in my lifetime. Sometimes I have been bored with people who have offered me love, or I have been unjust to them, or cruel, or negligent; but mostly, though not always with uniform intensity, I have tried to love them in return.

At this point of my life, I do not know of any other way to integrate my faith in God with my love for people than in my life as a priest. If I were younger, I might become a Christian doctor or psychiatrist or social worker, or even a millionaire who gives away money to the poor. But as a middle-aged man committed to Christ, I can only offer love to my friends, and sacraments for their healing, and kind words from the Gospel as best I understand those kind words after nearly twenty years as a member of the clerical establishment. I don't really mind being a priest; as a matter of fact, I rather love it. I find great truth and beauty in the church; and for all its failures as an institution, I really wouldn't know how to function without it. I would rather receive my absolutes from Rome, my dogmas from Paul, than from the faculty of the Divinity School at Yale.

Even as a priest to whom much love has been given, I am often bitterly lonely. I never caress other people's children without wishing they were my own. I never counsel couples in preparation for marriage without aching all over with hunger for a wife I could cherish as lover and friend. No seminary teacher ever told me the cost of the celibate life; perhaps my teachers had not lived long enough as priests to know the price: the empty side of the table in a restaurant; the empty side of the room in a hotel; the empty side of the heart where even God does not intrude, for that emptiness was not created to shelter him. Whom does a man give his treasures to, if he is a bachelor, or his watch, or his name? It is like losing part of one's immortality to have no one to whom to give one's name.

Despite the loneliness, celibacy has its values for me. As a priest who wants to give himself to people, I don't know if I could have done it in any other way than as a celibate. Perhaps that is due to some emotional imbalance on my part; more probably it is because of my training in the ascetical life; I suspect things would be quite different if I were a preacher among the Mormons. Celibacy is a necessary condition for the kind of priest I want to be, though some of the most Christ-like men I have met are ministers with wives and families. In their spiritual sensitivity and self-giving, they are the finest models I know of the ways a servant of God should act and live.

Though it is too late, I feel, for me, I hope that marriage will soon be part of the clerical discipline. Sooner or later, it has to be, whether the pope likes it or not. Otherwise the church will be faced with its own demise because of the shortage of priests.

As I finish this essay, I am about to go into a cold, half-empty church in Manhattan to say Mass. It is the Feast of the Epiphany, and the liturgy is apt to be a lonely dialogue between the celebrant and the God of celebrations. Other priests have said Mass today—those who have remained in the ordained life, and those others who have left it. In today's world, the underground church is growing, and ministries are not really ended with announcements of departure made at dinner.

I hope the priests whom I love are praying for me today when the bread is broken, and the cup is blessed. To know that they are praying is to know they are still my brothers, even though rectories are more lonely places because of their absence, and there are empty spaces at the altars of the church.

A LETTER TO THE CLASS OF '73:
DARBY AND I NEVER SAID
WE DIDN'T LOVE YOU

Dear Senior Class of 1973: On the morning after the election for the Senior Class Fellow, I was asked by the editor of *Notre Dame Magazine* to prepare an article "on what we can expect of the Class of '73." As the editor commented, "This is an impossible task. That is why I have asked *you* to attempt it."

The editor is right. The task is impossible even for me to whom you have given so much more than any man could have expected from any class at Notre Dame: years of friendship and love, confidence and trust, encouragement and support, and finally, at the end, the honor of being chosen Senior Class Fellow. Being Senior Class Fellow is the most beautiful gift I could have imagined; if you had elected me your pope, I could not be more honored. But Senior Class Fellows are not (that I know of) particularly notable as prophets. So speaking without prophetic insight, I offer you the following impossible remarks.

As I write these words, it is a lovely April morning at Notre Dame. The campus is very still, as though the Easter event of the earth's awakening were as peace-filled as the conversation of women greeted by angels in the garden of the Resurrection. Occasionally, this morning, students walk by my window, and once, a few moments ago, there was a great whirring of wings out of the hedges in front of Keenan as my dog, Darby O'Gill, startled a bird from its occult errand in the bushes. But despite April and Easter and the tranquility imposed by nature as it sets its days and season in order according to the pattern of ancient rhythms in the earth, there is no real peace in the world today except in the lives of those who have made a separate, inner peace of their own. In Rome, an ancient pontiff broods alone in anguish as schisms topple the venerable structures through which Faith has built its kingdom on the ethics and command of Christ. In Washington, the chief executive of our government struggles to emerge with unscathed image from the corruptions and scandal of Watergate. In the South, there are floodings from the Mississippi; and there are Indians struggling for civil rights in South Dakota. The bombs fall on Cambodia, and this morning, for the millionth straight day, there was fighting reported in Northern Ireland. Last evening's headlines screamed of the spiraling prices in the supermarkets; and before evening tonight, five thousand pregnancies will have been terminated by abortions. Everywhere there is unemployment, deaths through the misuse of drugs, suicides, hunger, poverty, the decay of cities, the pain and grief of the world.

The world is as bedeviled now by human mischief as it has been at almost any point in the last sixty years. I suppose none of us can say with certainty of any generation that has lived in this century that things were easier for them than for us; that the people newly grown into adulthood, for example, before the outbreak of World War I, had greater freedom from fear or felt less threatened by extinction. Each generation faces its own kind of fear and its own kind of despair. Gertrude Stein said to the young American expatriates of the Paris of the Twenties, embittered into cynicism by a war intended to make the world safe for democracy, "You are all a lost generation." Apparently the phrase was appreciated, for it managed to stick, although it reflects an enormous self-pity on the part of those in the generation who considered themselves "lost," as though they, among all the generations who have lived, had a special right to be bankrupt of hope.

When we consider the evils that threaten us, I suppose we do grow moody with the thought that we seem to be living in the twilight time of human decency, and that moral and physical deaths hover over our civilization like dark angels serving as acolytes to a night that can have no ending. But I don't think the world is more afraid now than it was thirty years ago, in the midst of World War II, when, for a time, all the news seemed bad, all the battles seemed lost. Each generation in its own time, facing its contemporary crises, has as much fear as it can handle and more problems than were ever solved.

So I don't write you now as boney Isaiah or a crotchety Jeremiah, warning of the judgments of God that will fall like fire from heaven upon a wicked, adulterous generation. But I do wonder how you, as decent, sometimes Christian, men will behave in a world of despondent popes and presidents who fail to bind up our wounds as a nation. Have there been special insights given you and a special strength communicated, in your Notre Dame education, in virtue of which you can contribute to the redemption of age? Are you about to become the victims of the world, or its saviors? Or are you as resistant to being messiahs as you are to becoming slaves? Will you save your own souls while others all around you are losing theirs? Will your moral victories be personal, or local, or cosmic? In the battles of Armageddon, will you make a private armistice with terms for your private security? Or will you plant the peace gardens of the Lord in a time of war, like vinedressers who invite the poor to the abundance of their table?

The questions I ask of you represent the traditional reflections that are annually gathered into messages to be delivered at commencement time. I suppose that every graduation class that has ever marched to the drumbeat of "Pomp and Circumstance" has been asked, in one way or another, whether they will light one candle, or curse the darkness. But now I have been asked to say whether I think you, the Class of '73, will be candlebearers in the long, dark night of the world.

Of course as a class, you are not going to do much of anything together except pay dues, and gather for reunions, and drink beer on the quads on lovely June afternoons. But as persons, anyone of you could become Schweitzer or Tom Dooley, Dr. Salk or Bobby Kennedy, Einstein, Daniel Berrigan, or Martin Luther King. Or on the other side of the angels, you could suffer the moral tragedy of a Lt. Calley, or you could grow shabby in politics in the shadow of the White House.

Let me say now that there are members of this Class of '73 whom I know personally—and there are many, perhaps the majority, whom I don't know at all—who are among the best and brightest souls that earth has seen. They give every evidence that they have fallen in love with God, or with humanity, which is sometimes all we can see of God when Omnipotence plays his game of divine masquerades. They have put their energies on the line in the places where children suffer, or adults weep. They have worked as undergraduates at Logan Center or the Children's Hospital. They will work during the summer in the ghettos of the city, or with CILA [Council for the International Lay Apostolate, a student missionary and service group]. Next year, they will go on duty with VISTA or the Peace Corps.

"Narrow-minded priest," you are perhaps saying to yourselves, "who praises first his friends with their religious and philanthropic commitments, as though it were the wound-healers of your own persuasion who are the first sons of heaven."

In honesty, I am delighted by people, especially when they are Notre Dame students, who speak, by the idioms of their actions, with the accents of Christ. But I say to you, as I say to them, be loyal to the truth you have recognized, whether its source be in Buddha, or Jesus, or the songbook of the Campfire girls. What do I hope for or ask of the Class of '73? Why only this: that using your private sources of grace, you establish absolutes of decency, gentleness, and service; and then that you live as witnesses of the truths you could die for.

In the past four years, I have talked with many of you about God. You admired Jesus, you said. You weren't exactly sure whose Son he was, but that didn't really matter. The dogmas of the church you dismissed as the metaphysical conundrums of the clergy. Your most enduring memory of the church was that of having your hair pulled by a neurotic nun with hang-ups on the Baltimore Catechism. You weren't going to send your own children to the Catholic schools, you said; you would let them grow up and choose their own religion. But you believed Jesus when he preached the doctrine of love, and love was what your religion was all about. You really believed in love, you said; and as long as you were honest, and tried to love everybody, that was as much religion as God could expect of you. Often, you said, perhaps even once or twice a week, you went to Communion, though there were months when you didn't go to Mass at all. But you felt you belonged at the Supper of the Lord, because he said to love everybody and you tried to love everybody; love, taught by him, practiced by you, was the force that bound your lives together.

Others of you said that you had given up Christ altogether; but you also believed in love, you said. Love was the highest principle any man could live by; and its practice gave integrity to the rest of your life.

I also believe in the doctrine of love, though in my faith God taught us the disciplines of love by shaping his body to the wood of the cross, and dying. I hope that you understand that love is more than a glow of fellowship and wine after a dinner with Poopsie, or taking little orphans for walks, or eating dinner with the Pullman car porter at separate tables in the Elks' Club. If you love your wife, love could mean that you live for years as a celibate, if her mental or physical condition demands it. If you love your children, you may spend the best years of your life drinking beer instead of Scotch, as your own father did, to pay for the cost of their education. If you love your friend, you will be loyal when the hate mob turns against him; and after the hanging, you may inherit the care of his widow and children as your own responsibility. If you love your enemy, he may consider you a fool, and your only reward may be the sound of his laughter.

But if you believe in love and make it your religion, it is in these services to mankind that your fidelities lie; and independent of your commitments to the Trinity, you will be recognized as a disciple of the Lord, whatever your self-labels of agnostic. That kind of discipleship is what I hope for and expect of you, if you say you believe in the gospel of love. With or without a reliance on Jesus, you will often fail, just as the priests and bishops, and the brothers and sisters of the church fail daily, but the Lord measures growth by the depth of our trying.

During the past four years, some of you made a religion of the ways of gentleness. You read Gandhi and Merton, Thoreau and Berrigan. With or without a Christian reference, you have admired pacifism, and opted for the nonviolent approach; and if you have liked Jesus, it is because you have seen in him a paradigm of the peacemaker who will inherit the earth. In the name of peace, you have dragooned archbishops into saying Mass for you, you have marched on Washington, you have campaigned for presidents. Now, when the draft has ended, and you are no longer threatened by the local board, is it vulgar of me to remind you that there is still fighting in Southeast Asia, and that there are conflicts in the Middle East, and that our nation is still building weapons that may incinerate infants as they sleep?

Do you really believe now in peace, or was that mostly a group activity, reserved for youth's exuberance, when kids burned their draft cards, to the twanging of guitars, in the presence of the mosaic of Christ of the library? If the bombs start falling one day real soon, will you demand of your employers at Price Waterhouse that they give you two days off with pay from your $20,000-a-year job for a peace moratorium, so that you can picket the White House in your Brooks Brothers' suit?

Do you still wear the peace symbol on your T-shirt, even when you play golf at the country club with the military-industrial complex? Or do you make the peace symbol on the walls of the executive washroom of the company where you work, as you once did with paint on the religious statues at Notre Dame?

I ask these questions not to sneer at the past, but to remind you there was a past when some of the members of your class and generation went into exile or jail; and to insist that in the crusade for peace, this is not yet the time for a passionate neutrality on your part.

One custom of your subculture that I have found most endearing is your sense of community in the ways you have of gathering together and belonging, for a time, to each other. At the center of the gathering is always an event, a person, a beach, a cause, a bottle of wine, a pot of coffee, a keg of beer, a guitar, or a cigarette I care not to think about. I have seen you gathered in my room. I have heard of your immense gatherings at Woodstock and the Washington Monument. I have visited a few communes off campus. In my preachy way, I would remind you that the home and the church are two of the most important communities ever established. It is essential for Christians, as people who love each other, to gather at times like a family, to share in the symbolic events of the redemption, when the Lord himself is pledged to be attentive, with gifts in bread and wine, to the hunger of our loneliness and to the thirst needing the greetings of love. Not all of our worship can be conducted when we are alone in places known only to stars, not if our homage is to the God of the people who arranged for his own best sacrament to be a celebration in togetherness of the life of the Vine and the branches.

These, then, are some of the things I expect from you as the Class of '73: love, community, sacrifice, peace.

For a long time now, my graduating friends, I have looked into your faces and seen there the beauty of Christ. I suspect that thirty years ago, some priest looked upon the face of my generation, and he felt that Christ had looked back at him in the beauty of youth. I think that as children are born and grow to manhood, Christ pays a visit to every generation. He comes as the Messiah, offering the gifts of salvation.

Reflect on the following story:

One day a young fugitive, trying to hide himself from the enemy, entered a small village. The people were kind to him and offered him a place to stay. But when the soldiers who sought the fugitive asked them where he was hiding, everyone became very fearful. The soldiers threatened to burn the village and kill every man in it unless the young man was handed over to them before dawn. The people went to the minister and asked him what to do. The minister torn between handing over the boy to the enemy or having his people killed, withdrew to his room and read his Bible, hoping to find an answer before dawn. After many hours, in the early morning, his eyes fell on these words: "It is better that one man dies than that the whole people be lost."

Then the minister closed the Bible, called the soldiers and told them where the boy was hidden. And after the soldiers led the fugitive away to be killed, there was a feast in the village because the minister had saved the lives of the people. But the minister did not celebrate. Overcome with a deep sadness, he remained in his room. That night an angel came to him and asked, "What have you done?" He said: "I have handed over the fugitive to the enemy." Then the angel said, "But don't you know you have handed over the Messiah?" "How could I know?" the minister replied anxiously. Then the angel said, "If instead of reading your Bible, you had visited this young man just once and looked into his eyes, you would have known." (From *The Wounded Healer*, by Henry J. M. Nouwen, published by Doubleday).

I think that each of you alone is like that minister reading his Bible. I think if each of you could take a long moment and look with love into the eyes of your brothers, you could recognize the Messiah whom the world in its ignorance would sacrifice.

A group of men with the zeal of the apostles—sixteen hundred of them—recognizing their strength in brotherhood, moving against the world to present the Messiah's gifts: love, community, sacrifice, peace.

It is a possibility which could be reality for you, O Class of '73 . . . except that, already, the gifts have begun to slip from your hands.

But Darby and I never said we didn't love you.

AN EVERLASTING MORNING

Close to the gray, jutting rock of the Maine Coast, in a grave that the sea mist loves to touch, my father sleeps in a plot of earth he shares with his father, his mother, and his infant son. In other parts of the cemetery, the brothers and cousins of my father are also at rest with parents, and sometimes infant children, of their own. In life, most of the men and women of my family buried there made their living from the sea. Now, in death, they wait on the shore for the winds and tides of eternity and the clear skies of an everlasting morning. Then, at the burst of trumpets, their journey will begin on unchartered seas, and the captain keeping the watch will be the Lord God Almighty.

Tonight I sat in the basement room of a 42nd street rectory in Manhattan, and listened while a young man told me (as other young men and women have often told me in recent years) that he wanted to die. In March of this year, he said, he had gotten out of prison after serving a three and a half year sentence. The crime as charged was an ugly one, for he had been arrested as a child molester. But things had not been as gross as his accusers claimed, he said. He had been a young soldier, alone in a far-off state; in his loneliness, he had hugged a little girl, and touched her in an intimate place. A lady had been watching, and two days later he was put in jail.

The incident need not be sentimentalized, for the young man had a history of sexual misconduct. At night, he said, he regularly looked into bedroom windows in search of excitement. Often, in the daytime, he rode the subway in the rush hour when it was impossible for bodies not to be crushed against one another.

Now, in an agony of self-loathing for a sexuality he couldn't control, the young man wanted to die. As I listened, I knew that some evening, he would attempt dying; and perhaps, if he were unlucky, the sleeping pills would be strong enough, the razor blade would be sharp enough to perform its mischief, and a father and mother would be left to mourn the loss of a child they never knew how to help.

It is now nearly thirty years since my father's soul drifted away on the dark waters that carry the cargos of life into the snug harbors of God. But my father's death still seems like a rude, unnecessary intrusion by powers that have promised to temper the wind to the shorn lamb. My father was only fifty-four when he died, and I was a boy of eighteen. I needed my father, and my brother and sister needed him, and my mother was left with duties that drained her of her strength. For more than a year before my father's death, he and I had been bitterly quarreling, and it seemed unkind of God to reclaim him before I could say I was sorry.

It always moves me to think of my father asleep with his little boy, my brother, beside him. In heaven, it seems, my father has found a son who can say, "I love you," which is an affection I refused to express to him for many months before he died so unexpectedly during my first semester away at college.

On another evening in Manhattan, I sat outside on the rectory steps and talked to a male prostitute whose wrists were bandaged with gauze. For eight years, he had been hustling on 42nd Street, he said. But for the past nine months, he had been sick, and he was living in constant pain, and doctors and operations had not been able to help. In eight years of hustling, he said, he had turned more than six thousand tricks, not counting the regular customers he had lived with. Out of all that trade, he said, there was not a single person he could telephone on a night when he was suffering, and ask for help. "It's not fair," he said. "All of *them* have families—their mothers, their wives, their children—they can go home to." He had no one to go home to, he said. Now he was broke, and growing old, and his body was too damaged and full of pain to be of use to him. So in despair, he had done tricks on his wrists with a razor blade. At the age of twenty-five, all he now asked from life was to die, and he had been denied even that. But one day soon, he said, he would try again, and this time he would not be denied.

Often I think of my father on those nights when I listen to the sad, shabby stories of the street people of Manhattan or to those other sad stories, mostly without the shabbiness, of the girls and chaps at Notre Dame who seem so much in love with easeful death. It is their despair, their loss of hope that frightens me, as though in the face of the absurd, the player has the right to quit the game, thereby denying life's abilities to correct its own mistakes in a redemption that leads to heaven.

I remember the final moments of my father's funeral, when our good-byes as a family were made to him. My mother leaned down to kiss a much-loved cheek.

"Good night, Jerry," she said.

It was a caress between lovers, separated by sleep, who will wake in the morning to the singing of birds. I suspect that for people who have known bluebirds and loved robins, heaven will always have the promise of the singing of birds. Why else would we need a resurrection, if it were not to continue with the unfinished business of life? I know nothing of heaven (except bluebirds), and might be tempted to skip it, except I know I shall see my father there, and my friends who died in the war, and a little girl named Alice who died at the age of nine from leukemia. I have loved these people too much for there not to be unfinished business between us. I know very little of God except what I have learned of him through people. I might be terribly afraid of God's holiness if I had not seen it first in the beauty of a child's face, or remembered how it looked when I brought cups of cold water to people who were thirsty or in prison. That is why I think that the earth we know and the heaven we dream of touch one another; and the touching point begins in the unfinished business of life.

I have many memories of death as a Manhattan experience: the time, for example, when the police came at five o'clock in the morning to lead me up the dark stairways of a tenement house into a shabby room, to anoint a body which was three hours dead. An old man in need of a shower lay naked on the floor, and the flies crawled over him as though he were garbage left in a dump. As I was anointing his hands and feet, an alarm clock rang, ignorant of its inability to awaken the dead. I left the room alone, embarrassed at having seen the dirt and flies on an old man's nakedness. I guess all of us would die with dignity, if we could arrange it. Death asks no appointments; and unlike clocks, it keeps no man's schedule.

There was another night when I was led by a policeman to the home of a woman who had been suffering for years with cancer. The battle against illness had been long and difficult. There were dark purple scars on her arms and face, and all her woman's beauty had been starved by sickness into skin and bones. But there was a crucifix over her bed, and a rosary on the pillow; and it seemed reasonable to hope that her surrender in death was not to darkness, but to Jesus.

The surprise to me in recent years has been the number of young people who seek death as a surrender to a darkness without ending. Theirs could be the ultimate sin, which not even the Holy Spirit has the power to forgive. Maybe our capacities for life are like the energies hidden in a seed. We, like seeds, may not appear to look like very much, and even the dirt may be prettier. But under the gentle washing of a summer rain and a touch of sunlight on August afternoons, seeds become chrysanthemums blooming as the chief glory of the autumn garden. Chrysanthemums, if they could, would be us, who are intended to bloom as God's children, and the energies of our souls are from God, and our sunshine and rain are his grace.

But even God cannot force life upon us, either on earth or in heaven, if we choose darkness instead of the light.

To all the sad young men on 42nd Street . . . to all the men and women at Notre Dame who talk wistfully of their need to die . . . Christ spoke these words: "I come that you may have life, and that you may have it more abundantly." The life he was speaking of is already here. The eternity which seems to come like an interruption to life has, for us, already begun.

This is our faith: if we are presently alive in God, and are responsive to love when given or love as gift . . . if we can (or want to) find God in sacraments and/or rosebuds . . . if we can make sacraments out of coffee breaks, or find Christ in the eyes of the boss . . . if we can do some of these things, or all of them, or make private lists of our own of the symptoms of immortality . . . then we march in the company of saints who live by the heartbeat of Christ.

But if we are not alive in God, but merely dead, nothing less than a resurrection can force eternity upon us . . . and resurrection can be arranged only with the prior consent of the corpse.

By ordination, I am committed to the care of gardens where the grapes have tender vines. That is why, like other Christians, I am constantly aware of the dark shadows where death waits like a mugger to strike down all things that breathe. But I write these words to you neither as a philosopher nor as a theologian. I am writing as a human being who has been asked once again to say what he feels about death as a mystery he has sometimes dealt with.

Sometimes at night in the dorms of Notre Dame, when death seems to beckon students in the direction of graveyards, I see him as an enemy whom I fear very much, and I am grateful I do not face him alone and without power. When I see him on 42nd Street, I judge him to be a fool with lessons to learn; for on 42nd Street, I suspect, all the ultimate victories belong to Christ, who was always concerned about the loss of his sheep. When I see death visiting the sickbeds, I look him in the eye and sometimes find that he is a friendly jailor unlocking doors.

And for nearly thirty years, I have resented him as a bully who took away my father too soon. By faith, I know I shall see my father again, and it is death that will lead me to him. Then, I think, I will neither fear death nor hate him . . . for in the brightness beyond shadows, in the light beyond the dark, I will understand that there is no death . . . there are only pathways, seaward and landward, that bring me to the infinite shore where all my fathers are waiting.

CHRISTMAS ON 42ND STREET

The world at Eighth Avenue and 42nd Street is quite remote from the villages dreamed of in the ballads of the white Christmas. Often the carols of redemption are heard there playing on someone's transistor or picked up by a car radio, or as tunes offered to the neighborhood in the seasonal drumbeats and trumpets of the Salvation Army. But that intersection is a grim and busy place; and after the working day is over, the traffic to and from the skin flicks, the massage parlors, and the porno shops is very heavy.

Then the street scenes seem etched in gray, edged in black and framed for death.

On one corner, there is a Childs' restaurant; almost next to it, there is a sign advertising a blood bank where a donor is offered money for his sale of blood. It is an open invitation to exchange blood for the price of booze, though it seems there could be no health, no healing in the blood offered for sale by the winos and addicts of 42nd Street.

Sometimes, on the sidewalk outside Childs', a street preacher will proclaim redemption to sinners whom the Lamb's blood has washed; but in these sad neighborhoods, even God's Son seems powerless to offer the transfusions of grace from which our immortal hopes are sprung, and the crimson sufferings on the Cross seem no more efficacious for life than do the commercial transactions taking place at the blood shop next to Childs'.

Truly, the world at Eighth Avenue and 42nd Street is quite remote from the villages dreamed of in the ballads of the white Christmas. In its intense commitment to the World Made Flesh, 42nd Street is quite impervious to the holiday mood celebrating the birthday of the Word Made Flesh in Bethlehem.

I am spending Christmas this year, as I did last year, and as I spent a month this summer, at Eighth Avenue and 42nd Street serving as a priest at Holy Cross Church, located near the infamous corner just one block west of Times Square. If you ask me why I go there, I will tell you: there are children there representing everyone's hope for innocence; there are old people in love with Christ; there are working people who come into the parish daily from elsewhere; there are men and women who live there as parishioners, raising families, struggling to be decent, loving God faintly or as fervently (like the rest of us) as their sufferings and joys permit.

Only on the surface is 42nd Street a jungle, though I may appear a fool to say it.

Behind every switchblade, there is a human being. Behind every street mask of pimp and prostitute, there is a face that tells its own story of the need for being loved. Under the debris and decay of every life, there is a human innocence to be restored. There is a Shepherd searching for every lamb that strays, and some of us who are hirelings will find our own salvation only in the company of other sheep led back to the fold.

My room in Holy Cross Rectory will be a basement room with barred windows that look up at the street. When I leave the venetian blinds up, it is invitingly convenient for panhandlers. They can come up, knock on the window, and arrange (if they are lucky) for carfare to all the mercy joints—Salvation Army in Paramus, the welfare office in White Plains, St. Christopher's Inn at Graymoor—where, they will claim, work and a fresh chance await them. On any given evening, all that ever stands between the skid-row types and their immediate rehabilitation is the priest's willingness or ability (I must, by now, have turned down half the undesirables in the Times Square area) to pay the transportation to hobo havens that cost much money to reach. "It's only three-fifty to

Graymoor, Father; I'll send it back as soon I'm working." Priests have died in abject poverty, waiting for those checks that were never mailed by winos who were never reformed.

I once thought of opening up a walk-in confessional at that basement rectory window. I would merely have to announce the hours when confessions would be heard; then I would sit there and wait for the street penitents to come out of the skin flicks. They would scarcely have to interrupt their walk to the subway before they found a penance tossed at them and an absolution delivered. In the end I didn't do it. I thought it might seem tasteless to the Cardinal Archbishop of the city if he should hear of all those errant Catholics whispering their sins into a rectory window. Still, at a parish church like Holy Cross, the search for relevance must go on.

The rectory above the basement stairs is an old-fashioned type of house, nearly a hundred years old. It is the kind of place where Bing Crosby as Father O'Malley might have served Irish coffee to Barry Fitzgerald, while the Dead End Kids hummed Ave Maria as a background. The dark wood paneling of the dining room and the huge china closet shelving the monogrammed crystal and dinnerware of a departed monsignor reflect an elegance and affluence now vanished from the life of this very poor parish.

The central decoration of the dining room is a painting, notable for its shades of red, showing Cardinal Spellman kneeling before the pope, upon the occasion of Spellman's receiving the red hat of the cardinalate. Also pictured, as a principal witness at this investiture, is the same monsignor whose monogram is emblazoned on the dishes. Every morning at breakfast I will be offended by the painting, seen on an empty stomach, with its sycophantic overtones and its depiction of the smug intimacy existing among priest, prelate, pope, and God. One fears the simple arrogance of office of those so highly placed in the power structure as to play about at the papal feet. The papal court has never been healthy for American churchmen struggling for humility. Monsignors searching for virtue would do better to pitch horseshoes with representatives from the Longshoremen's Union.

My rectory duties at Holy Cross will consist mostly in periodic marches to the front parlor where various indigents, for a variety of reasons, will be on the search for money. It will nearly always be the same story: an epic of innocent travelers newly arrived in the city, who had their pockets picked in the subway; or else they were rolled in the streets, or perhaps betrayed by prostitutes with whom they had spent the night. Some will arrive with gaping holes in their clothing where their jacket or trouser pockets have been slashed open with a knife, so they will say, while they were slumbering at the movies. None of them will have identification or phone numbers of relatives with whom their identities can be checked. Their needs will be piteous, and every welfare station in town will be disinterested in them, closed, or out of business.

Only the priests can help them; but all the other priests, out of meanness, have refused them, and their only hope is in your Christian kindness. Otherwise, when they leave the rectory, they will die in the streets.

Sometimes, out of pity, you will give them the last dollar you own in the world, for it is not easy to see a grown man cry. Only afterwards will you wonder: Where did this destitute and starving derelict get the money to buy the cigarettes he was smoking? Destitute and starving derelicts can't afford cigarettes in New York City, not at sixty cents a pack. Now it is your turn to cry, because this Marlborough man has your last dollar and you're almost as destitute as he claimed to be.

By now, it should be clear to you that, at Holy Cross, the cry for money is more often heard than the cry for salvation. Poverty is the nagging, daily problem of the pastor trying to finance a church, a rectory, and a grade school attended mostly by children from outside the parish. Poverty is the problem of the parishioners to whom the pastor might appeal for money. Many of the younger families have moved out of the parish, and only the old people are left. They live on small, fixed incomes which are mostly paid by the city or the state. Finally, poverty is the problem of the crushed and needy who ring the doorbell of the rectory with legitimate needs which truly should be met in no other place.

Despite the suggestions of the chancery, bingo cannot save the church, not in a parish of old people who have neither the money to spend on games nor the inclination to venture out into the viciousness of a New York night where they could get mugged for the very turkey they have just won as a door prize.

I make such a big point of the appeal to the priest for money, because in a parish like Holy Cross, such appeals, uninterruptedly made, can create a vocational crisis. The priest constantly feels the irrelevancy of his vocation in a neighborhood where he could, he feels, make a bigger impact as an altruistic banker than as a dispenser of Christ's mercies or as a witness to eternal mysteries. It becomes a serious problem for a priest, making him feel psychologically shabby, when he is everlastingly harassed for money he does not have, especially when the askers are professional beggars who make their living moving from one rectory to another with stories that, if true, would break a priest's heart. The problem is knowing which tales of grief are true, and which are not.

The street population in New York seems to assume that in every rectory, there is a great pot of gold, the church's treasury, stocked with inexhaustible funds. All a priest has to do is reach his hand into that pot, and he has the price of meals, hotel rooms, plane tickets, bus fares, and Brooks Brothers' suits available to any Catholic in the state of grace.

The trick is, of course, if you're begging, to authentically appear as a Catholic in the state of grace. So winos come in clutching rosaries; atheists appear, asking to be invested with the scapular; pimps drop by, wanting to renew their baptismal vows in an obvious passion for restored innocence. The most fervent confession, whether in the church or at the rectory, can turn out as the first step on the way to a touch. Last Christmas morning, at an early Mass, a panhandler interrupted me, with hosts in my hand, on my way back to the tabernacle. He asked me for the train fare to Scarsdale. It wasn't enough, at that point, that he had just gone to Communion; the gift from the Lord that he really wanted was money.

Balance all such demands against the limited funds of a priest who needs to know that his few dollars given in charity are received by a sick husband out of work, or a grandmother suffering from malnutrition, and not by a professional solicitor for whom begging has become a game or a way of life. Because the mythical pot of gold, the church's treasury, is assumed to exist, no priest is ever credited as being generous enough to have exhausted his personal resources through trips to the rectory door. There is often the hint that the Father could be bigger-hearted with his alms, if he really wanted to.

I remember an old man, last year, to whom I had given my last two dollars because he said he needed food. He sat there before me, money in hand, making noises that said he had expected a deeper dip into the till. In a sudden fit of anger born out of a mood of hopelessness, I tried to snatch the money back, to keep it for myself. My fingers never stood a chance. The man, thinking I had gone crazy, was out of the chair, out of the door in an instant. His last words were, "You priests sure have bad dispositions."

A question that must be asked is: Why do these ghost parishes continue to exist? The large parish plants, once useful before the parking lots replaced the tenements, are expensive to maintain, and they do nothing to reform the moral tone of the neighborhood. One feels that if Jesus Christ is going to renew the human shabbiness of 42nd Street, he is not going to do it through priests used up in a ministry of almsgiving, and the place where the sinners will be gathered should be more personal than the marble auditoriums built for the worshipping crowds of the Catholic Church's ghetto years. That is why each time I offer Mass at Holy Cross this Christmas, before a congregation hardly bigger than the cluster of Apostles who first gathered for Eucharist in an upper room, I will dream of a storefront church, located on the corner between Childs' restaurant and the blood bank, where the priest can be as much in competition for the souls of men as are the porno shops and dirty-movie houses.

Storefront church or not, this once wonderful parish is dying. One day soon, the last little old lady is going to light the final candle before the Virgin's statue. The last old man is going to bless himself with holy water as he finishes the visit made on the way home from work. Then there will be the darkness of a building closed, the sadness of a sanctuary lamp extinguished, and the present structure of the parish will be dead.

At Christmas I must remember that Holy Cross Church is not my work, but Christ's. One of the first lessons of Christmas is that God is born at midnight in the heart of darkness. Even on 42nd Street, the Lord will prefer to light one candle than to curse the darkness.

It was Walter Winchell who wrote the epitaph for the showgirls who never made it big on the Great White Way stretching from 42nd Street to Paradise. "For every bright light on Broadway," Winchell wrote, "there are a million broken hearts." I wish Winchell could have met

Edna Thayer. He might have forgiven Broadway all those bright lights, all those broken hearts.

Last year, Edna was just another broken-down hoofer who attended daily Mass. One day she came into the rectory during the 12:15, pale and trembling with chills. She thought she was dying. We wrapped her in a blanket, and I held her in my arms while the housekeeper called the ambulance.

Edna didn't want the ambulance, "I don't have enough money for food," she said. "I can't afford no ambulance." Eventually, we found out that Edna's most serious illness was hunger. After that, the word was out: keep an eye on Edna.

Last August, when I returned to the city, Edna was the toast of Broadway. Three nights a week, she sings for her meals at the Times Square Automat, the star of Horn and Hardat's. At age sixty-five, in the first stages of Parkinson's disease, Edna belts out the tunes like Merman, and the crowds love her. She's been written up in the *Times*, and she's made an appearance on the Cavett show. At five-foot-two, weighing 165 pounds, Edna, that round, little dumpling of a woman with golden hair and Kewpie-doll face, is no pinup girl, and her voice in the lower registers sounds like Durante. But when she walks up Broadway these days, Edna owns the street.

Then there is Forty-second Street Joe. I met Joe last year, just after he had had an operation for throat cancer. An ex-wino, Joe was killing himself with cigarettes. I would see him at night in Childs', chain-smoking and gagging on the phlegm, with a plate of mashed potatoes and gravy in front of him, and a pile of napkins he could spit into. When I left New York last Christmas, Joe's weight was down to eighty-five pounds, but he still preferred cigarettes to food. When I returned to New York in August, he was dead. Joe was a sad little man, divorced from his wife, separated from his kids, and, in the end, he starved himself to death. The beauty of his life was to see how the winos loved him. They watched over him in the street at night, and they kept him alive with coffee. On the day Joe was buried, every wino on the block kept sober until after the funeral. The winos put him to rest at Gate of Heaven cemetery in a $1200 casket, and God alone knows where those derelicts got the money. It certainly wasn't from the priests at Holy Cross rectory.

Stanley was one of Joe's best friends; they had been classmates together at Bellevue. Stanley began drinking at the age of fourteen. He did the drug scene and hustled for trade on 42nd Street. At nineteen, he went for three years to Bellevue. Stanley knows every sad story 42nd Street has to tell, for he has lived them all. Only, he says, "I never murdered anybody."

Today, at thirty-seven, Stanley, the Augustine of Eighth Avenue, is the most cheerful man in New York, and he preaches cheerfulness to everybody. In the morning, he cheers up the curates at the church where he works as a custodian; at noonday, he cheers up the pastor; in the evening, he cheers up the housekeeper, whom he secretly hopes to marry.

On Saturday night, he dresses up like an alderman and goes over to Roseland Dance City, walking as though on broken glass because his feet suffer from bunions.

"Stanley," I say to him, "how do you dance on those sore feet?"

"For everybody else," he says, "it's a dance. For me, it's a concert."

I smile knowingly. I know something about the concerts in New York, especially the summer concerts, where the symphony of the city is played.

I once knew an old lady, faded in beauty and down on her luck. She was shabby and toothless; her shoes were run over at the heels, and she walked with a shuffle, though she had once been a dancer. There were old men who loved this lady, because they remembered her as she had been when she was young. Instead of the wrinkles and sunken face, they recalled dimpled cheeks, rounded into loveliness. Instead of white, straggly hair, they thought of sunlight playing in and out of golden hideaways.

Holy Cross Church is like that old lady and still desirable for her departed glories. This church was once the parish of the Fighting Father Duffy, whose statue now stands in Times Square. This was the church of Monsignor McCaffrey, called *honoris causa* the Bishop of Times Square, who during the years of World War II brought over twenty-five thousand people a week into the church to pray for the servicemen at the weekly novenas. The mayor of New York used to come to the rectory for dinner, to eat off the McCaffrey monograms in the dining room. The rectory is shabby now, and the church is chintzy with forms of piety now out of date—the Infant of Prague honored as the Christmas Child comes to mind. But for the old people, it is their spiritual home. It is the Lord's house, the sanctuary of the Eucharist in the land of Sodom. Many of them made their first Communion here as children; it is the place from which the priest will one day bring them Viaticum.

At Christmastime, I will be with those old people, saying Mass in a sanctuary full of poinsettias, struggling to help them believe the story of God's love revealed in the birth of an Infant. It was not always easy— for them or me—to believe in God on the corner of Eighth Avenue and 42nd Street.

Sometimes, it is not easy to believe in God in any neighborhood, when all the world looks like Eighth Avenue, and all roads seem headed toward 42nd Street. That is why there must always be churches that survive to remind us of Bethlehem in the places remote from the villages dreamed of in the ballads of a white Christmas, so that the birthdays of God may be celebrated, the candle lit by Christ in the heart of darkness.

In the symphony of the city, new movements are being written every moment. I pray that I will find music in the street sounds of 42nd Street this Christmas. I hope it sounds a lot like the carols of redemption.

ABOUT FRIENDSHIP

"I am looking for friends," said the little prince. *"What does that mean—'tame'?"*

"It is an act too often neglected," said the fox. *"It means to establish ties."*

"'To establish ties'?"

"Just that," said the fox. *"To me you are still nothing more than a little boy who is just like a hundred thousand other little boys. And I have no need of you. And you, on your part, have no need of me. To you, I am nothing more than a fox like a hundred thousand other foxes. But if you tame me, then we shall need each other. To me, you will be unique in all the world. To you, I shall be unique in all the world. . . ."*

(from *The Little Prince*)

Jamie Quinn is the son of two dear friends of mine, Judy and Charlie Quinn, and the youngest of three children. I became aware of Jamie's existence about two months after his conception, before we even knew he was a Jamie. Judy called up one morning to announce: "Hey, guess what? I'm pregnant." For the next eight months, at candle-lit dinners and in conversations before the blazing logs of the Quinn fireplace, the three of us, Judy, Charlie, and I, would be thinking of the little life being shaped for birth; and as in religion, we blessed mysteries we could not understand and were silent before them. For ten months, so it seemed, we awaited childbirth, for Jamie was not one bit considerate in observing timetables set by doctors. For ten months, or even eleven, I looked forward to the news of delivery. Finally, weeks after I had written off the stork as shiftless, Charlie called up to say: "It's a boy."

The priest who baptizes an infant gets off to a very bad start with the child. For years afterwards, the baby associates the priest with the indignity of having water splashed on its head . . . and in church, of all places; how chintzy can the guy with the turned-around collar get? Friendships have to begin more gently than that. There had to be a faux pas like that, I said to myself, to explain Jamie's resentment toward me, because the kid's attitude was a distinct disappointment. Here I had been waiting all these months for him to be born. Afterwards, I had drunk vintage wine in his honor. I had made telephone calls 'round the countryside announcing the happiness of there being a new Quinn. Yet Jamie would not tolerate my holding him for more than a minute. I would take him in my arms; and just as soon as he found out the tweeds weren't Daddy's, or the shaving lotion wasn't his mother's Chanel, his mouth would pucker, his eyes fill up, his face turn red; and if I didn't instantly deliver him into less alien auspices, he was very apt to spit up all over the clerical black. As a new person to be cherished, James Quinn turned out to be a total flop; even his parents were embarrassed by his rudeness.

I would like to report that as Jamie reached the age when he was beginning to walk and talk that we became intimate friends. I would like to report it; but if I did report it, I would be speaking lies. At age one, he grudgingly endured any familiarities from me, like a hug or a kiss. Bedtime affections were exchanged between us only as the result of a direct command from his father or mother: "Give the priest a kiss," or "Show Father how much you love him." Even then he would not surrender his aloof cheek for more than a quarter of a second. Sometime I would swoop him up for a closer look; but he would squirm his way down again with his independence intact; and as a punishment for my impulsiveness, he would afterwards ignore me until I finally went home.

Gradually, however, I began to feel I was taming him, when he began to offer me cookies he had no use for, or to show me a toy that needed fixing. One day, he stood in front of me for three minutes, making faces of welcome; and the following Sunday, his father announced, Jamie made the discovery that the celebrant of Mass at the Urchins' Chapel and the fat man who came to his house to eat dinner were one and the same stranger.

Now that Jamie is two, the friendship between us still proceeds according to his agenda, for he is still learning to trust me. He doesn't want to be surprised into doing my thing, especially if it is kissy-face and affectionate. Restraint is a necessary discipline of any taming. But I think he has begun to recognize me as his friend, capable of comforting bruises or chasing lions, real or imaginary, out of his playroom. I have learned to be consistently gentle, attentive, patient, solemn, and serious before all the ways in which he is a child. It helps to make him laugh, if we can share the laughter, as long as it isn't tenderness he needs at the moment. To tell the truth, I am never sure about the laughter. I just have to wait and see if it is tolerated.

Now that Jamie has begun to accept me as a friend, the next question in my mind is: when will he become a friend to me? There is a point, with a child, when his cuteness is not enough, when patience with aloofness begins to wear thin, for an adult has his own need of being noticed. We can love children who are very distant; but our favorites— those we would like to keep—are the youngsters who can give love and accept love. I think to myself: Jamie must become aware of how he is affecting the guests who come to his house. When he begins to care how he is affecting them, he must do some taming of his own, if he decides there is a value in having friends.

I don't know what age Jamie will be when he formally decides—if he ever does decide, if not about me, then about some other uncle-type— "I want Griff to be my friend." But even now, I think I see some of that need of friendship in him. Every time he does a somersault at my feet, or throws a block into my lap, he is looking for my attention; and there are entire moments when he seems to be using all his gifts as a charmer to make me like him. I think: it has only taken two years, but it is really nice to have a friend like Jamie Quinn.

It must be obvious to any parent that I am just a bachelor, without training, who practices child-watching; and I'm writing of one small boy and of my expectations from him as a child I will watch growing up. I have always known it is not necessary to Jamie's happiness for him to love me, though I now think that he does, at least a little. But he must learn to love someone outside of the family that gives him his security if he is not going to grow up as a very lonely child.

Someday, I hope, Jamie as an older child is going to ask me about having a friend, or being a friend; then I will teach him of the need of taming.

"There is a certain little girl," he might say, "and I would like her to be my friend, but she doesn't notice me very much."

"Maybe she does, or maybe she doesn't," I reply as one thoroughly acquainted with the ways of little girls. "There is a certain corner of the eye that little girls watch a fellow from, so you can't tell if they're noticing, or not."

He sighs. "I would know if she were noticing," he says.

"Jamie," I say, "you've got to let her see that you are interested. You've got to show her by the things you do."

"Like bringing her peanut butter sandwiches, and stuff?" (Note the Charlie Brown influence on this scenario.)

"Peanut butter sandwiches, indiscriminately given, can cause a weight problem," I say, "and, later on, acne. Say: 'I'm Jamie Quinn, and I just want to say hello.'"

"'I'm Jamie Quinn, and I just want to say hello,'" he repeats.

"After a few days, you can stop telling her your name. After a few days, she will know that."

"She already knows," he says. "We're in the same class."

"Let her see how important it is for you to speak to her," I insist.

"She knows that," he says, "but sometimes when I speak to her, she gets embarrassed and looks as though she's going to cry."

"Maybe you're coming on too strong, Jamie."

"Oh, sure," he says. "She thinks I want to be her boyfriend. She thinks she's too young to have a boyfriend."

"How do you know?" I ask.

"My father told me," says Jamie. "He knows a lot about things like that."

"I thought you said she didn't pay much attention. I need the facts, Jamie, the facts."

"She doesn't speak to me," he says. "How much less attentive can she get?"

"Taming, Jamie," I say, and almost add, "as in the *Taming of the Shrew*"; but don't, because it seems unfair. "Taming," I say again as an instruction, meaning nothing more by the word than the slow educative process by which the heart and mind learn trust and faith, which are the companions to love. Sometimes such taming is a courtship; at other times it is a ministry, but it is always gentle, courteous, patient, and reticent.

"Some of the best taming is done by leaving the other person absolutely alone," I say. "Some living creatures want to be, need to be, shy; then you can't intrude. Friendship never frightens, or takes by surprise, or gets pushy in its demands for attention."

"Taming," Jamie says, "seems like very lonely work."

"It's especially lonely," I answer, "when you lose the game."

It is silly, perhaps, for a middle-aged man, if he is not Saint-Exupéry, to be writing about taming; but I have been asked to say what I might tell a child about friendship. I would like to tell him this.

"One only understands the things that one tames," said the fox. "Men have no more time to understand anything. They buy things already made at the shops. But there is no shop anywhere where you can buy friendship, and so men have no friends any more. If you want a friend, tame me. . . ."

When the child is old enough, or even before then, when he is too young to understand anything, I would like him to hear these words:

Love is patient; love is kind and envies no one. Love is never boastful, nor conceited, nor rude; never selfish, not quick to take offence. Love keeps no score of wrongs; does not gloat over other men's sins, but delights in the truth. There is nothing love cannot face; there is no limit to its faith, its hope, and its endurance.

Tamers can read, with profit, the words of St. Paul; if they are true about love, they are true about friendship.

Jamie Quinn, together with his brother, Charles, and his sister, Sarah, are children I love very much. Year after year, as I watch them grow up, there has been a constant mutual taming going on among us. I have watched Charlie and Judy being parents. Sometimes, in their family life, there is annoyance or anger on the parents' part at the naughtiness of a youngster in bad temper; corrections have to be made, and I wonder what I would have said or done if it had been my child. Then, I go home and read a favorite poem called "The Toys," by Coventry Patmore. The poem, while not saying everything, tells me as much about fatherhood as I need for now to know—the kind of knowing I would have to have if ever I were to teach a son or daughter anything about the ways of caring that God's love teaches us.

My little Son, who look'd from thoughtful eyes
And moved and spoke in quiet grown-up wise,
Having my law the seventh time disobey'd,
I struck him, and dismiss'd
With hard words and unkiss'd,
His mother, who was patient, being dead.
Then, fearing lest his grief should hinder sleep,
I visited his bed,
But found him slumbering deep,
With darken'd eyelids, and their lashes yet
From his late sobbing wet.
And I, with moan,
Kissing away his tears, left others of my own;
For, on a table drawn beside his head,
He had put, within his reach,
A box of counters and a red-vein'd stone,
A piece of glass abraded by the beach
And six or seven shells,
A bottle with bluebells,
And two French copper coins, ranged there with careful art,
To comfort his sad heart.
So when that night I pray'd
To God, I wept, and said:
Ah, when at last we lie with tranced breath,
Not vexing Thee in death,

And Thou rememberest of what toys
We made our joys,
How weakly understood,
Thy great commanded good,
Then, fatherly not less
Than I whom Thou hast moulded from the clay,
Thou'lt leave Thy wrath, and say,
"I will be sorry for their childishness."

I REMEMBER THE FIRE

Monday evening, I came back with friends from a dinner that celebrated my birthday. There was a note awaiting me that Bob Rieman had been killed in an accident a few hours earlier. "It's impossible," I thought to myself. "People like Bob have too much life in them to die." But friends began dropping by. The news was true, they said: Bob Rieman was dead from an accident. "Incidentally," they said, "Happy Birthday." There was a new kind of specialness to the date of October Seventh; now it belonged also to Bob, and I wished with all my heart that it had belonged only to me. I thought of Bob walking through the Keenan-Stanford lobby with the little blind girl he tutored, and of the sadness she would feel, and it was difficult to keep back the tears. At midnight the Club O'Gill (Chez Darby) opened for the first time. There was a graduate student there who had seen the accident. He had touched the body and felt the pulse die under his fingers. Now, hours after the death, he seemed to need the physical closeness of people, as though afraid to go home and be alone with his memory. A group of Bob's friends from the Innsbruck program were there also, huddling together and talking. One of them said: "I know you can't solve the mystery of why it should have happened, but would you mind trying?" Again it was difficult to hold back tears when I saw the grief of Bob's friends.

On Tuesday evening, at a memorial Mass for Bob, I used the story (from *The High King*) of how Fflewdurr the bard had splintered his harp into firewood on a bitter, stormy winter night to keep his friends from dying of cold and exposure. Miraculously the fire kindled from the ruins of the harp burned all through the night.

The flames had now spread to all the fragments, and as the harp strings blazed a melody sprang suddenly from the heart of the fire. Louder and more beautiful it grew and the strains of music filled the air, echoing endlessly among the crags. Dying, the harp seemed to be pouring forth all the songs ever played upon it, and the sound shimmered like the fire. All night the harp sang, and its melodies were of joy, sorrow, love, and valor. The fire never abated, and little by little new life and strength returned to the companions. And as the notes soared upward a wind from the south, parting the falling snow like a curtain, flooded the hills with warmth. Only at dawn did the flames sink into the glowing embers and the voice of the harp fall silent. . . . Of the harp nothing remained but a single string. . . . Fflewdurr knelt and drew it from the ashes. In the heat of the fire the harp string had twisted and coiled around itself, but it glittered like pure gold.

Our lives are like Fflewdurr's harp, I said. The heart has its tunes, the mind has its music. When mortal life has finished with us, these are the melodies of our song before God, played from a harp string of the purest gold. In the choruses of eternity, nothing that our animal minds have known of truth, or that our hearts have known as beauty, is ever lost. That is what I said, and I hope it is substantial enough for faith.

Afterwards, I was sorry I had not added lines from Housman's "To an Athlete Dying Young":

Smart lad, to slip betimes away
From fields where glory does not stay
And early though the laurel grows
It withers quicker than the rose.
[. . .]
Now you will not swell the rout
Of lads that wore their honours out,
Runners whom renown outran
And the name died before the man.

Close to the mind also were the insights of Masefield's "On Growing Old":

Be with me, Beauty, for the fire is dying;
My dog and I are old, too old for roving.
Man, whose young passion sets the spindrift flying,
Is soon too lame to march, too cold for loving.
I take the book and gather to the fire,
Turning old yellow leaves; minute by minute,
The clock ticks to my heart; a withered wire,
Moves a thin ghost of music in the spinet.
[. . .]
Only stay quiet while my mind remembers
The beauty of fire from the beauty of embers.

Beauty, have pity, for the strong have power,
The rich their wealth, the beautiful their grace,
Summer of man its sunlight and its flower.
Springtime of man, all April in a face.
[. . .]
So, from this glittering world with all its fashion,
Its fire, and play of men, its stir, its march,
Let me have wisdom, Beauty, wisdom and passion,
Bread to the soul, rain where the summers parch.
Give me but these, and though the darkness close
Even the night will blossom as the rose.

To be taken at noon from the business of life into the high ecstasies of heaven, with its possibilities of passion, can be a tragedy only in the eyes of the beholder. To think that life must have its fourscore and ten years is to forget that God may need a life still in the beauty of its fire rather than the beauty of its embers.

With thought based on reflections such as these, I avoided quarrels over Bob Rieman's death with the Father of beauty who shatters a life as easily as Fflewdurr splintered his marvelous harp, confident of the fire and music that the instrument can sustain. One of Bob's friends said to me: "Your words help a little bit in speaking of Bob. But what about the others who die in innocence, who never achieve his passion for life?" Thoreau, on his deathbed, was asked if he was prepared for the next world. He said: "One world at a time." I, asked about the terms of being reconciled with heaven over the death of the young, can only reply: "One death at a time. That is all the heart can deal with." As other deaths come, knowing the details of the summoning, I can try to be reconciled; but then, as now, I must insist, one death at a time, please, God.

Bob was so alive, so curious, so anxious to experience, that at times it required patience to deal with him. He was a difficult chap to meet at breakfast, if you merely wanted to doze over the early cups of coffee. But I loved him because he was good and eager, bright and kind, thoughtful and gracious, inspiring and encouraging, gentle and beautiful. Now, after three days, when I realize that an only half-awakened man will never again meet the breakfast table cheerfulness of the inquisitive lad, it is once again difficult to hold back the tears.

But nothing is ever lost—never! Not the least drop of ocean, the humblest speck of dust. The tulip bulb is ugly in winter, but April confirms it in glory. The grain of wheat falls into the earth and dies, but its death brings forth new life. If the earth is so careful of its beauty, are there no cherished futures for the sons of heaven whose lives are like the songs and poetry our best hopes are made of?

Bob Rieman, your silence at this moment does not frighten me of death. I remember the beauty of fire. That beauty, whose loss I mourn at your funeral, is the best promise you could have given that immortality has overtaken you.

ON ANCIENT RITUALS AND
MODERN YOUTH

One evening last semester, I made arrangements to deliver a manuscript to one of our young campus leaders named Tom before or after the 11 p.m. Mass in Farley. Tom came into the chapel after the Mass had started, sometime around the Gospel; at Communion time, he received the Eucharist with the rest of the group. Immediately after the liturgy was completed, he came into the sacristy to see me.

"The Mass was very moving," he said. "I'm always deeply stirred by the Mass. Its age and tradition make it a very special form of worship."

I was pleased by his enthusiasm because I knew his devotional life had been in a state of drift. I said, "I am glad you came over to join us."

"So am I," he said. "It's the first time in over a year that I've gone to Mass. It's been a lot longer than that—years maybe—since I went to Mass as a matter of choice . . . without doing it to please my family, or as an accommodation to help out a friend."

Since he seemed willing to talk about it, I asked: "Could you tell me the reason why you don't go to Mass?"

"Well," he said, "I guess I really don't believe any of it."

"Are you telling me you're an agnostic?"

"I prefer," he said, "to call myself an atheist. It seems more honest."

"Tom," I said, "if you are an atheist, why did you just now go to Communion?"

"I don't know," he said. "I just felt moved to share in the ancient ritual of the Christian faith."

Months later, we talked of the matter again; I was still taken aback as to why a professed atheist would want to receive the Eucharist. I recalled for him the conversation in Joyce's *Portrait of the Artist,* after Stephen Dedalus has refused his mother's wish that he make his Easter Duty.

> *Do you fear, then, Cranly asked, that the God of the Roman catholics would strike you dead and damn you if you made a sacrilegious communion?*
>
> > *The God of the Roman catholics could do that now, Stephen said. I fear more than that the chemical action which would be set up in my soul by a false homage to a symbol behind which are massed twenty centuries of authority and veneration.*

"I fear that too," Tom said. "I don't live without fear."

"Then why did you go to Communion, Tom?"

"I don't know," he said. "It's just one of the mysteries of doubt."

It is my opinion that Irishmen have more difficulties of faith, either of losing belief or of finding it, than any other group I know. "There is more faith in an honest doubt than in all the creeds of man," Tennyson once opined. Maybe so, but I always feel like a dishonest fool when I try to turn a chap's opinion inside out, insisting on the paradox or irony that sees the libertine's lechering as his wistful quest to become pure, or that judges the blasphemer who burns down the temple to be acting from motives of the heart's having reasons that the reason knows not of.

I am too old, you see, to need to kid myself, or to want to kid myself, about matters like faith, or religious experience, or theology, or the role of God in human affairs. I've been a priest for nearly twenty-two years; I've been a Catholic for over thirty years; before that I trudged in and out of Protestant churches as though they were supermarkets. Baptismally speaking, I have been sprinkled, poured on, and totally immersed. Twice, under the hands of bishops, Catholic and Anglican, I have sacramentally submitted myself to the Descent of the Dove. From the earliest remembered moments of my life, there has never been a time I wasn't, in some way, conscious of God. From the age of four or five, when I sang the anthems of salvation at my grandmother's knee, I have been stirred in my emotions by the stories of the Lord who commanded the wind and the sea, and who rose from the dead on Easter morning. There was a time when I ran after faith experiences; now, I don't have to run anymore. Christ is happening all around me. In the ordinary events of life, I find the Lord busily revealing himself in the simple gifts, as in liturgies where he is recognized in the breaking of the bread.

Every year or two, some group, or some campus publication asks questions about the state of the Catholic religion at Notre Dame these days. I am too old to need to pretend that I understand how God and our campus people are dealing with each other. To me, Notre Dame seems to be one of the most religiously exciting places to be found anywhere, more exciting even than the Vatican (if I may be whimsical), where the Holy Spirit is at work night and day, keeping the pope infallible in matters of faith and morals.

Mass attendance is high—higher, I think, than it has ever been in recent years. The candles at the Grotto are continuously blazing rack upon rack. Theology is one of our most respected disciplines, and some of our brightest students are running around with Bibles under their arms, talking of Reuther and Rahner. Practically every sensitive Christian in town is involved in some project intended to save the community, the country, or the globe. From many visible signs, Notre Dame, Our Mother, is still flourishing as a Catholic institution.

Only sometimes I remember that once, during the Ages of Faith, there was a beloved priest and counselor and confessor on this campus. For seventeen years he was the prefect of religion; later, he became president of Notre Dame, and at the time of his death he was the cardinal archbishop of Philadelphia. His name was John Francis O'Hara.

Sometimes on Saturday afternoons after the 5:15 Mass at Sacred Heart Church or on Sunday afternoons when I have had baptisms, I pause for a moment to pray at the tomb of Cardinal O'Hara. I feel that I have a special need of Father O'Hara's prayers because, through a kind of apostolic succession, some of his pastoral cares as prefect of religion now belong to me. In the evolution of office, the prefect of religion became the university chaplain, then the university chaplain became the director of campus ministry. Now, by title, I am the university chaplain, and Father Bill Toohey is the campus ministry director.

There are many of us walking in Father O'Hara's footsteps and living in his shadow. And his zeal and effectiveness are the standard against which his successors must measure themselves, as later football coaches must surely measure themselves and be measured by the greatness of the incomparable Rockne.

None of us can keep Notre Dame Catholic as it was Catholic in the days of Father O'Hara. For example, he disapproved of the works of Ernest Hemingway, and would not allow them to be placed on the library shelves. (There were other proscribed books and authors also.) If a chaplain tried that today, he would be giggled at as silly.

Father O'Hara may have felt competent to take after the loose-minded professors; few of us today feel qualified to take after the loose-minded professors, whatever their discipline of study. But neither can a chaplain announce, as O'Hara announced in 1921, that each student was averaging 3.5 Communions per week; or to rejoice in the statistics of a later year that the number of daily Communions was averaging a high of 1,910 out of a student body of 3,000.

For O'Hara, the boy who was receiving Communion daily was constantly living in the state of grace; therefore his other problems would take care of themselves. To encourage daily Communion, he would distribute the sacrament until noonday to the late risers who had missed attending Mass. He dismissed the criticism that he was making Communion too easily available: "While part of the grace of Holy Communion depends upon the sacrifice made by the individual, the great grace of the sacrament comes from Our Lord Himself working in the soul."

In other words, he was relying on a sacramental efficacy that theologians call the *ex opere operato* effect: that is to say, the spiritual benefits of a sacrament come from the sacrament itself, and are not dependent on the fervor and zeal of the recipient, granting he is already in a state of grace. Contemporary chaplains do not have the peace of mind that arises from so simple a view of the sacrament because modern theologians tell contemporary chaplains the *ex opere operato* formula makes them nervous, suggesting, as it seems, that the effect of the sacrament is automatic and magical. Sacraments, the modern theologian says, are not something we receive, but something we do, celebrating our own existence as Christians.

Considering the more sophisticated theology in use today, I say again that none of us can keep Notre Dame Catholic as it was Catholic in the days of Father O'Hara.

There are verbal portraits that have survived of O'Hara among the students: quick-motioned, energetic, smoking heavily, taking time out of his eighteen-hour day to match wits, besting the students in their own kind of game. But what would have converted us to O'Hara, as it converted our fathers, was his unflagging love and devotion to students; uniting that love to the nimbleness of his wit and the depth of his faith, he brought all his sons home to their Father's house. He would rouse them out of bed to attend Mass; he would note the students who were absent from chapel, and he would send notes reminding them of Easter Duties to be made, of confessions that seemed overdue, of Communions that had been neglected. He knew every face, every name, every hometown, every personal history; and quite simply, nobody has ever matched his success. That is why, as one of his successors, I am haunted by the memory of the chaste, gleaming marble of his tomb, with its Meštrović statue of the Prodigal Son and the red roses that the alumni send twice a week, as though for their own peerless parson they were matching the romantic legends of the roses left by lovers on Valentino's grave. I remember with emotion O'Hara's homecoming, when he returned in death to Notre Dame, where his sleep in the Lord seems like a ministry of caring from the best of all the Notre Dame chaplains.

I think to myself: if the judgment of other chaplains were to be given into his hands, as the judgment of Irishmen has been promised to St. Patrick in that day when all flesh shall see their God, what can we say of the Notre Dame of these years as evidence we have stood by the Faith?

Were there 1,000, 2,000, 5,000 students who went to Communion today, last Sunday? I believe that the number is very high; I know also there are hundreds who never go to Mass at all. Is Hemingway on the library shelves? It would be absurd not to place him there; but O'Hara knew that. O'Hara lived to see Hemingway win the Nobel Prize; the Cardinal and the laureate died within a year of each other. Are confessions being heard in the hall chapels? I would guess that Father O'Hara heard more confessions in a week than most of us now hear in a year. This is not from neglect of chaplains; it is due to the changes since Vatican II. As Father Thomas McAvoy, who was university archivist for many years, remarked: "O'Hara did not belong to the *aggiornamento*."

These are the easy questions. But how does one render an accounting of the Christianity of a place where the numbers game with the sacraments does not necessarily mean anything, because faith and a reception of the sacraments do not always go hand in hand? There is a whole group of Notre Dame students who attend the celebrations of the Eucharist, not out of a belief in the mercy of Christ (though they are perfectly assured of the mercy of Christ); but out of a belief in their own goodness and the goodness of their friends assembled together (as they might say) in a community of love and sharing.

It is a trite trick to talk of a place as though one were giving an account to some figure out of the past. But for me, as for everyone, O'Hara is the symbol of a great tradition of Catholicism at Notre Dame. If I could explain to him how we too have a great tradition of Catholicism, differing from the past, yet related to the past and growing out of it, I could be more at peace with myself as a campus minister not needing to live with a sense of the past betrayed. A two-thousand-year tradition of Christianity should not have changed very much from one decade to another. Yet, it has changed. Notre Dame has changed. I would have to say that the campus, like the country and the world itself, has suffered a loss of innocence. For me, it is the innocence that is so characteristic of all those religious bulletins, all those students averaging 3.5 Communions a week, all those confessions whispered into the prefect's ear, morning and evening, for seventeen years. The other quality of our contemporary Catholicism is how much more involved we are with the Mystical Body of suffering in the world. There has been an abandonment of the theology urging students to "hit the box" and "hit the rail" before you hit the road, because death waits at the crossroads, and you may be in a state of mortal sin. Mortal sin seems a more remote enemy than the famines in Africa and Bangladesh, or the loneliness and neglect that make old age so terrifying to so many, or the varied illnesses of children, or the abortion laws that help doctors and parents destroy more than a million half-formed infants a year.

This is a generation of students who have grown into adulthood since Vatican II, and it is a generation with global concerns. Not only has there been a relaxation of the moral and canonical legalisms within the church, there have been all those other events of history that have revealed the world to itself as a wounded, bleeding place. Priests, nuns, and lay journalists have been busy for ten years pointing out how a politically minded church has been dragging its feet in helping out at the crises centers. The ancient institution is suffering a loss of credibility in being accepted as a Community of Those Who Care.

Would it be a weak answer, then, to say to his venerable eminence: Notre Dame is a fine and Catholic place, and its happiest manifestation of religion is the intensity with which the young people care? The young people care; the priests care; the faculty care; the administrators care; the secretaries care; the hall staffs care; the maids and janitors, the maintenance men and the security guards all care; and the Greatest Carer of Them All is Father Hesburgh, who comes home to campus to give us lessons. We care not only for Biafrans, Cambodians, Chileans, Guatemalans, and Vietnamese; sometimes, incredibly and beautifully, we even care for one another. Notre Dame people have always cared about one another, even when they hurt each other with vicious or careless behavior. That caring, sinewed sacramentally in the life of the church, is what binds our generation to O'Hara's generation. It is the quality of caring that was in O'Hara that makes him a folk hero to us chaplains today.

It is the union between the caring and the service, to the faith and the liturgy, that gives such vibrance to the Catholicism that works and plays on this campus these years; that union is felt in every Mass that is said here, which is as it should be in an age when theology stresses the social character of the sacramental graces. You should see how beautifully this union is happening with the freshmen, who are experiencing it as a heritage of the special place called Notre Dame.

Of course, I can't prove any of these things to you, but I can't prove the presence of the Lord in the Eucharist, either. To tell the truth, I don't even want to try. That is why I have avoided cataloguing the prayer groups and the service organizations which are the visible signs of an invisible grace.

PREMARITAL SEX:
THOU SHALT NOT?

In August, I met a girl, and we immediately hit it off. A few weeks later, we moved in together into a place which I had lined up. We do and have slept together, made love, or however you want to state it. I realize I was brought up that this is morally wrong. I was not a virgin before this relationship, but I by no means slept around town. I do believe I love this girl, however I don't believe marriage is the answer in the immediate future— she is only nineteen, and I know we have some things to do before it would make sense. Now, Father, I just don't feel like I'm sinning or doing wrong. I have thought about it and I just don't feel wrong. . . .

My family and I have always been extremely close. I don't want to hurt them, but I just don't feel wrong . . . I guess I don't know what to think. Thus this letter to you. . . .

The last place I went when I left Notre Dame was, of course, to the Grotto. I do miss it.

(from Rick, a Notre Dame grad, class of '77)

Sometimes, I don't like my job. Sometimes, I don't like being a moralist or a preacher who is forced, out of duty, to frown on cozy, comfortable life-styles that nice people have adopted in forgetfulness of commandments and moral upbringing. Two young people—alive and beautiful and decent—give themselves to each other in a temporary intimacy that leaves them comfortable, happy, and protective of the other's existence in essential ways. Then, because of their families' anger at the choice they have made, the priest, the clerical bachelor, the celibate, is appealed to: "Is it a sin, Father? I don't feel like it's sinful, but my family says it is a sin." And the priest can answer only with the rules that begin "Thou shall not. . . ." But what do rules have to do with anything? What do Mount Sinai and the tablets of Moses have to do with the caresses made to a young girl's loveliness in a fishing shack on the tip of Cape Cod? Rules are a matter not of life, but of language, cold, dead, prohibitive, inhibiting. Anyway if God wants Rick to know the rules, why did He deliver the message to Moses or to me, instead of telling Rick? Rick is the guy with the girl in the sack; she is warmth at his fingertips, feeding hungers that are immediate and consuming. Embrace a girl, and you can be at peace with energies of your human nature. Embrace a rule, and you have to cope with loneliness of an unshared bed, an unshared room, an unshared life.

Let it be clear: as a priest, I stand with the commandment and tradition that begin with the prohibitory words: Thou shall not. . . . But I am uncomfortable trying to offer the church's teaching (it is always easier, telling folks what they want to hear) which prohibits people, unmarried to each other, from keeping each other's company in a sexual way, when each other's company, enjoyed in all possible ways, is what each one wants most in order to live contentedly. Where I fail most egregiously as a teacher of the church's logic is not so much in counseling the young, but in instructing the old; as, for example, a widow and a widower, aged sixty-five, who, for reasons having to do with income needed for survival, are prevented from being married; but who, nevertheless, are trying, in each other's company, to go not gentle into that good night.

Having sneered a little at commandments and the lifelessness of rules, maybe we can look for a moment at the Sinai side of the law. "Everything I ever wanted to do," says the cynic, "is illegal, immoral, or fattening." It does seem, in this perversely ordered universe, that every time I'm really enjoying myself, I look around and find someone shaking a finger at me, saying "It's a no-no." That is why I hate temperance freaks and the Hunger Coalitionists (but not really) collecting money at the doors of the dining hall. How can I enjoy eating two desserts, when I've just been reminded that some child is starving to death in Bangladesh?

Believe it or not, the commandments on sexuality (the Sixth and the Ninth, I think, though I may have forgotten, since I don't break them much), were not the life project of some Jewish, cosmic spoilsport. Jehovah did not—in consultation with the angels, who have no bodies, and so could hardly be expected to know—think to His old testamentary self: "Sexual indulgence is fun; therefore, I'm going to pass a commandment making it a sin." I think God let human beings discover for themselves that sexual energies, indiscriminately indulged, can be so mischievous and destructive, that it destroys all possibility of community life or personal integrity, just as murder and theft and perjury against one's neighbor can make life generally miserable for everybody. A woman sleeping around, a man who is a sexual predator: their offenses against the decencies of life in the tribes of Israel were judged harmful enough to deserve stoning. I think it was man who said to God—and not God who said to man—"Adultery and lustings are sins," and God said: "I agree." Thus, it was out of a community's experience, I think, that the commandments began.

Six thousand years later, the commandments still encapsulate wisdom for the fishing villages of the Cape as well as for traveling campsites of the tribe of Judah. The wisdom says: "Man bears in his body a fire sinewing the loins. There is warmth in that fire to be used as a blessedness by a man and woman who have become endeared to each other; out of it, all human life comes. Watch the fire; it is never to be used casually or without commitment. It can consume the ignorant and the innocent who would make it a toy."

Young friend Rick, freshly graduated, writer of letters, lover of a girl: tender relationships like yours would be insensitively described if I dismissed them under the moral rubric of sin. But is the relationship wise, or thoughtful, or responsible? Are you prepared for all the possible consequences, e.g., if that nineteen-year-old girl were to become pregnant? Can you ever, ever be sure she won't? Can you be sure she does not—or will not—want marriage, even though you decide there are other lives you must lead before becoming anyone's husband? When you drift off, will she then settle in with another young man, and then another until, finally, one of her young men decides to marry her? What is the decency in this for her? What possible cheapening and humiliation is she exposed to?

I know that lots of men and women have affairs before marriage; and I know that young women, if they get into difficulties, have abortions. I am soiled enough in my own life so that I try not to make judgments. But each time you have ever received the Eucharist—and I have given you the Eucharist often enough—you have registered your fidelities as a Christian. Part of your Christian fidelity (I assume) implies a care not to hurt the little ones of the Kingdom; specifically if it implies that you should not give or accept the intimacies belonging to marriage when you intend the relationship to be nothing more than a winter's tale told by an amiable idiot, plotting his flight like the swallows when the springtime comes back to Capistrano.

Rick, I believe that every sentiment and emotion you feel for this girl is clean and honest. I'm sure you don't lie to her, or promise her anything when the intention is to give only Arpège. I am sure you are happy together, and that your love would protect her; but you won't marry her (and she won't marry you; I have not overlooked that), though marriage is the game you are playing. Christians don't play games with relationships Christ has made into sacraments.

When you wrote me, Rick, I am sure you expected traditional answers. The hard principles of the Christian tradition can never be as comfortable to live with as the warmth of a woman whom you love to caress. But loving a woman doesn't mean taking all that she is willing to offer; because when you take that much from any person, you become responsible. Married responsibilities are spelled out in vows and promises made before God. If you don't feel willing to assume responsibility for a lifetime, then don't accept the favors symbolizing the deepest gift of self that this woman will someday owe, as a debt in justice, to the husband she will belong to until death.

I don't like my job at times; it makes me defend viewpoints that are not fashionable. It is very old-fashioned to say you don't sleep with a girl until after you've married her. Such anachronisms are part of the faith that has lit candles at the Grotto for a hundred years.

I am glad you remember the Grotto, Rick. I am glad you visited the Grotto as a final event of Commencement Day before leaving Notre Dame.

I will light a candle there for you . . . and for the girl. Remember me to the ocean off Cape Cod, and I will remember you at the lakeside amidst the glow of candles.

THE HOLY FOOL

I have a red rose, a little faded by time, ready to fall apart if I touch it. It is a Christmas rose, and it was once part of a young man's scheme to convince New Yorkers with shabby life-styles that Christmas is a love story that promises redemption. I keep the rose as a gift of Christmas past, wondering if it symbolizes guilt more than innocence, sickness more than generosity. I hope never to know the answer, because if I did, I might no longer have a reason to keep my Christmas rose at all.

There is a kind of character, known to every rectory and convent, whom the Irish call "the holy fool." This character is not exactly a saint; sometimes, in fact, you wonder if he is not the devil. On good days, however, when the tides of grace are in, you feel willing to concede that this neighborhood nut will be sipping from Waterford crystal in the bosom of Abraham while the rest of us are still in purgatory, clearing our way through customs. Holy fools have more to be said in their favor than my doubts will admit. Some of them are lovely people to meet, but they are more difficult to argue with than atheists.

Bernie Halloran is the holy fool I have known best. I am not sure whether he is holy or just a madman in need of forgiveness. But I was completely convinced he was a fool, liable to be confined as an idiot, on the day he announced his decision to give roses as a Christmas gift to every hooker on the streets of Times Square.

Roses, for heaven's sake; red roses that can cost $1.50 apiece if you buy them from a florist. Not even the angels can count up the number of hookers in Times Square. There must be at least five or ten thousand of them. Hanging roses on their blouses is the least of their needs. Samaritans could buy toys for orphans. Philanthropists could send turkeys to tenements. Roses to the Rockettes, I could admire. Posies to popsies, as Bernie wanted to give, I thought a sin. I would rather see them get pairs of warm stockings.

Bernie first came to New York during the Vietnam War from one of those classless little towns in Ohio where culture reaches its high-water mark when Bobby Fields (gender unspecified) plays the piano at the Holiday Inn on Saturday nights in the Starlite Lounge. Bernie came to New York as a war protestor. He had protested the war in his Ohio town, but nobody had gotten excited when he burned his ROTC uniform in front of the restaurant where the Rotary Club held its weekly meeting. In Ohio, if you can't impress the Rotary, what's left? So Bernie came to New York with a plan for smiting the nation's conscience.

In a shop on 42nd Street, he bought a used sword, probably the unredeemed pawn of a lapsed Elk. Then, carrying the two-edged tickler and a sledge hammer on a sightseers' boat to the Statue of Liberty, Bernie enacted a biblical image. He pounded the sword with a hammer, breaking it into pieces, leaving it to other craftsmen to shape the shattered metal into ploughshares and pruning hooks, as certified messiahs are supposed to do. Now statesmen and militants would know how Bernie Halloran felt about Vietnam. Johnson and Nixon could consider that the Messianic hope had its living witness. The nation would understand that the Ohio farmboy wasn't fooling.

Crazy stuff it was, and it eventually landed Bernie in a psychiatric hospital. In talking with Bernie, you might think him crazy, but he would not let you fail to take him seriously. He would talk at you and talk at you, never interrupting himself, until you felt suffocated by words and schemes. I wished he could stop looking as though he were being measured for a halo as he told me about wanting to buy roses for the street girls at Christmas.

"Bernie," I said reasonably, "where are you going to get money to buy flowers? Keep away from the street life. Some of those girls are dangerous. They'd just laugh their heads off at you."

"But don't you see, Father Griff?" he said. "Once I took advantage of a girl like that. Now I want every prostitute in New York to know that Bernie Halloran is sorry for what he did. I want every one of those girls to know that Bernie Halloran loves them, and that Jesus Christ loves them, and that at Christmas, a boy loves them enough to give them roses."

"Bernie," I said, "wouldn't it be enough if you just gave flowers to the girl you took advantage of?"

"I already did give her flowers," he said. "I told her I was sorry I took advantage of her. I told her that Jesus loves her. She said that no one had mentioned that to her in her whole life. Now I want to give roses to all those girls at Christmas. Then they'll know that Jesus loves them. Then they'll say: 'Bernie Halloran gave us Jesus Christ's love as a Christmas present.'"

"Bernie," I said, "I don't know what happened to you in Times Square, but I doubt if it's possible to take advantage of a New York streetwalker."

"I didn't want to do it," he said. "All the time it was happening, I kept saying: 'This is crazy. I don't want to be doing his. I don't want to be taking advantage of this girl.'"

I honestly believe he could go through an experience like that without once shutting his mouth. I really think that the grossest advantage Bernie could take of a girl, on or off the streets, would be to talk her to death.

For a while, I thought I had talked Bernie out of giving Christmas roses to the hookers. I knew that he was working, but it never occurred to me that he was salting money away, because he had a habit of giving his paychecks to street beggars. I hadn't heard from him in a while, and if I thought of him at all when I came to New York, I was probably grateful that he stayed away. Then, a year later, on Christmas Eve, Bernie showed up at the rectory carrying a huge flower box full of red roses. "They're for the prostitutes in Times Square," he said. "I've got more in a truck outside."

"Bernie," I said, "you are crazy."

He evaded the opinion. "Father Griff," he said, "I want to give you a rose."

I said: "Where did you get the money?"

"I saved over $1,500," he said. "I earned it all myself. I have a truck full of roses now, and I'll have another truck at midnight, and I'll have two more trucks tomorrow." He looked at me to see if I was angry. "Do you think I'll have enough flowers to give roses to every prostitute in Midtown?"

"Bernie," I said, "I don't know how many girls will be working the streets on Christmas. Even prostitutes have places to go on Christmas."

He said: "I want to give you roses, too."

He must have guessed that I was thinking it was no compliment to be included with the hookers. "It's in return for a favor," he said. "Would you bless the roses for me?"

So on one lovely Christmas Eve and all day long on Christmas, at a time when even Manhattan is a suburb of Bethlehem, the holy fool gave away his roses in Times Square. Some of the girls thanked him. Some wouldn't take the flowers. Some took the roses and immediately threw them down on the sidewalk. Some simply said, "Why are you doing this?" Bernie told them his story of how he had taken advantage of a girl, but that at Christmas, he wanted that girl to know, and all girls to know, that Jesus Christ loves them, and that Bernie Halloran loves them. I have no doubt that the good news cheered them up considerably, quite making their day, but I've never heard that any of those girls joined a church or went home to Minneapolis as an aftereffect. And I doubt that any other person could have expressed so much love in so short a time as Bernie Halloran did that Christmas when he tried to speak to prostitutes in a language he hoped they would understand.

Bernie ended his day by giving armfuls of leftover roses to some cloistered nuns on the East Side who had probably never set foot in Times Square in their adult lives. The Mother Superior told Bernie she was sure Jesus loved him because he was a cheerful giver.

Bernie said to me: "Will you send the story of my roses to the *New York Times* so that people can read about nice things for a change, and not just about crime and sadness in the newspapers?"

"The *Times* would think me a fool if I expected them to print a story like that," I said. I thought: they might even think of me as a holy fool. A priest has enough worries these days without being thought of as a holy fool. The *Times* probably wouldn't believe the story anyway. But the story is true; holy fools are characters you can't invent.

I couldn't invent a Bernie Halloran. Bernie Halloran is his own idea. I hope he is also God's idea. Even as a holy fool, Bernie Halloran couldn't make it without God. Bernie Halloran seems like an idea whose time has not yet come. Except for one day of the year, Christmas also seems like an idea whose time has not yet come. I think Christmas and Bernie Halloran, in his best moments, deserve each other.

A MASS FOR THE LITTLEST CHRISTIANS

An *urchin*, by Webster's definition, is "a small boy, or any youngster, especially one who is roguish or mischievous." (Webster adds, as an obsolete definition, "an elf.")

A *moppet*, says Webster, is "a little child or young girl: a term of affection."

Urchins and *moppets*, a Catholic encyclopedia might tell you (if one treated of urchin and moppet lore instead of wasting pages defending the Spanish Inquisition), are "frequently found in delightful clusters in the homes of Roman Catholics, though other sectarians are equally blessed."

So much for reference books. Their shallow scholarship would never be needed if visitors to Notre Dame did not often ask: "What on earth is an urchins' Mass? Who are urchins, and where do they come from? What in heaven's name is a moppets' Mass? What are moppets, and how do you get rid of them?"

"Urchins and moppets are simply children," I explain. "Where they come from is God's mystery, though their origin may be in heaven. Getting rid of them is simply not allowed."

"But why," the visitor may ask, "an urchins' or moppets' *Mass*?"

"It's a way of housebreaking the youngest Christians," I reply, "making them feel at home with the faith of their fathers."

Let's face it, folks. Sunday Mass is not guaranteed to be a box office success. We priests often play to a bored house, and half-empty pews accuse us of dullness. Insist that a child share that dullness; then wonder, when he is old enough to make the choice, why he never wants to go to Mass at all.

Even when the liturgy is superb, facing God as He is formally worshipped by adults must seem like a chore for the youngest Christians. The gentle Jesus, met at bedtime, seems as comfortable as old pajamas. The God applauded on Sundays, in doxologies that deafen church mice, is as stiff as a starched linen T-shirt: He hates it when you wiggle, scratch, squirm, whisper, sit next to kids your own age, or get silly enough to giggle. Sometimes foolish parents make Him seem like a sneak ("God is watching you, Margaret Mary. You can't hide chewing gum from God"), or a bully ("God knows how to punish mean little boys. How'd you like it if your face fell off?"). I wonder if the youngest Christians at times don't want to grow up agnostic out of sheer revenge.

Urchins' Masses were begun as a way of helping children enjoy their church simply by keeping them informed as to what the liturgy is saying and doing. It doesn't hurt reverence to tell the youngest Christian what the priest is up to. Let them know that bread and wine are being consecrated. Let them touch the hosts that are to be blessed as their Jesus-bread. Let them smell the bouquet of wine made of grapes that have lain in the sun. Sunshine will be like darkness compared to the glory that will come unseen, overwhelming the substance of bread and wine. Teach them of Christ hiding the immensity of His being in a snowflake of wheat.

This teaching is what I try to do at the Mass for moppets and urchins, explaining to them what is happening as they stand with me at the altar, in a catechesis that runs the length of the liturgy.

Give them a gospel story they can watch unfold; let them hear the account of the prodigal's return as the priest reads the story, while students use mime or puppets to illustrate. On Palm Sunday, we have shown urchins the whole grief of the passion on a marionettes' stage. During Advent, we have used masks to represent the prophets, thereby adding pageantry to the prophecies and deepening the sense of mystery that surrounds the Messiah's birth.

Once, in my ignorance, I thought if you were to enter a child's world, you needed the company of Puff, Winnie the Pooh, Smokey the Bear, and all the other cuddly creatures that make cuteness a cult. I was mistaken. In a faith that uses symbols that touch the senses—water, incense, candles, colors, gestures, bread, wine—you need only God's heroes: David with his sheep, Noah with his menagerie, Ezechiel in his valley of the dry bones, Joshua toppling the walls of Jericho. God has given to his church every truth and beauty and example that a priest needs to lead a child's imagination into a first experience of heaven's mysteries. The dragon and the Poohbear may still come to Mass, but they are expected to sit quiet and not make a fuss, like the adults assigned the back pews where they must wait without fidgeting until the urchins need them for a ride home.

The urchins' Mass can be outgrown in a summer like an old pair of sneakers. Urchins go back to their parishes knowing what a gospel is, and what a canon and a consecration are, and at least having heard of an epiclesis, though I hope they never admit it to the pastor.

Parents tell me that the urchins' Mass has helped; and helping was all I ever meant to do. Nine years, almost, have passed since I called the first youngest Christians to be urchins and moppets at a worship that is almost playing games in the presence of the Lord. Some former urchins and grown-up moppets are now beginning college. The urchin congregation renews itself year by year as the youngest Christians come, refugees from homilies that were never meant for them.

I don't think it would be obsolete usage to admit that often the youngest Christian has the face and features of an elf. Elfin or not, it's enough to call all the urchins moppets, because moppet, says Webster, is a term of affection.

YOU CANNOT SING A NIGHT SONG

I don't want to pretend to know more about loneliness than I have actually experienced. People have died of loneliness, and it would be cheap to praise it as some kind of spiritual desert where the pilgrim soul finds God brooding in solitude. In places of great aloneness—the polar caps, the Himalayan peaks, the Sahara sands—travelers describe an experience of feeling befriended, as though God were more accessible in wastelands than in crowded cities. But for an invalid without friends, a hotel room can seem as bleak as Siberia, and the silence can seem like death without burial.

In my life, God, in some of His best appearances, is a quiet joy felt after great loneliness at night on crowded Manhattan streets. The Lord whom I preach as a crucified Galilean risen from the dead belongs to a faith that depends on the imagination, not the memory, for its images. I believe in the miracles, the cross, and the resurrection. But faith needs to be supported by its own immediate experience if it is to sing songs to the Lord in the time after midnight.

You cannot sing a night song until the hour before dawn, when the darkness is nearly ended. Then, when loneliness has worn you out, you understand, in an insight as spontaneous as laughter, that God has been keeping watch. There is no existence outside Him, and all the life of the city is like a single note that could never be sounded outside the symphony of God's being.

Randy was a second-grader who used to follow the bigger kids around, pleading to be allowed to play kickball with them in the 43rd Street school playground. If you've ever been the junior member of a street crowd, organized for summer games and mischief, you'll realize how often Randy was reduced to the role of spectator, grumbling at the fate of never being wanted. Once or twice, I interceded for him, testing Irish logic and the persuasive force of the Roman collar against the organized self-interest of the youngsters' Mafia, on a Catholic playground in Hell's Kitchen.

"It's Monsignor McCaffery's playground, named after Monsignor McCaffery, as a memorial given him by his friends," I said. "Monsignor McCaffery would want you to let Randy play kickball."

"Aw, Father," the impish lads chortled in a rich blend of accents, "he's too small, and he gets hoit"—which means hurt, if you understand these things—"and he starts to bawl, and he runs home and tells his grandmother we're killing him, and the old lady comes out and starts knocking on us with a broom."

"Nevertheless, this is the church's property," I insist. "The church wants you to let Randy play kickball. Otherwise Cardinal Cooke will be very upset, and he might mention it to the pope." I shuddered as though I could already feel the papal anathemas turning the 43rd Street kickballers into ice.

"He can't play kickball worth garbage," they objected.

I could persuade them that an inability to play kickball was only a slight concern compared to the cardinal's grief, if I also hinted that in the fall I would encourage Sister Athanasium to flunk all of them back into fifth grade. Unfortunately for Randy, he really couldn't play kickball worth garbage and after being in the game with him for about ten minutes, the older boys decided to leave the playground and go off and talk about holding up Tiffany's, which was the midtown Manhattan equivalent of playing Star Wars.

I was left to cheer up Randy, by then a basket case of rage and disappointment. One day he told me about his family. His mother was dead, and his father was in Chicago, living with another family. He had older sisters who didn't want him around because then they couldn't talk about the boys. The children lived with their grandmother who had a reputation around the neighborhood as being slightly crazy.

"I've got no one to play with," he said, "and no one to talk to." Even as a second-grader, you need someone to talk to. Having no one to play with seemed as sad as a run-over puppy.

"How about the other children in your grade school?" I asked.

"Oh, they live Uptown or Downtown, somewhere out of the neighborhood," he said. "Their folks send them to summer camp to get them off the streets."

"Do you watch much television?" I asked.

"My grandmother doesn't like kids staying 'round the house all the time. She says it isn't good for kids to be 'round the house all the time, when they could be out playing. Anyway, she says it's *her* TV, and she's going to watch *her* programs."

"What do you do when she sends you outside to play?"

"I go to the movies on Eighth Avenue," he said. "The guys let you in free if you do stuff for them. It's okay if the cops don't come and chase you out. The cops don't like to have kids going to the movies on Eighth Avenue."

"Do you understand those movies, Randy?"

"I understand them okay," he said, "but I don't like them. The only time the big kids want to talk to me is when I tell them about the movies on Eighth Avenue. They won't let the big kids in those places, but the guys let me in because I do stuff for them. The big kids want me to tell them what happens in those movies." He made a gesture with his shoulders as if to say, "You have someone to talk to if you've seen a movie on Eighth Avenue."

"Randy," I said, "what do you enjoy doing when you must stay by yourself? Do you like to read stories? Is there a children's room at the public library you could visit?"

"I don't read good," he said. "I don't like books much 'cause they make my head ache."

"But what do you like doing best?" I asked. "How do you spend the days when you're happiest?"

"Sometimes, I go down to see the boats on the river," he said. "When the boats are going somewhere, I wish I was going with them. Sometimes

I wish I was a boat, and I'd travel on and on. Then somebody would miss me, and Grandma would say: 'Where's Randy?' and the kids would say: 'Randy went traveling on the river, and he may never come back if he doesn't want to.'"

"If you were a boat traveling on the river, do you think maybe you wouldn't want to come back?"

"Well, I guess sometimes on Sunday I'd want to come back," he said. "I like going to church with my grandma. They don't let kids into church if it isn't Sunday and you're not with somebody. They say kids break stuff and steal things, but I never did."

"Why do you like going to church?" I asked.

"Well, I sit there, and I'm not alone by myself, and nobody's yelling and nobody's trying to hurt you, and nobody's saying, 'No, you're too small, so you can't play.' I think of being alone by myself, and I think, God knows what it's like, 'cause he's been by hisself and all alone. I say to God: 'How did you like being by yourself, and beat up on?'

"And God answers: 'It was awful.'

"I say: 'I thought maybe being God it wasn't as awful staying by yourself as it would be for a kid staying by hisself.' God says: 'It's worse, because if you're a kid staying by hisself, I'm staying there with you. But when I'm staying by myself, I got only me. That is why I wish sometimes you'd come and stay with me, if you'd like to, and then I wouldn't be alone as much.'"

"Randy," I said, a little nervous at the precocious mysticism, "are you making this up?"

"Well," he said, "it's kind of like making it up, but it all happens real inside my head."

"What else do you think about at church?" I said.

"Well, God says: 'Randy, what have you been up to lately?' I say: 'Not much,' and God says: 'You've been going to the movies again on Eighth Avenue. Now you know that's not right, Randy.' Well, I say, 'You know it's been lonesome alone by myself.'

"God says: 'Being by yourself isn't the worst thing, Randy. It's never having anybody ever to be with at all that makes you want to cry. You got me, and I got you. We just gotta think of each other, and that makes it nice.'"

"Going to church," I said, "thinking about God, and going down to see the boats on the river sound like happy things to do. But I think it would be healthier if the kids would let a second-grader play kickball."

"Don't lie to the kids," he said. "They know you're lying. They know Cardinal Cooke wouldn't tell the pope about a garbage player like me."

"How do you know?" I said.

"You just know things," he said.

All of it was the fantasy world of a child, making up games about God. But I wondered what Randy meant when he said that God told him: "I wish you'd come and stay with me sometime, if you'd like to."

One summer day, weeks later, Randy found an old boat on the river. He got into it, cast it loose, and started floating with the tide. A day later, the Coast Guard picked him up. For a week, he was kept in a children's shelter. Finally, his father came and took him to live with his new family in Chicago.

I've often wondered where Randy thought he was going when he went traveling on the river. I wonder if he thought he would ever come back to New York. I wonder if, in his new neighborhood, the older boys ever let him play kickball with them.

I don't want to pretend to know more about loneliness than I have actually experienced. I don't want to tell you more about Randy than I actually heard him say. But that is what his words sounded like to me, after I thought about them.

Of all the creatures God has made, only man can be lonely, and reflect on his loneliness. Only sometimes, in the solitude, one meets a friend who seems like God. Travelers in the Himalayas tell you it can happen. Children on 43rd Street tell you it can happen.

As for me, I can only say that sometimes, after great loneliness, I can sing a night song of faith. I can only trust that God gives other people their own night song, at the times when they most need to know that they are notes in the music that is piped by God.

SIMEON'S CHRISTMAS

Simeon was a clean, respectable old gentleman who lived in a neat room next to a Catholic school on Washington Place in Greenwich Village. He loved the schoolchildren as though they were family; they adored him as the neighborhood grandfather.

Some widows he met at the market admired his politeness and manners, and they would laughingly invite him to lunch with them on bagels and rice pudding, assuming that he was Jewish. Simeon never said he was Jewish, though it was understood that his wife and children had died in a prison camp in Europe. Simeon never spoke of his griefs to anyone; he kept all his secrets to himself.

The old gentleman was good at fixing things, especially if they were toys made of wood. His hands touched woodwork so lovingly that he was believed to have made his living as a cabinetmaker or a sculptor.

But woodworking, for Simeon, was merely a hobby he was good at. Like others, I never knew if he was Jewish, but I did know what his profession had been. The first time I met him, he sat on a neighboring bench in Washington Square Park, watching me struggle through the Italian text of *The Divine Comedy* with the help of an English translation.

Finally, as I was leaving, he came over to speak. "Do you like the Sinclair translation?" he asked.

I, surprised, replied: "Do you know it?"

"Very well," he said. "I have a translation in the Scots dialect I would like to show you. Do you come to the park often?"

I arranged to meet him the next day, when he read me in Scottish dialect Dante's meeting with Paolo and Francesca on the second circle of hell. Then he showed me the structure, grammatically and poetically, of Saint Bernard's prayer to the Virgin at the end of the *Paradise*.

Virgin Mother, daughter of thy son, lowly and exalted more than any other creature . . . In thy womb was kindled the love by whose warmth this flower has bloomed thus in the eternal peace.

"Do you read Hebrew?" he asked. I shook my head. "Ah, it's a pity," he said. "I have things I would like to share with you."

There were other things he wanted to share with me, in a variety of languages, until finally I asked: "Are you a teacher?"

"No," he said, "I was a linguist working as a translator at the United Nations. Next to Hebrew, I have always loved Dante best."

Now my desire and will,
like a wheel that spins with even
motion, were revolved by the Love
that moves the sun and the other stars.

"Magnificent poetry," he said, "but absurd theology."

————

The Holy Spirit's first gift was the gift of languages, whereby apostles could speak in assorted tongues to ethnics living in Jerusalem. Simeon enjoyed a personal Pentecost through his command of languages; he would speak to children of an international community in their native speech, sharing their familiarity with Spanish folktales and Russian nursery rhymes. He would tell the Br'er Rabbit stories in a Cajun dialect. He would wait for them after school, when he would lament with them over bruised knees or encourage them to hope for lost teeth to replace themselves quickly. In a few homes, where the fathers had moved out, he brought a man's love.

The children sometimes wondered about the life of their international grandfather. They guessed he was sad sometimes when he hugged them, as though he were embracing, through them, other children whom he hadn't hugged in a long time. They comforted him for a sorrow he never spoke of, that was as much a part of him as his laughter. They kept with him a conspiracy of silence, as though they had never heard of horrors that could leave an old gentleman childless.

––––––––

Simeon kept another secret that probably wouldn't have shocked those children, mostly Catholic, even if they had known it. Simeon, that gentle, tender old man, denied fiercely and passionately that their God existed.

He did not practice the faith of a Jew. He did not believe in the God of Judaism, and he took no stock in the God of Christians. He hated the lies that supported religion. He cherished and protected gentleness in all the ways that gentleness needed his help; but he was sure, from the deepest experience of his life, that heaven offers no gentleness.

He had expected heaven to be gentle, but his expectations had betrayed him. "If gentleness were there," he said, "I would have found it. God, if He existed, could not have refused my prayer."

He spit on the faith that says there is a love that moves the sun and the stars.

––––––––

Perhaps because we had read Dante together, Simeon mentioned to me how much he hated Christmas.

"When you think of what it does to the minds of children," he said. "Even Christians doubt the truth of a virgin birth."

"That is the way the story has come down to us," I said. "I'm not comfortable with scholars who try to explain it away."

"Are you telling me, as a reasonable man, that you believe a supreme being slept on filthy straw?"

"I'm sure they would have laid him on fresh straw," I said. "It's a faith I share with Dante, and Dante was a reasonable man."

"Dante was writing allegory," he replied, "and he used the images of allegory. He wrote of sinners being boiled in rivers of blood. He had a whole torture chamber that he wrote about. But if you believe it literally, you contradict all your theology of a God who loves you."

"You are a scholar at home in literature," I said. "You certainly know that Christian faith doesn't have to defend itself against the creature-features of a medieval imagination."

"You defended yourself with Dante," he said, "not I."

"That's because I knew that you love him," I said. "At least as a poet."

"I also love Grimm's fairy tales, but I don't think they're going to take me to heaven."

"I'm sorry we're quarreling," I said. "I believe that children would be impoverished if we never led them to Bethlehem."

"Couldn't you just give them their toys without asking them to trust in a legend that will betray them, about a God so nonexistent that a belief in Him will break their hearts?"

"From the moment of his birth," I said, "the child Jesus was promised heartbreak."

He looked at me as though I had rebuked his life's suffering with a cheap remark.

Simeon, I think, had a special tenderness for the children attending the Catholic school. Perhaps the reason he lived so close to the church was to keep his eye on the children, protecting them as much as he could from the superstitions of nuns and priests.

He wouldn't harm their faith; he just wouldn't encourage them in it. He wouldn't let them think he found it interesting to hear that they were making their First Communions or that the archbishop was coming for Confirmation. His only weapon for saving them was to display his indifference to their spiritual nurture.

As Christmas grew closer, he found it hard to ignore their happiness and excitement. "You Catholics are such fools," he said, "celebrating feast days of deception instead of teaching your children to use their strength against heartlessness."

The children seemed to understand the old man's doubt; they listened carefully to the words he didn't say. They noticed that he did not live religiously as other Jews did; he did not keep the holidays or observe the Sabbath. They expected he would ignore Christmas, lighting neither a tree nor a candle, refusing to open a gift or a card that looked suspiciously holiday-like. On Christmas Day, he would sit alone in his room, not even answering a knock on the door.

Simeon, depressed by the season, seemed to avoid the children; he shrank from playing their grandfather. If they asked his help, he would say: "I can't do it now, go off and play." Then he would hug them, as though to take away the gruffness from his words. Their parents would tell them: "Simeon is always depressed at Christmas. Maybe he's remembering a happier year."

––––––––––

Simeon brooded alone, tormented by the season's silliness, until finally the time came when, literally, the sky fell on the children at the rehearsal of their Christmas pageant.

Actually, the part of the firmament that fell was the star, the official star of Christmas night. It narrowly missed braining the holy infant, and in its wooden clumsiness, it bent his halo. He cried, and it was obvious to everyone that he had wet himself, becoming a symbol of a soiled humanity and a dented divinity.

"Well," said Saint Joseph, "that settles it. We need a new sky."

"Where are we going to get a new sky?" asked the Virgin Mary. It was obvious to her that you can't pull a new sky out of thin air.

"Look how it's sagging," said Joseph, a bit sharply. Indeed, there was a new dip to the Big Dipper as though it were being lowered into a well.

"We've got to fix it," said the First Wise Man, with obvious wisdom.

"But how?" said the Second Wise Man, showing a passion for truth.

"Simeon!" said the Third Wise Man, as though he had seen the light.

Three kings and two shepherds, in the company of Joseph and Mary, trooped through the streets in search of an old man as their originals had once searched the earth for a child.

When Simeon saw them, he said: "Who is this?"

"I'm Caspar." "I'm Melchior." "I'm Balthasar," said three young voices. Simeon shook his head. "I gave at Halloween," he said.

"We want you to fix our star," said Mary.

"We want you to make us a new sky, because the old one fell," said the kings.

"Who am I," said Simeon, "that children should ask me to give them heaven? Go back to playing your games. When the holidays are over, we will go to the zoo."

"Simeon," said a boy's voice speaking through the black whiskers of Joseph, "we need you now. The scenery's falling apart for our Christmas play, and we need you to fix it."

"No," said Simeon, "I'm busy. Ask one of the priests. I'm too busy to help you."

"The first grade is going to sing carols and the mothers' club sewed our costumes," argued Joseph, "but nobody knows nothing about making a star that moves across the sky. But you could do it, Simeon. You could make a star that moves."

"I'm sorry," Simeon said. "I can't help you. I've had no experience with traveling stars. Perhaps your fathers can help you."

"Oh, Simeon," said the dark-faced child playing Mary, "we don't know anyone else to ask."

Simeon was still shaking his head in refusal when she began to cry. Joseph moved to her side, and he was crying too. Soon the wise men and the shepherds joined in.

Simeon stood there watching. Then he spoke.

"Too often I have heard children weeping in places where I couldn't help them. What do you want me to do?"

———

He fashioned the children a moon and stars and hung them on a firmament of midnight blue. He made a crystal star, and as it moved across the sky, it seemed to sing; it danced down the Milky Way before coming to rest over a manger where a Spanish baby represented the hope of Israel.

Simeon, when asked how he did it, said: "Love makes the star. *L'amor che move il sole e l'altre stelle.*"

He continued: "'The love by whose warmth this flower has blossomed thus in the eternal peace.' Eternal peace seems possible, if you are with children when they are happy."

Then he pointed to a dark-faced child playing the role of a mother on a Christmas stage.

Simeon, as usual, was being himself, keeping secrets.

BEFORE THE DAYLIGHT FAILS

"Last week he tried to commit suicide," one waiter said.
"Why?"
"He was in despair."
"What about?"
"Nothing."
"How do you know it was nothing?"
"He has plenty of money."

(from Hemingway's *A Clean, Well-Lighted Place*)

A number of years ago, I stayed in a home where I found every morning that my razor blades had been taken away.

The first several times, I explained to my hostess that, packing too carefully, I must have hidden the blades from myself, and asked if there were a razor in the house I could borrow.

Finding on the fourth day that the Gillettes were missing again, I suggested to my hostess that her relatives were having some fun. "Even if they were gay blades," I joked, "they didn't run off by themselves."

Apparently embarrassed, she apologized and said she would find out what was happening. The next morning, when she served me my razor blades with the breakfast coffee, I realized she had been playing games with me. When I teased her, I understood the game wasn't funny.

"I hid them because of Henry," she said.

Henry was her son, an alcoholic who had developed manic-depressive psychosis. He once had been hospitalized for a couple of years in a state hospital.

"A month ago, he tried to commit suicide," she said. "Now I hide everything he could harm himself with."

One morning she had found blood all over the bathroom. She had followed a trail of blood into Henry's bedroom. Henry had slashed his wrists and lay down on the bed, expecting to die. He didn't die, but his mother wasn't sure when he might try to kill himself again.

Henry, fearing his mental illness, preferred death to the ordeal of the state hospital. One could say of him: "He must have been crazy, trying to kill himself." One can also remember saying, after seeing certain sick wards: "I would rather be dead than in a place like that."

The couple, after fifty years of marriage, "were going home," as their note put it, "on a flight we've booked ourselves." The note continued: "We've had our wonderful lives, and no one should mourn our leaving. We want it this way: being together, taking passage before the daylight fails. We do this because we love each other, and we love our children. We want them to know we are very happy, moving outward on the evening tide, together even in death, for as long as death shall last."

All of us say, almost as a reflex action, when we hear of a suicide: "The guy must have been nuts."

De facto, you can always find a reason: a man punishes himself because he cannot live with guilt; because he cannot live with failure; because he cannot live with fear; because he cannot stand waiting; because he would punish his family, his friends, the girls who wouldn't date him; because he believes his sexuality is wrong; because he figures he has damaged himself with drugs; because he is sickened by the thought of living in institutions; because he is afraid of being afraid; because he is tired of being alone; because he is tired of being tired.

The suicidal person, we believe, always has a reason involving drugs, defeat, discouragement, or disease, which he cannot handle in a healthy way.

But as I grow older, I find myself wondering if life is really worth the battle. Are there circumstances when a person could rationally and cheerfully say: "It's dull, and it's getting worse. I'm giving it all back, Lord, before it turns to horror."

I mean, really, why should we put up with the general indignities, with our personal share in the tribe's sufferings? Life gets to be a fight for survival, from the petty pain of corns and the humbling curse of hemorrhoids to the daily depression of seeing the faces of unhappy citizens coming home from work on the subway.

Could not one, with logic and dignity, achieve a detachment that seeks the solace of a dreamless sleep rather than a shabby dawn?

She was only fifteen years old, and she hanged herself, and it all began with drugs. She had a fight with her father, and she must have thought they'd find her before she really hurt herself. Perhaps she was unlucky; but if killing herself was what she wanted, she got her way. "What a terrible waste of life," said the nurse. "What a horror it must be for her parents."

You murmur protestingly about the truth and beauty of life. The truth is summed up nicely in an Ash Wednesday ritual: "Remember, man, that thou art dust, and unto dust thou shalt return." Even on its best days, the beauty of life limps around on a clubfoot. The poet Keats notwithstanding, the nightingale, not an immortal bird, was certainly born for death.

One night, a student visited my room at midnight, to join a group of students discussing their days in Catholic grade school. By four o'clock, he was back his own room in his hall, where he cut his throat.

Hours later, his roommate found him, still alive but weak from the loss of blood, and took him to a hospital. When I saw him in the afternoon, with huge bandages covering the veins of his neck, I asked, "Why did you do it?"

He said, "It was a bad day yesterday. In the morning, the car wouldn't start."

"Can you think how your family would have felt," I asked, "if you had died?"

"I would have been sorry to have bothered them," he said, "but I didn't think about it."

I am not convinced by the logic that begins with a sick car and ends with a sick, and almost dead, person. The life force, the survival instinct, should be healthy enough to survive discouragement.

I've usually been impressed by the hardiness of the life instinct. Old codgers in flophouses, who have been killing themselves for years with the more lethal forms of alcohol, resolve, on the brink of death, to give up smoking and get more exercise. Old ladies who sleep under park benches and make their lunches out of garbage cans carry vitamin-enriched bread in shopping bags and energize themselves regularly with afternoon treats at fruit-juice bars.

Seeing them dogged by poverty and old age, you would guess that they would be waiting for the sweet chariots to swing low. In truth, they don't want to go anyplace they can't get to, and back, on a subway token.

It feels freer to use a doorway as a night couch than to sleep on starched sheets in a home that has rules. The final sleep in the grave, as they see it, is the freedom to go no place in particular on tufted taffeta.

He was a big, good-looking Irish kid and he had a great Irish grin. He was sensitive and intelligent, and very serious when he talked. Even when he was serious, I never worried about him because of the grin. There was mischief in that grin; the mischief seemed to say: "I can handle anything." I thought he could handle anything. I never recognized the sadness in his face until after he died.

Life persists. A single blade of grass cracks the surface of a highway. Flowers break through the ruins of a building. Golden shafts of wheat push through the bleached bones of a cemetery. And the bread of a Eucharist has its source in grain growing from a calf's skull.

A young man dies from the ravages of cancer, but against all odds and expectations and planning, a child is conceived before the disease makes its final onslaught, and the infant is born healthy as a miracle child, as though chemotherapy had never threatened her graceful formation: one life exchanged for another, as a kind of proof of the order behind the world's meltdowns.

One speaks from the evidence of his own experience, from the stirring within him that loves a life. More profound than commandments from heaven is the instinct within one's being to preserve one's being, to which every heavenly hope directs its promise.

> *Do not go gentle into that good night,*
> *Old age should burn and rage at close of day;*
> *Rage, rage against the dying of the light.*

Even beasts do not go gentle. If you trap a butterfly, it struggles, to its peril, in your hands. A moth beats its wings against imprisoning glass with all the fierceness it knows. A moth does not go gentle into its loss of light.

> *He was a fourth-grader. He made himself and his sister sick by turning on the gas in the kitchen. The landlady insisted that he had been trying to kill himself and his sister, but he didn't look like a killer to me.*
> *"What you did," I said, "could make you die. Do you really want to die?"*
> *He looked away from me. "I wouldn't mind," he said.*
> *Oh, do not go gentle, kid. There's no coming back.*

In Hemingway's story, an old man tried to hang himself, because he was in despair. Life was nothing, and all that was left him was to drink until daylight in a clean, well-lighted cafe.

The old man, clean and polite, has the dignity of a hero. Hemingway, killing himself like one of his best characters, was a casebook study of illness.

> *He was standing on a bridge, trying to decide to jump. The police had a name for his kind. They called him a "jumper" as though he belonged to some class of people the police had a lot of experience with. Jumpers are certainly not heroes to policemen.*

Of persons I have known who have taken their own lives, I am sure: "They did the best they could. They made a private, separate peace, and God consented to their decision. He alone knows the terms of their arrangement."

But I've never seen a suicide of which I could say, "It was good, it was right, it was better this way."

If I were to kill myself, I think I would tell God: "I could not finish the work you asked me to do. I made too many mistakes, and the circumstances were too hard."

The Father, full of pity, would hug his humiliated child tenderly and lovingly. But I think he might tell me: "It could have been otherwise."

Who am I to judge who the heroes are? Maybe it's an act of high courage to give back a life. Maybe it's a way of dealing with dullness and pain.

She sat there talking about wrapping her car around a tree. "They couldn't ever be sure it wasn't an accident," she said.

She asked me if it wouldn't be fun to play Russian roulette. "If the gun is loaded," she said, "it's a game that has no losers."

When I asked her to explain, she said: "Figure it out."

She was undoubtedly putting me on, but how could I be sure? After she left, I gave her mother a call. The craziest things happen these days.

Do not go gentle into that good night.

A TRUE CONFESSION

Sometimes, when I'm hearing confessions, the confessing Christian with his cargo of sins moves me onto heavy seas before I've gotten the tip of the paddle into the water. I am caught totally by surprise, not because some mean form of human indulgence is being offered to me for absolution, but because of an assumption that the penitent makes that my view of things coincides with his view of things. On this particular day, in New York, the young man began with a declaration I always find saddening.

"I am a homosexual," he said.

Homosexuals I have known live more difficult lives than the rest of us. I wish it were otherwise; but when a person tells me of being homosexual, I know that the person will frequently be dealing with a special kind of pain.

The young Christian continued: "I'm living with a guy. We've been together now for three years, keeping very faithful to each other. Last night, I met a fellow in a bar. I went home with him and spent the night with him. This morning, I was very ashamed. That's why I've come to confession."

I don't think any sensible priest is going to hit the ceiling at this point. But he might be taken aback at the circumstances of the living arrangement. He might be upset by an association that he is expected to treat like a marriage in which one of the partners is admittedly adulterous.

Easy now, I thought to myself. Give yourself a moment to think.

"How old are you?" I asked. Whenever I'm waiting for the Lord to help me out, I always ask penitents: "How old are you?" It gives me, as a confessor, something to do while stalling. Anyway, the information is necessary and helpful.

"Twenty-three," he said. "My roommate and I have been very happy for over three years now. That's why it was so dumb of me to go home with a pickup."

"Why did you do it, then?" I really had no previous confessional experience of an affair like this from which to approach him with a prepared reaction.

"I was just curious," he said. "I feel very shabby, because I know that he would never cheat on me like that."

"What would he say if he found out?" I asked.

"Oh, he already knows," he said. "I woke him up to tell him when I came in this morning."

"How did he react?" I asked. "Was he deeply upset?"

"We cried together," he said. "It brought us closer. It won't happen again. I told him that, and he knows it's true. To show him how sorry I am, I told him I was coming to confession."

"What did he say when you told him you were going to confession?" I asked.

"He said that if that was what I thought I should do, then go ahead and do it. He isn't a Catholic himself." He looked at me as though he thought I might object to the union on religious grounds. "He comes to Mass with me nearly every Sunday."

"What age were you," I asked, "when you decided you were a homosexual?"

"I've known it since I was a kid," he said. "It became clear to me in high school when the guys would make jokes about fags. I decided to live openly as a gay when I was eighteen. That's when I came to New York to live. If I had stayed home in Massachusetts, it would have hurt my folks too much."

"Have there been other gays that you've lived with?" I asked. "On a regular basis, that is."

"I don't consider myself promiscuous," he said. "In my first days in New York, I nearly ruined myself with one-night stands. I guess I was looking for someone who could love me. One-night stands can kill you. After a couple of years of one-night stands, I was practically a street-walker."

"Do you and your roommate intend staying together permanently?" I asked.

"Neither of us has anybody else," he said. We don't even want anybody else. That's why I was such a cheap fool, messing up last night."

"Did you ever talk about your life with your roommate with any other priest?" I asked.

"I've never needed to," he said. "I was never unfaithful to him before."

While we were talking, I had been reviewing options in my mind. As a priest, I know that the sacraments belong not to me but to the church. A good many hours of my life are spent in offering sacraments as redemptive signs to sinful people. The church expects me to be her faithful sacramental minister. Administering a sacrament is not like buying a drink for a pal: you don't do it because you're a good fellow, and someone you're sorry for is feeling blue.

A Catholic is expected to be in a state of grace when you give him the Eucharist. A Catholic should be contrite, with a purpose of amendment over his serious sins, when you give him absolution.

The young homosexual confessing to me was living in a secular, unsanctified, and unsanctifiable union; in traditional language, objectively (though seemingly not subjectively) in an occasion of sin, which I could not bless in the church according to any tradition that I was aware of. Of course, I was not being asked to bless the union, but only tacitly not to condemn it, leaving it unchallenged, uncriticized, and unexamined. I sensed that he was unaware that I might object to the way he was living.

I'm thought by my critics to be liberal, and by my friends to be sentimental, but I can make hard-nosed decisions when hard-nosed decisions are called for, for I take my church's teaching very seriously. I thought: This is not a hopeless case. In some confessions of this genre, I've met hopeless cases: people utterly without discipline or principles to keep themselves from self-destructing. In talking to them, you grasp at straws, trying to get them to assent to principles you know they could never live by, so that you will not have to dismiss them, deprived of the mercy they have a claim to as Christians.

The church never told me that I can't rely in an emergency on my gut feelings. On that afternoon in New York a few years ago, I decided it was wisest to respect the love and fidelity that seemed to bind two problemed lives into a relationship of respect and caring. For all I could see, they were doing the best they could. Every human being needs to find some decency that he can cling to. Decency, in its ways of being loving and faithful, is an absolute that becomes relative to the strength that is given us to survive with grace.

I dealt with his sin as the young homosexual confessed it to me. I accepted the purpose of amendment in the terms that he promised it. I forgave him for the guilt he experienced. I did not try to make him see sin in a relationship where, apparently, he found innocence, because I wasn't sure I could convince him to live heroically as a celibate.

The church, in ordaining us priests, takes a chance on our prudence. At the moment we enter the confessional, we *are* the church as healer; those whom we try to heal are also the church in its failing, faltering human element.

Within those rooms set aside for reconciliation, movements are not absolved or recognized; organizations are not told whether they are good or bad. Lifestyles reflecting philosophies of liberation are not submitted for judgment. In confessionals, the encounter is one on one, with the Holy Spirit assisting: a sometimes foolish person talking to a sometimes sinful person, with the penitent and the confessor judging each other.

The church, so far as I can understand the church, is willing to let its gospel and creeds be personalized in me. The church trusts me with its traditions and sacraments, to speak with authority in the name of Jesus. Christianity, at the grassroots level of its organized structure, comes down to the parish priest helping a soul toward heaven, tempering the winds of doctrine to the human nakedness of the shorn lamb.

My shriven penitent, having heartily resolved with the help of God's grace to do penance and to amend his life, said: "My roommate is thinking about becoming a Catholic, and he would like to talk to a priest. Could he come and talk to you?"

"Actually," I said, "I'm not here regularly, but I'd be happy to give his name to one of the other priests. The pastor would be very happy to help him, I'm sure."

I feel certified as infallible when I proclaim God's mercy in the context of a sacrament. But I get nervous as a teacher of God's truth in situations when I'm not sure my gut feelings should be relied upon as the inspirations of the Holy Spirit.

A STORYBOOK MARRIAGE

He was an executive in his company, so his secretary placed the call. She gave me the caller's name and asked me to wait until he got on the line.

When, after fifteen seconds, he spoke to me, he was businesslike. He was a man of affairs, and he knew I was a professional; I would know how to deal with the business he would lay before me.

"Padre," he said, "my son Rick is a freshman at Notre Dame. He's a good kid, he handles himself well. My wife and I recently decided to divorce. We told the children over the weekend. Rick can take care of himself, but I thought one of you padres ought to keep an eye on him."

There is a grace under pressure called "poise" which is needed by the sophisticated priest in the 1980s. It helps him not to yell when the saddening announcements are made: "I've decided to leave the active ministry" or "I personally don't believe in abortion but the two of us have decided we have no other choice" or "My wife and I recently decided to divorce."

Poise had its masterpiece in me as I murmured: "I'm sorry for your trouble. I know Rick well; we have talked often. He has mentioned he has several brothers and sisters."

"We have five children," he said. "Rick is the oldest. There's no way to spare them pain, of course; but my wife and I think it would be best for everyone concerned if we separate. Our marriage hasn't been working for some time."

I could hear weariness in his voice. He's not a bad man, I thought, but if his marriage were a business deal, he would know how to straighten it out.

"Is there someone you could talk to," I asked, "who might help you?"

"Thank you, no," he said. "It's been over between us for many years. My wife and I are tired of living the lie of being happily married. Our children are bright enough to understand there's a deadness that's as real as a wall between their mother and me."

"I'm sorry," I said.

I have sat at dinner tables where couples try to push conversation through a wall that separates them. Words don't get through unless they're fired like bullets. By the end of the meal you believe the cloth must be littered with words, fallen like birds that have smashed against the sound barrier.

"I wanted to tell you about Rick," he said, "in case he doesn't talk to you himself. I don't want his grades to suffer. He's been doing so well. I would appreciate it if one of you padres kept an eye on him."

He clicked off, and the "padre" in me made me wonder if I shouldn't look up Rick and offer to do something archetypally priestly for him, like teaching him to play baseball. Unfortunately, I am not an archetype, nor a padre, either, except to some former servicemen who date themselves with the Catholic chic of Hollywood in the 1940s.

I hoped Rick would drop by my room to talk, but I didn't hear from him. A few days later I got a note from his mother:

> I understand that you talked with my husband. I don't know what he could have said about me, but I hope that he mentioned we have a storybook marriage: a lovely home, five lovely children. We have good times together.
>
> Only I worry sometimes at my husband's silly talk. He gets some silly idea, and I put my foot down. It makes a marriage strong and Catholic when a woman knows how to put her foot down. . . .
>
> Please don't worry Rick with this. I hope you don't mind his father's calling; he shouldn't have bothered you. It's so immature to bother people with silly, crazy notions. . . .

I'll have my husband call you in a few days to invite you to come and see our wonderful family. . . .

The next night, Rick's father called again.

"Padre," he said, "I feel trapped. I thought we had agreed to a separation, if I promised not to ask for a divorce right away. Yesterday, when she found out I had gotten an apartment, she got hysterical. It was the worst scene of our whole marriage."

"I was wondering how she was handling things," I said. "She sent me a letter."

"She wrote Father Hesburgh, too," he said. "I found it and tore it up. She wanted him to talk to me. She wanted him to tell me that I couldn't leave her, that Rick would get kicked out of Notre Dame if I left her."

"Father Hesburgh gets lots of mail," I said. "Nothing surprises him."

"She sent for Rick," he said. "She told Rick she would kill herself if I left the house."

"How's he doing?" I asked.

"He's trying to protect his mother," he said. "He made me promise I wouldn't leave. I told him, 'Kid, I'm not going anywhere until your mother calms down.' "

"I'm sorry he's involved," I said.

"She dragged him home," he said. "She kept threatening to kill herself."

Rick stayed home for more than a week. When he finally came to talk to me, I asked, "How are your parents doing?"

"My parents have such a wretched marriage," he said. "Dad wants to leave. He's been wanting to leave for years. Mom kept on having babies, I think, as a way of holding him. He kept getting more involved in business, as a way of escaping."

"Why does he want to leave?" I asked.

"Mom thinks he has another woman he wants to be with," he said. "It probably isn't true. There probably have been many women in his life, but no one in particular. My mother's jealous of some imaginary redhead."

"Do you think they could live together successfully," I asked, "if your mother wasn't jealous?"

"My mother has a problem in the head," he said. "One week she's imagining that she has the perfect marriage, with her playing the Catholic mother of the year. The next week she's complaining to the kids about the silly bitch that their father is having dates with."

He looked at me as though he were declaring a moment of truth. "Do you know what I wish?"

"What do you wish, Rick?"

"I wish to God there *were* another woman," he declared. "I wish he would get out once and for all! I wish they would end the marriage, so all of us could have some peace."

"What would happen to your mother, Rick," I asked softly, "if your father left her?"

"She says she would go crazy," he said. "She says she would kill herself.

"If craziness is what she chooses, let her have it. If dying is what she wants, let her die. If she could forget the self-pity and think of her kids, we could get along pretty well as a family." At this point, he was fighting back tears.

"It hurts to love people so much," I said.

"I hate them as much as I love them," he said. "Mom's got this obsession about Dad's leaving. Dad is in love with long distance. My brothers and sisters and I don't know where we're supposed to fit in."

The next day, I tried to make arrangements to meet Rick's father for lunch in Chicago.

"Well, padre," he said, "I don't know if it's convenient to do that. Maybe we could visit in the spring when I come to the campus to bring Rick home."

If he wanted to deal with me as the padre, I was willing to play the game. I was willing to chew him up with the charm, wit, and wisdom of all the clerical curmudgeons he had met in the movies. I was willing to bully him with talk of his immortal soul while using an Irish brogue, just like Barry Fitzgerald. I was willing to have the last word, after which further speech was nonsense.

The last word can be a gentle word; it can be the essence of calm common sense. Cardinal O'Hara, I thought, is one of my fathers in faith. I want to be as authoritative and as sensible as he would have been.

"I want to talk to you," I said to Rick's father, "and I want to talk with your wife. I'm going to shove you together or I'm going to push you apart. I'm going to talk to you about your souls and I'm going to talk to you about your lives. I want you to listen to me, to listen to each other, and to listen to a marriage counselor.

"I want to remind you that you have made covenants registered with God. You don't mess around with covenants promising to watch over children. You've got to honor your covenants no matter how tired or bored you get doing it. You've got to learn once again to cherish each other, before you ruin your children as well as your marriage."

"Padre," he said, "we've talked to some of the best. My wife and I are as uneasy together as two victims nailed to the same cross.

"I love my children, but they'll get along. Keep an eye on Rick. That's why I sent him to Notre Dame, so that you padres could keep an eye on him. I can't keep the world safe for him, any more than my father kept the world safe for me. Hell, when I was his age, I was in the Marines, fighting on Iwo Jima."

We had that conversation a year ago. I haven't heard from him since.

Rick didn't come back for his sophomore year. I've heard his mother is sick and is being taken care of in some home or hospital. I tried calling his father, but his secretary told me he was working in an office overseas.

Rick, I gather, is home, playing temporary parent to his siblings. From what I hear, he's making out all right. Eventually he hopes to come back to Notre Dame and finish his degree.

I'm sorry the padres couldn't do more to help Rick. At least we had a chance to keep an eye on him for a while. There are students like Rick, living through similar problems, that you never get to keep an eye on at all.

Padres are not as omniscient as they were in O'Hara's day. Enemies are not as identifiable as they were on Iwo Jima.

A BROTHER'S REQUIEM

All my life, I have spent time with friends who were mourning the deaths of brothers.

When my own brother died in June this year, it was my turn to play the role of survivor, and I felt embarrassed. People, trying to be helpful, wanted to talk about my brother. I did not want to talk about him. I could not discuss the pain of his life which was very personal to me. I felt it was unfair that he should have died as he did. Yet perhaps death, when it came, arrived for him as a kindness.

The phone rang at 2 a.m. in my New York rectory with the news from the hospital. I spent the hours remaining until daylight planning the funeral. I didn't think it would be kind to telephone other people in the middle of the night. No one else needed to know until morning, not even my mother. What could the poor lady do except grieve? It seemed unnecessary to wake her up so she could cry.

I hated the thought of mentioning my brother's death to anyone. I didn't want people offering condolences. Nothing about death is unusual, after all. Death, like birth, is as predictable as the seasons.

People seem called to moral attention when you tell them of a death in your family. I didn't need attention. I just wanted time to figure out a mystery which had overtaken me.

Yet death is too shattering an experience to keep silent about it. You cannot let friends think that life, for you, is the same today as it was yesterday. And it seemed wrong to let a soul slip away into eternity without fanfare, as though my brother were a spy escaping from one country to another, not wishing to call attention to himself.

"Early this morning," I finally said to friends, "my brother died up in Maine."

"We're sorry for your trouble," everyone said in the polite, kind words people use when they hear of death. "Is there anything we can do to help?"

"No, nothing, thank you," I said. Each of us had said the necessary thing. In telling them, I had taken part in a universal experience.

———————

There is something epic about the journey you make in going home for a family funeral. It is one of the inevitable scenes, if you are the youngest child, like the initial awareness that innocence has been lost.

In Maine, I talked to a young undertaker whose father and grandfather had handled the mortuary services for my father and grandfather. I wanted to make the simplest arrangements possible. He wanted to make detailed explanations of the prices he was charging.

"Can you arrange for a minister to conduct the burial service?" I asked.

"Oh, certainly," he said. "Can I give him an idea of the readings you want?"

"He'll know what to use," I said, "I'm sure he will include 'Sunset and Evening Star' by Tennyson." (I know these New England ministers. They always include "Sunset and Evening Star." No one in our family has been buried without those verses.)

"We'll play tapes of sacred music," this undertaker said, "unless you prefer the organ."

"My brother never cared for organ music," I said. The undertaker seemed doubtful until I added: "My brother wasn't Catholic." That seemed to satisfy him. He was a nice chap, anxious to please.

At the nursing home where my mother lives, I decided not to speak of my brother. Last year, during an illness when we thought we would lose her, she entered a world between life and death where she keeps company with a whole troop of people I believe to be in heaven. Now, almost blind, she lives a reality that seems close to dreaming.

"It must be raining cats and dogs," she said. "Did you ever in your life see so much rain?"

"Mama," I said, "the sunshine is streaming across your bed. Can't you feel how warm it is?"

"I can't see a bit of the weather because of my eyes," she replied.

I raised the shade so the light would bathe her tired face. After a while, she said: "I hope you have an umbrella. You could catch your death of cold on a day like this."

"Mama," I said, "do you know who this is?"

"No," she answered. "Who is it?"

"It's your son Robert," I said.

"Oh, no, dear," she replied, "Robert died." Just when I was thinking how confused she was, she asked: "Are you still losing your hair?"

"No," I said, "not really."

"You should get a haircut, dear," she said, "unless you're trying to look like a hippie."

Neither of us ever mentioned my brother's name.

———

On Wednesday, at the funeral home, the undertaker kept waiting to usher guests who never arrived. A few of us from the family were there, and some old neighbors came.

The minister read scriptures which, as I expected, had nothing to do with my brother. He did not recite "Sunset and Evening Star." The service was dignified but impersonal. I felt it would have been an insult for me, or for anyone, to try to be personal about my brother's life.

We brought my brother to the cemetery, where he sleeps close to my father in a lot open to the sea.

Earlier, riding in a car up to Maine, I had examined the deed to the burial plot; it was dated 1919. My father, as a newly married young man, had bought this land for his family not far from the burial place of his own parents.

I felt blessed to think of my father's foresight. As I said the prayer committing my brother's body to its eternal rest, I felt at peace for the first time in this whole experience of death, knowing I had brought him to a place where, finally, he was home, as he would have wanted and as my father had intended a long time ago. Burial in such sea-girt, sky-touched, blessed New England earth gave a dignity to my brother's dying, as though he had lain down to sleep with patriarchs and kings.

I thought of words which were not Lord Tennyson's.

Under the wide and starry sky,
Dig the grave and let me lie:
Glad did I live and gladly die,
And I laid me down with a will.

This be the verse you grave for me:
Here he lies where he long'd to be;
Home is the sailor, home from the sea,
And the hunter home from the hill.

That was the kind of life my brother led. For this day, Stevenson's "Requiem" felt appropriate.

THE BAG LADY'S WINDFALL

On New Year's night, riding the subway shuttle from Grand Central to Port Authority, I saw a shopping bag lady whose appearance shocked me.

She was asleep and incredibly dirty. Her hands guarded four or five plastic shopping bags, as begrimed as herself. Her legs were bare and scabbed above filthy ankle socks. Her skirt, if she wore one, must have been very short; I thought it was possible that, beneath an old black coat, she wasn't wearing anything at all.

Oh my dear, I thought, how can I possibly help her? She was only one of thousands, I knew, who were without shelter that night. But how could I leave an old lady to an uncertain sleep on a subway train? What rest could she get there? What proper rest did she ever get? How weary she must be, I thought, with never a place to lie down in winter that was free from cold and danger.

I was on my way home from an excellent New Year's dinner with friends in Westchester, and although I didn't want to walk away, I didn't want to touch her either. I would have been afraid to try to lift her to her feet and take her to a place where she could have been washed and fed and put to bed and looked after for the night.

I would risk getting lice, I thought. No one would be pleased with me, if I brought home lice.

I have a terrible fear, when I'm in New York, of catching lice. I am more afraid of catching lice than I am of being mugged. Most people I know in New York have never gotten mugged, but a few have caught lice.

A lady who teaches grade school in Manhattan told me of a girl who brought lice to school in November, and they infected the whole class. "I'm fifty years old," she said, "and it's the first time it ever happened to me. Special soaps and shampoos were necessary, and every article of clothing had to be washed or dry-cleaned. It was the most terrible feeling to know I had lice."

A number of years ago, I spent a few days visiting a mission house on the Bowery. An old actor named Mark complained to me of being lousy. An aged lady named Julia told me of discovering lice crawling in her hair at the nape of her neck.

"Don't you get them," she warned me. Some of these dirty men are alive with them." Fearing the possibility, I itched imaginatively for a week.

A nurse from Beth Israel Hospital who made regular visits to the mission suggested precautions I might take.

"Never leave a coat or hat lying around," she said, "and if you must sit down, choose a straight wooden chair placed at a distance from the walls. Always shake every article of wearing apparel before you put it on.

"At the hospital, they warn us to do these things when we're visiting the neighborhoods, though it is not always possible, and you can't embarrass people by being too obvious."

"How do workers who live in this place manage to avoid being infested?" I asked.

"They do get infested," she said. "Dorothy Day's friends say she sometimes got lice from the homeless men at the Catholic Workers. She had a horror of lice, but they were one of the crosses she accepted in showing her love for unfortunate people."

As for myself, the smallest louse would defeat me.

I was sure there must be lice living off the unwashed woman who sat sprawled on the seat across from me on the subway. Unwilling to get close to her body, I did the only thing I knew how to do: I gave her some money.

I slipped a bill into those fists twined around the handles of a shopping bag. I did it gently so as not to awaken her. It would seem an unkindness to awaken her, because God knows when she had slept before or when she would sleep again.

If she awoke, seeing me with money in my hand, I thought, she might accuse me of robbing her. If I had been wearing a Roman collar, she might have accepted me as a person to be trusted, but seeing me in my Harris tweed jacket, she might have considered me an intruder on her privacy.

The train was nearly empty. No one had noticed us. Still, because I was afraid that someone might take the money away from her, I waited for her to wake up and take charge of her tiny windfall.

I've made an investment, I thought, as the train shuttled back and forth between stations, and now I have to watch my investment. I hadn't given her a lot of money, because I didn't have a lot to give. But since I had nothing else to give her but pity, I didn't want her to get ripped off before she even knew she had a grubstake in her hands.

Passengers got on or off at Grand Central or at Port Authority. No one ventured to get close to the sleeping woman. A policeman walked through the train, glanced at her, shook his head, and moved on. I had no way of knowing whether he would let her stay there for the night.

To entertain myself, I began thinking of Saint Francis of Assisi. After his conversion, they say, he embraced lepers whom he had previously feared as loathsome.

I have never seen a leper, I thought, but I doubt if I would want to embrace one. I could never embrace a leper, or a derelict either, because of my fear of lice and disease.

Most derelicts don't want your embraces; some want your money, and a few want to shake your hand. I'm brave enough to risk a handshake, though I am careful afterwards not to smoke until the hand is washed.

Derelicts are not lepers, though I treat them that way, and I am not Saint Francis. I am an imperfect Christian who now travels through the Bowery in a car, and stays away from the missions on Second Avenue as much as he can.

When the train lurched to an abrupt stop at Grand Central, my shopping bag lady was finally rocked into wakefulness. She checked her bags and her person. Noticing money in her hand, she looked around. Then she let it flutter to the floor as though it were a gum wrapper.

She took a cigarette butt and match from her coat pocket. The cigarette had seen service before; I guessed that she had lifted it from a public ashtray. She finished it in a half-dozen puffs and threw it on the floor not far from the money. Then, gathering herself up, she moved herself and her bags to the far end of the car, and I could see she was wearing something as abbreviated as a luncheon cloth wrapped around her in place of a skirt.

I picked up my bill from the floor and got off the train before it started to move again. It's God's money now, I thought. I will give it to the friars at the Franciscan church in the morning.

If I had truly seen the features of Christ on that old black face, I would have offered her something more helpful than money which, for her as she was, would have opened few doors. In trying to give her money, I wanted to feel virtuous, and she disappointed me by not accepting it.

I could have handed it to her when she was awake, I thought. But she might have bitten me. Some of the street people are crazy enough to bite. Then I would have ended up with hepatitis as well as lice.

It is not comfortable to be a Christian who is selectively charitable. Still, as a priest unconverted to the social gospel, I had done the best I could.

I decided to walk the two blocks from Grand Central to Port Authority, where I would catch the A train down to the Village. I had seen enough of the truly needy for one New Year's evening.

PART OF THE MYTH

I watch them through the door of my room, working out in the lounge beyond the lobby; lying on their backs, scissoring the air with their legs, arching their bodies for a pelvic twist. Aerobics, they call it—a physical quest for the perfect form, adding graces to a loveliness exquisite enough already to take my breath away.

I see them on their way to dances, gowned and elegant, sometimes wistful, always lovely; needing approval, praise, reassurance. "You're a knockout," I say, and they smile. They have grown up to wear their mothers' dresses and are ready to burst into the flowering of young womanhood. For that passage, they have come to Notre Dame.

Young women, here and elsewhere, are always full of the mystery of being themselves. Seeing their windburnt faces and loving their barefoot innocence, I feel warmed by their company, as though the sun were visiting some hidden rim of earth. I can add nothing to their grace as women. Their youth is their own, waiting for the years to confirm or diminish their loveliness.

I see them watching attentively at Mass, listening, hearing, learning, believing; wanting to be loved and hoping to find love here. I overhear them talking among themselves, and sometimes they talk to me. They always tell me more than I ever tell them.

Now and again, I can help these young women of Notre Dame. I let some lovely homesick child lean for a while. I try to be the cheerful chaplain who knows when a compliment or an opinion or an objection is needed. I make myself available during the times when love has failed. Because of age and experience, I tend to play a father's role, to act as a parent figure in this home away from home.

Last fall, when I moved into Pasquerilla West, I was greeted by a note: "Blessed art thou among women." For a decade now, I have been among these women of Notre Dame, like a thorn among roses, a kindly toad in a rosebud garden of girls.

In 1972, when the first women arrived, it was like we men had adopted them. No matter how nice it was to have them here, no matter how kindly we treated them, those first women were still a bit like Little Orphan Annie. They felt it; we felt it. We praise them as good, intelligent, and self-reliant, and then we offered them hand-me-downs, because that's all we had to give. We expected them to be grateful, because they were orphans, dependent on the kindness of strangers who said, "You belong to us now."

Ten years later, I still meet some jealous siblings, older brothers who think the birthright—the tradition—belongs only to them.

But it doesn't. No administrator can hand on a deed of ownership to the Notre Dame tradition, as though it came with the class schedule and the football tickets. The birthright has to be earned.

I heard it said of some of those first freshman women, "She had a father and brothers who came here. She knows the myth." At Notre Dame, it's as simple as that. If you want to belong, you have to learn the myth. You have to wrap your heart and mind in it. You have to believe the meanest rocks of the place tell a story.

The myth begins and ends with the church.

In the old days, Notre Dame was as mythical as Camelot in its fidelity to the beauty of the Latin Church. If you loved the Mass, you could love it here more than anywhere. The university, with its dozens of chapels where the Eucharist was kept and where the liturgy was celebrated hundreds of times a day, called itself a City of the Blessed Sacrament. On any floor of any dorm on campus, pardon and peace were available from priests. The place was so Catholic, it must have felt uncomfortable not to be a Catholic, or at least open to the truth and goodness of the church.

The Eucharist is still here. The dome still gleams in the light of the sun and moon. The altars, most of them, remain in place, and, though their numbers are sadly diminished, so do the priests.

Women now are part of the myth, the happiest development in our whole tradition. Their story is only now unfolding.

A number of books have been written about the history of Notre Dame, but the women have yet to write their own books. Will those who write know the myth? What will they make of a tradition that includes Knute Rockne and Joe Evans, Pop Farley and Frank O'Malley and the other bachelor dons?

Giants have lived here as saints and scholars. They entered the solitude, their personal share of the world's loneliness. The truth of their experience was wisdom, a truth they shared with their students.

By the time pens are put to paper in the third century of Notre Dame's existence, women will have their own giants, their own Rocknes and O'Malleys. The freshmen will be told in their first hours on campus of the rare characters who, in the 1980s, were the rectors of Farley and Pasquerilla. Legends will be repeated, and expanded in the telling, of those wise women, tenured in truth, who could show you the view from the top of the mountain, like the spies of Joshua scouting the Promised Land.

Outside my window, a girl with red hair is playing Frisbee with her roommate. The girl's name is Cathy. I saw her one day playing football with some lads. I asked her if, someday, she wanted to play in the Super Bowl.

"I'd prefer," she said impishly, "to become a priest."

"Maybe someday," I said, "you can take my place as the university chaplain."

"I don't know if I can wait that long," she said, meaning, I suppose, that she expected I would live forever.

Whenever changes are made, some will say, "Things are getting better." Others will say, "Things are very difficult." Both will have an eye on the truth.

In a hundred years, Notre Dame will still be Notre Dame. Some things will change; others will remain the same. Old faces will go away and new faces will take their place. Buildings will be built from the ancient yellow bricks of Sorin's time. The place will survive.

When an old order passes away, the rhythm of the change is gradual, like the ticking of a clock. When the earth is renewed each year, the beauty of the ways in which it is old increases, like the loveliness of Grecian urns.

If you are old yourself, you bless the Lord for the gifts of this day, without frightening yourself by looking backward or forward. If you live in the peace of an acceptance of here and now, the springtime is within you, flowering in the gardens and the orchards of the soul.

Down the hall, the aerobic dancing is beginning. Two doors away, chocolate chip cookies are being baked in the kitchen. A delightful friend sits across from me in a rocker; she is mending my shirt.

In the words of a New England transcendentalist: "I accept the universe!"

To which comes back the reply: "You damn well better."

LIFE IN THE BOOT CAMP SEMINARY

Notre Dame is justly famous for its football teams, but all my friends were surprised when I chose it as a place to study for the priesthood.

In Maine, where I lived, nobody had any idea where a guy went to school if he wanted to become a priest. If you had asked them, they probably would have said, "Rome."

Furthermore, nobody had any idea why I wanted to become a priest.

Some Protestant friends said: "A priest can't get married and have kids. Are you sure you want to be a priest?"

Some Catholic friends said: "It takes lots of brains. Are you sure you can make it?" They believed the myth that priests are smarter than everyone else. They knew I wasn't dumb, but they doubted I was enough of a genius to become a priest.

I would have walked through hell to become a priest. The idea seized my attention and imagination. I knew life would look cruel if I didn't make it; I would have felt that God let me ruin myself with dreams.

So with high hopes I came to Notre Dame. Before entering the novitiate, I was supposed to spend a year as a postulant at Holy Cross Seminary (now Holy Cross Hall) on Saint Mary's Lake.

I stayed there two years instead of one. Hell sometimes means having to do the things you hate for a second or third time, until they judge you've got it right.

Holy Cross Seminary—once called by Knute Rockne "the cradle of Notre Dame"—was an old, decrepit building that could not have been more cheerless. Living there, I felt like an orphan from the workhouse in *Oliver Twist*.

A third of the staff, two priests and a brother, wore hearing aids. Another priest, also wired for sound, would come in for weekly confessions. We used to joke that hearing aids would be given us as symbols of our final vows. (Now that I am older, with hearing difficulties myself, I am more sympathetic to the problem.)

The superior of the seminary was named Richard Grimm. We imagined him to be distantly related to the German brothers who wrote fairy tales. He was six-feet six-inches tall, and he could give you a look as stern as his name, He let you know from the beginning that he was serious about the business of making priests. You'd better be serious, too.

For the first month, I was constantly sweating from the high humidity. I was asthmatic from hay fever, and I was homesick enough to die.

Nobody had warned me about a rule of silence. For many hours of the day (when we weren't at the university taking classes) and all night long, we moved around in silence like Trappists, to help us become "interiorly recollected."

Interior recollection, as I understood it, was listening with an inner ear, in case God was kind enough to speak to our souls. With me, He never even cleared his throat. Interior recollection seemed as useless as sticking my ear against a seashell and pretending to hear the roar of the waves.

So there I was, a pleasure-loving American boy, living in a decaying building on the edge of a lake on the edge of a campus, with other lads as deprived as myself whom I couldn't talk to, even though we studied and slept in the same room.

After lunch and dinner, following a seminary tradition, we all walked to the community cemetery and prayed for the deceased members of the Congregation of Holy Cross. It seemed morbid to a lapsed WASP like me. It made me worry about my mental health. Let the dead bury the dead, I thought. They have nothing to do with becoming a Catholic priest. It didn't seem fair that I should waste my time praying their souls out of purgatory. (If I had been wiser, I should have asked them to pray for me.)

I've always hated doing things I wasn't good at, and I was never good at sports. Each day, for ninety minutes in the afternoon, we were expected to play games that would exhaust our energies. I hated it.

The alternative was plucking chickens, which was smelly work. I must have plucked a truckload, but we couldn't possibly eat enough chickens to keep me plucking through all the games I was otherwise expected to play. So I joined in, making a fool of myself with my clumsiness.

In the forty-five minutes of evening recreation after supper, a group of us would walk down the road, past the cemetery to the Dixie Highway, and stare across longingly at Saint Mary's. At 7:15, we would hear the lonely whistle of a train hauling freight to Chicago. We knew it was time to head back to the chapel for the rosary, after which the grand silence of the night watch would begin.

Everything that seemed pleasurable in our former lives was proscribed to us here as worldly. Black was the color of our suits, ties, and hats. It was a sign we had chosen the higher spiritual gifts that can be earned only through self-denial.

All the world was out there, beyond the gate, up and down the Dixie Highway, waiting to endanger our vocations: hit songs, popular magazines, milkshakes and Cokes at HoJo's, novels, newspapers, and drive-ins, where souls, not lucky enough to be Christ, watched Fred Astaire dancing with Cyd Charisse. The world seemed so attractive when so much of it was forbidden.

A classmate, worried about his "worldliness," went to talk to a priest.

"What's on your mind?" the priest asked.

"Wine, women, and song," the seminarian replied.

"Forget it," the priest said. But amnesia does not come easily when you're twenty-one.

Some went home. One or two left the first day. Others were gone by the end of the semester. A few were told to go home because they were in the wrong place.

The one thing I shrank from more than seminary life was the thought of quitting it. Everyone at home, Catholic or Protestant, would have thought they understood. No one would have suggested that I couldn't make it. But I wanted too much to make the team to even think of going home. Anything else I imagined myself doing seemed smaller than my ambition of being ordained. Life would have defeated me at the beginning, I thought, if I let myself become what in those days was called a "spoiled priest." Perhaps persistence is the essence of the grace of vocation.

When I left Notre Dame to enter the novitiate, I didn't care if I saw the campus again. I didn't know it, but I had been through boot camp. The toughest part was over; the rest of religious formation was relatively easy. After boot camp, nothing gets so grotesquely exaggerated again.

Silence became a habit, necessary for a young cleric who has chosen to be thoughtful and serious. I had learned that worldliness is no great fault, but I also had learned not to depend on superficial things. And I had made friends who would help me through. These friendships were the beginning of my community life in the Congregation of Holy Cross.

Notre Dame has meant many things to me. But before I could learn to love it, I had to survive it as a boot camp. Holy Cross Seminary was tougher than any spring training camp the football team goes through. We had a coach, as we used to say, who was Grimm.

BILL AND PAT

A dear friend of mine, now married, formerly a priest of my community, asked if I thought the church would ever call old veterans like himself back into service as married clergy.

"Bill," I said, "if the bishops tried to reestablish the priests who have left to get married, the ones who stayed—some of them, at least—would be livid with anger, like the elder brother of the parable for whom the father never slaughtered the fatted calf. If the matter came up, I'm not sure I wouldn't agree with them."

I sounded portentous and dismal, like a preacher trying to wing his way through an unprepared homily. Bill accepted my answer in a sweet-tempered way, a sign to me of how beneficial his marriage has been.

In his bachelor days, with nostrils flaring, Bill might have argued the matter until the last drop of Jack Daniel's had disappeared from the bottle. Soggy at sunrise, we would have said good night, our friendship strained to the breaking point, until sobriety replaced the unreality of the half-life of bourbon.

Bill and I have been best friends since seminary days. He had taken his ordination and his ministry very seriously. I know how he struggled as a priest against being misunderstood by superiors. Bitterness against injustices kept isolating him until finally, after years of pain, he felt he had no other option but to leave.

I hated to see him go, but I couldn't argue with his decision. Love, when you need it, comes as grace. The church should be grateful to the caring women who have become responsible for loving those priests whom the church has failed to love enough.

I would never be guilty, I hope, of the elder brother's sin toward Bill, or some of the other departed priests I know. If you love someone, you wish him well; jealously would be unworthy of the brotherhood. Bill is my boyhood chum. He will always be a part of my ordained life. Someday, if the shepherds are generous, we will again celebrate Mass together. The church, in its loving kindness, will not exclude Bill forever from participating in the eternal priesthood.

Even at this moment, as a married man in Westchester, Bill has not been excluded as a priest. As he says, "I am part of the married clergy, whether they recognize it or not."

Bill's wife, Patricia, is a treasure. Chautard and Tanqueray, in their books on the spiritual life, never did as much for Bill as Pat does. As middle-aged people, married four years, they seem like lovers who have been keeping their romance fresh and growing since they were young.

We often sit at the dinner table and talk. Conversation is Bill's delight. God furnished him with a wit that keeps the meal joyful, as though for him the table were an altar with rituals and mysteries symbolized in wine, which celebrate friendship in a liturgy of charm.

(Once, in leaden times, when an evening could turn into an ordeal, I told Bill he talked too much.

("Did you ever think," he asked, his face strained with pain, "that I wouldn't talk so much, if I met someone more often who would listen?" I understood how isolated he felt. I felt small for my criticism of a lonely man.)

Now, Pat sometimes says, "C'mon, Bill, you're not eating."

Bill considers how much food he has made disappear. "All right," he says, "I'll catch up in a minute." In a short time, he has again forgotten to eat. Pat, without a word, picks up his plate and carries it to the kitchen.

"That woman," he says, "is a wonder."

I know without being told that she is a wonder.

We then talked of families and of jobs, of the church and of the popes.

"God bless John Paul I," said Bill. "He was elected to do me a favor. Approving my papers was one of the few things he lived to do as pope. I must have been the last priest out the door."

This night seemed so beautiful because for years, when I visited Bill, I had listened to him dying.

Patricia had made the difference. Being with them together is comforting, as when you rest your weariness against a favorite pillow.

Remembering his old life, Bill said as I was leaving, "I did my best for them. After a while, there was no place left to go. I liked the life and I liked the people. I didn't leave them until they left me first."

He has no regrets. He is a happy man.

The church is not wholly to blame for its exiles. All of us are somewhat responsible for what happens to us. But I'll bet more priests are lost in lonely rectories than in crowded saloons.

Bill and Pat are an ordinary couple. They've had to help each other a lot to become so beautifully ordinary.

Maybe someday, all the Bills, with their Patricias, will be at work in the ministry where they began. The elder brothers will welcome them without rancor from the places where they have also tended the vines.

A PARTING GIFT

My mother, to her embarassment, took a long time dying. For two years, she seemed like a prisoner in the house of life, always on the point of leaving yet detained against her will, weary with waiting for the door to be opened.

Alone at the moment of her death last August, she slipped away while we thought she was sleeping. To all appearances, she joined the company of her loved ones. She had felt close to family members who had gone on ahead; she had spoken to them so directly, I could almost see their faces in the dimness of the sickroom. When her own moment finally came, death was gentle with her, coming like a playmate at noonday as the clock was striking twelve.

My mother always kept close to God, so I didn't hesitate to entrust her welfare to the prayers of the church. The metaphors expressive of God's love, full of assurances about peace and rest for the soul, are the kind of truth I have the grace to accept. "The shepherd is watchful of the flock." I trusted the shepherd to bring my mother through the valley of the shadow of death.

So, in a small parish in Maine, the requiem prayers were said. The church honored her body with its incense and holy water as a temple of glory that would be raised from the dust. Nine priests prayed for her soul to be graced with holiness from the Mass—that ancient act which remembers that the shepherd laid down his life for the sheep.

The Mass has a way of tapering its immensity to plainitive simplicity, minimizing the pomp and circumstance to fit the size of the need. My mother would have enjoyed this service. She never in all her life saw me active on the altar as a priest. Though she was a Catholic, she wasn't comfortable with playing the role of the priest's mother in the old neighborhood where we all had lived as Protestants. On the day of her funeral, when she would no longer feel embarassed, I had my final chance to bring her to church as a captive audience. I felt good about taking her there, as though I had done her a favor with a lot of class. Her Catholic funeral made me feel at peace with her death as nothing else could have.

At her burial in the cemetery close to the sea, she rejoined the Protestants, my father and brothers and grandparents, and I doubt that there was religious discomfort among them. The weather turned wet, and I stumbled through the final prayers in my hurry to get friends and relatives out of the rain. "Good night, Jerry," she had said when we buried my father. "Good night, Mother," I said in the rain, not knowing how long it would be before morning comes again.

"After great pain, a formal feeling comes— / The Nerves sit ceremonious, like Tombs— / ... First—Chill—then Stupor—then the letting go—." Sadness replaces the sweetness of nostalgia for memories as shy as ghosts. The long loneliness begins. It is part of an old, old story that most human beings come to know. For weeks after my mother's death, I was afraid to have a bad thought, for fear it would hurt her. She still stays on my mind, as though death were also a kind of bonding.

Death, when it keeps its appointment with old age, comes as a release that prohibits mourning. Forty years ago, I knew that my mother, so protective of her family, was afraid of death. She lived to be eighty-seven. Blind and lonely, she made her peace with fear. Without a backward glance, she became part of a universal experience.

Death affects you as a survivor even while you figure out the difference it makes. You keep your grief private, because others have their own problems; they have only a brief time to spare in mourning with you. You keep detached from the appearance of loss, though death leaves you scarred with insecurity. "My mother has died, and I'm feeling quite alone with the loss"—that would be in the worst taste to admit. Grief, like the late winter wind, is tempered to the shorn lamb. If it is not, you have a problem.

John Donne, meditating on "for whom the bell tolls," said that every man's death diminished him. I do not believe, though, that I was diminished by Christ's death. The veil of the temple was split, the sun hid its face in shadows, the cock crowed three times, but the dirge bell never tolled for Calvary with its three bodies and its weeping women. No man was diminished by Christ's death. Death itself was diminished by that victory over darkness.

Easter is the season for strengthening hope. When the alleluias are sung, they should be every Christian's alleluias, the victory song of those who trust the blood of the lamb. In celebrating the communion of saints, the church celebrates my mother's feast, too. With or without halo and harp, she lives in the country where the saints talk to God. I will keep as a parting gift the memory of her speaking with my father on her deathbed. The Lord talked with his father from his deathbed, too, saying, "Into thy hands, I will commend my spirit," and the gateway to life was opened.

Every Ash Wednesday, when I am marked with the burnt-palm cross of penance and *metanoia*, I will hug the memory of my parents, whose mortal bodies have put on immortality like a choir robe; they were flesh from which my flesh came, now vessels of clay wearing incorruption as though clothed in light. For forty days, I will try to keep close to the Lord on his way to the cross, accepting the archetypal death of every man's suffering and dying. In his burial, the Lord underwent a universal experience, to gather the lambs from the valley of the shadow of death. Because of his rising, the graves became gardens where grains of wheat were planted, awaiting the new life that comes out of dying, in the freshness of a never-failing springtime.

So say the church's imagery, its poetry and myths. The church sees the truth dimly now, as though in a mirror.

Saint Paul, who always was high on the experience of Easter, wrote: "Eye hath not seen, nor ear heard, nor has it entered into the heart of man to know what things God has prepared for those who love him."

In that case, I trust they will know enough to offer my mother a good cup of tea.

"YOU SHALL BE
MY SPECIAL POSSESSION"

The turkey salad and the potato salad at the Jewish deli on Seventh Avenue are fit for a feast of Elijah. In the summer, when I live in Manhattan, I stop there for supper. A big turkey salad sandwich with a kosher pickle, a side order of potato salad, and a dish of rice pudding is a better meal than the lamb chops served at Luchow's.

Jack, the waiter, comes on me like he's my father. He suggests the knishes, the chicken soup, the chopped liver, the corned beef served on a roll. I stick to my favorites. Jack figures we don't grow turkeys in Indiana.

He once asked me if I'd ever been to Israel. I told him I'm saving my pennies in a mayonnaise jar decorated with the Star of David on masking tape, lettered with the words MOUNT SINAI OR BUST. I was kidding him—I'm too much of a religious snob to go as a tourist to the Holy Land which, I'm told, has been vulgarized by commercialism. I hate the clink of coins in places rumored to be holy.

"It's the Promised Land," Jack insisted, "the land of milk and honey." He got a faraway look in his eyes as though he were seeing fields of grass for the cattle or clusters of flowers for the bees. "Ask the Cardinal to send you. Tell him you want to study the Torah." Then Jack made a big show of pulling out his pocket change to give me pennies for my trip.

One night, I could see Jack had something on his mind. At the end of the meal, he brought a cup of coffee to my table and sat down to talk.

"You've seen the Jews for Jesus hanging out in the streets?" he asked.

I had. The Jews for Jesus are a familiar sight in the city, preaching the gospel and handing out literature urging people to convert to Yeshua, son of Miriam. As Jews, they feel enfranchised to give witness as blood brothers of the Savior.

"You think well of them?" Jack asked.

I told him I didn't have much of an opinion—although I admire fundamentalists who have the courage to be heckled by crowds. I knew, however, that the Jewish community saw this group as traitors.

"They're bending the ear of my youngest boy, Nathan," Jack said. "He's a bright Jewish kid, fourteen years old, and they're bending his ear with a name we don't talk about at home. I tell him, 'Nathan, if you make the mistake of joining this outfit out of conviction, you're out of the family.' His grandparents would go through the mourning rites as though he had died."

"Jack, would you be that hard on a fourteen-year-old going through a phase?"

"I would have to do something. He's bar mitzvah, a Jewish adult. He's studied the Commandments at the yeshiva." Jack hunched his shoulders in a gesture of helplessness. "I might refuse to see him or speak with him. But I myself would never mourn him as dead."

It's not easy listening to a Jewish father talk about disowning his son, his Isaac. Abraham's face must have shown the same kind of grief.

"These Jews for Jesus are slick operators," Jack continued. "Nathan meets a bunch of fellas, nice and friendly, near his school. He's wearing the *kippah*, the skullcap. They say, 'See, we're wearing *kippahs*. We are Jews, too.' They frighten the boy with pictures from the death camps. They tell him. 'This is the price the Jews paid for not accepting Christ.' I tell him, 'Nate, Christian theology does not teach such hate.' He answers: 'Then why do they hate us so much?'"

"Theology would never be so unfair," I agreed. "Theology would always favor the justice and mercy of God." Theology, I know, is not the business of amateurs, and I am not a theologian. But Christ couldn't have wanted guilt passed down as his inheritance.

"To tell the truth, Father," Jack went on, "if they're Jews, they are very ignorant. The Messiah isn't in the Jewish Old Testament; it's an idea that comes later. My boy doesn't know how to answer them when they tell him David and Moses were waiting for the Messiah."

Jack asked me to talk with Nathan; he trusted me not to brainwash his son as the fundamentalists had done. "As a Jew, he thinks he has blood on his hands," Jack explained. "A rabbi trying to tell him different would blow his stack. Anger wouldn't help to untrouble his conscience."

A few nights later I met Nathan, a dark-eyed, serious-faced lad wearing a skullcap, sitting with his father at a deli table. I asked him if he had read Chaim Potok, Isaac Bashevis Singer, Elie Wiesel, or Alfred Kazin, all of whom I had heard speak at Notre Dame. He knew who they were. He was reading Joseph Conrad's *Lord Jim* for school.

I asked him if he had read the entire Old Testament. He said he hadn't.

"You need a lot of patience to go from Genesis to Malachi," I said, and told him my own impressions of a sacred history full of stories about desert sheiks making covenants with Yahweh, and tribal fathers who wrestled with angels in the dark of night, and prophets who promise vineyards whose fruitfulness symbolized blessings of a world at peace.

"God really put his word on the line to take care of the Jewish people," I said, "in poetry as tender as love letters. Jews, in times of trouble, read the letters and believe in the love that was promised them. Even when God is silent, they hold onto the letters as though they were contracts."

I looked at Jack and Nathan, descendants of the survivors of a hundred pogroms. Some of their fathers most likely were holy rabbis in Eastern Europe, hurrying ahead of slaughter, carrying with them into exile only the sacred texts and the matzos for observing the Passover. I wondered if Jack and Nathan, who knew these stories better than I, were skeptical of me as a prophet.

"I like being a Catholic," I said. "But it's more of a miracle being a Jew. Nothing could be more of a miracle than holding onto a four-thousand-year-old tradition of trusting the God of your fathers and being faithful to his will, remembering the lightning over Sinai and manna in the desert. Maybe the survival of Israel's faith is the greatest of all the miracles that glorify God, surpassing even the miracle of the dead being raised to life."

I could see as I spoke that they were holding hands; I don't know who had taken whose. Maybe they were protecting themselves against being talked to death.

I put a question to Nathan. "Do you think God was indifferent to the prayers that came out of the ghettos when Europe was burning?"

He shrugged as though shrugging were a gesture of the perplexed taught at the yeshiva.

"Don't you think he felt honored by the family of Anne Frank, living in fear, living in an attic, happy when good luck brought them mouthfuls of honeycake with raisins to celebrate the Sabbath, the day of rest, which was a gift from the Master of the Universe to people who had once been slaves?"

I waited for Nathan to ask why the Master of the Universe hadn't saved Anne Frank. But he wasn't listening to me. He must have been reminded of something he knew better than I, something the Jews for Jesus couldn't have told him. He spoke to his father in Yiddish; they talked for a while back and forth. Then the two of them started to sing.

I have been at prayer meetings where the Holy Spirit has come and filled the air with music, as though he were using people's prayers as his wind chimes. In the same quick, unexpected way, the two of them started singing in a language I didn't know, swaying back and forth, singing a song. They both knew the words, the text of a covenant as full of love as a marriage proposal:

"You have seen for yourself how I bore you up on eagles' wings and brought you here to myself. Therefore if you harken to my voice and keep my covenant, you shall be my special possession dearer to me than all other people, though all the earth is mine. You shall be a kingdom of priests, a holy nation. . . ."

When they were finished, Jack brought a bottle of wine to the table so we could have a drink. He thought Christian Brothers was a wine I would be pleased to receive from him.

"Next year in Jerusalem," he said with hope.

"Next year in Jerusalem," I echoed.

YOU GET WHAT YOU NEED

Some conversations about last spring's events and attitudes on campus got me thinking about fathers and paternalism.

One was with a graduating senior. "What does Father Hesburgh care about this place?" he asked. His tone was bitter, as if he could answer his own question: "Obviously nothing."

I thought, youngster, you've been listening to too much dormitory griping; you should know better. You should know that Father Hesburgh is proud of Notre Dame, that he uses his best energies to make the place wonderful. You should be ashamed to be so shallow.

Another was with a freshman who complained the priests are "out of touch with the students."

"You meet them every Sunday night, saying Mass in the chapels," I pointed out. "You see them hearing confessions in the church, drinking coffee in the Huddle, walking the halls. You can tell that the rain and snow around here are as depressing to them as to you. I know of colleges where students can go for four years without ever laying eyes on a president or vice president."

Father Hesburgh doesn't need me as his defender, and it is no great accomplishment to get in the last word when a student makes a thoughtless criticism. Still, I felt compelled to remind these young people that love keeps this place going, and that love wears a father's face.

Paternalism has become a dirty word, and not just around here. In what students like to call "the real world," it has come to be regarded as the last refuge of the male chauvinist.

Still, I feel at peace with authority and responsibility that is shaped in God's image. Christian theology says that the world was created by God the Father; everything that exists owes its being to his paternal will. He knows the destiny of the stars and creatures, for he is the caretaker of the universe, maintaining order, consenting even to chaos, to which he sets a limit. According to traditionalists, fathers, as progenitors and patriarchs, are godlike men.

According to cynics, all the gods have gone to their graves. I hope they're not right, because if they are—if we have no gods or fathers left—then heaven has been left to rot like an abandoned estate, and our heroes are as small as our egos.

I saw a picture once of an old man from a nursing home, leaning against an oak, touching it with his forehead and hands. For him, I thought, the tree endures as a symbol of the elders he can no longer touch, of the fathers he can no longer lean on or rage against. How sad it would be to survive to become the last of the patriarchs, having said good-bye to all the fathers who have gone before.

My own father knew about the real world before I did. It was the only world he ever knew. He grew up during World War I and died soon after World War II; between the wars, he had the Great Depression to contend with. Through all the years when there was never enough money he provided for his family, and just as he was getting prosperous he left us. He had lived his whole life in worry and fear because he had seen American children with rags for shoes.

Toward his three children he was clumsy in showing love. I was the youngest and the one who made him angry; he felt I was spoiled. Being spoiled for him meant undisciplined, living beyond your means. The world could ruin you if you were spoiled. In time his face showed nothing but anger for me.

I remember, one year, wanting a Boy Scout uniform. "Other kids have uniforms," I told my father.

"Their fathers have money," he replied. "If you want to dress up as a Boy Scout, you should get a job and earn yourself a uniform."

"By the time I get enough money I'll be too old for scouting."

"I'm sorry I can't help you," he said.

I undertook a sympathy campaign with my mother, who understood my frustration at being a Boy Scout out of uniform. She gave up personal things and put money away so I wouldn't feel humiliated as the poor boy on the block. Finally, after months of sacrifice, she had saved over $20, enough to buy me a uniform for my birthday. We were to keep it a secret from my father. She didn't agree that the uniform was a useless, unaffordable luxury, but she didn't want to fight with him, or to hurt his feelings.

I loved the uniform, although it never looked great on me, because I was a fat and lumpish kid. Carefully, protectively, I kept it out of my father's sight through most of a winter.

One day he found it. He understood immediately how I had manipulated my mother's sympathy. He loved her too much to scold her, but offered a terse commentary: "A fool and his money are soon parted."

A few years later we clashed again over money. I had just gotten my first real job, making $56 a week working for the gas company during the summer. On my first payday, while I was busy planning how to spend it all, my father notified me that he expected me to leave part of my wages on the kitchen table.

I became angry and indignant; I felt he was taking advantage of me. What good was it for me to work if he was going to take the money I should be using to buy clothes?

I must have sounded to him like one of those little brats you see in stores, kicking and screaming, trying to get his own way, furious at his father for not buying him a toy. A right-thinking father will just stand there waiting for the storm to pass, a monument to patience, and then hug the child while pointing out the hard lesson that none of us can have everything. The world isn't accommodating; it sometimes denies us toys.

My father didn't give me a hug, but he did teach me a lesson. "You're not giving the money to me," he said. "You're giving it to your mother for ironing, cooking, cleaning, and taking care of you. When you need money for college, I'll give you back every dollar doubled or tripled. All I want is for you to learn to save money."

I know now that it was a privilege to have a father whose love takes you in like a harbor, who tempers with kindness the winds of your emotional tempests in teapots. In the real world, as Yeats knew, "Things fall apart; the center cannot hold; / Mere anarchy is loosed upon the world." But for a while, at least, a father's love can furnish a center that holds steady for you.

My father had his prejudices. He needed my forgiveness, as I needed his. He thought I spent a long time growing up. I never made a career decision he agreed with. How would he expect more of me, as selfish as I was?

By the end, there was always anger on his face for me . . . except for the last time. I was leaving for college; we were saying good-bye after a year in which silence had stood like a wall between us. This time, though, I saw tears on his cheeks.

He died while I was away that first semester. I missed him; I hungered for his respect. I still do. We had forgotten how to talk, and then we ran out of time.

———

Years ago, I knew a group of seniors, an intellectual elite, who were bitter at Notre Dame. They all lived in a hall that was considered a grooming place for campus leaders, and they all were graduating with distinction. A month before their graduation they got together to exchange complaints about the harmful effects of the university's shortcomings.

It had no women; that was unhealthy. It did your laundry, cooked your meals, and even made your bed; the real world would never spoil you like that. It was too Catholic, dominated by the narrow thinking of clerics who relied on catechisms for answers. It was too upper middle-class, an Irish ghetto, as bad as anything in James Joyce, where originality of outlook was discouraged and scholarship was impossible. These seniors sat through the night drinking wine and describing how their college education had warped them.

They graduated into the decade of Vietnam, Watergate, political assassinations, violent revolutions, and mass murders. I wonder what happened to them. If they turned out like most of their fellows, they got their wings clipped early; they learned that even on Easy Street, life doesn't pamper you with caring.

The Best and the Beautiful often come back to campus, but they rarely come back still perfectly beautiful, because they've suffered; the world with its cheap tricks has disappointed them, and it shows. At this year's reunion, a group of graduates within earshot of me kept comparing themselves to the characters in *The Big Chill*. The highlight of the movie, they said, was the funeral scene of a suicide victim, where they played his favorite song: "You can't always get what you want. . . ."

Campuses are places were boys and girls are supposed to grow up; they may look like rose gardens but they aren't meant to be ones. Students get tired of standing in line for meals and of trusting their health and sensitivities to the indignities of communal bathrooms. Few realize that they'll get a lot more tired in the years to come.

You can't make rules compelling students to love a place, or forcing them not to blame it for their restlessness, and not to feel suffocated by its paternalism.

Some do grow up and get over their bitterness. Others, after half a lifetime, still wince at the sight of a priest, still recoil at the guilt of growing up with a Catholic conscience.

This past spring, the students rushed by me at midnight, shouting their battle cries, celebrating their rites of spring. The administrators kept their cool, prayed that the property and the people stayed safe.

Administrators like to hold themselves still. It's the way they win. Like parents, they wait for the shouting to stop. Nothing is negotiable in the noise.

Papers across the country were filled with letters criticizing Notre Dame students as spoiled. Collectively, with their rampaging in a minor cause, they acted spoiled. Individually, the worst they seem is immature.

In this ritual administrators performed their part. Following the commands of caution, they avoided a confrontation and left the emotional outcries to the students. By and by, they reasoned, the students will get tired, tempers will cool, and demands will disappear. They all will go back to their residence hall rooms and fall asleep remembering the good feeling of righteous indignation.

If they're looking for comfort, perhaps they can find it in the knowledge that love is patient, and patience is fatherly, and the nights they spent shouting slogans were really family affairs. On most nights, nothing really ugly happens here, nobody gets manhandled, because the figures of authority don't need to be reminded, as the police in Chicago did in 1968, that the game should not turn rough; that, as the protestors shouted to the cops that night, "We are your children."

I don't like to admit to students that I believe that some adults have a legitimate claim to stand *in loco parentis,* to point out the paths of discipline and virtue to the young. But I feel compelled to remind them, when they turn cynical or bitter, that this community is more caring than the real world, and that our quarrels are family ones.

A BROKEN-DOWN HOLY MAN

I'm always shocked in New York when I see the street people in line to go to Communion. Dirt seems so offensive when it's caked under the fingernails of a hand reaching for the Eucharist. Some priests refuse to serve them, insisting that they clean up as preparation for receiving. Any priest would guard against a wino wanting to drain the Communion cup. I've never had the heart to turn them away—if they seem to know what they're doing.

Peter was a street person, and, in a funny sort of way, he always knew what he was doing. I would tell him to clean up before coming to Sunday Mass and he would answer, "I *did* clean up." He *had* changed his pants, combed his hair, and wiped the grime off his face, but he still looked like a bum. In contrast to the half-naked, savage look he had on the days when he worked the crowd as a panhandler, however, he was dressed like a Christian gentleman.

Peter was no ordinary rum-dumb skid row dropout. As a beggar hustling for change, he was a streetwise professional, a loner who found the daily grace under pressure he needed to survive.

He had his shortcomings. He was a loudmouth, always getting into shouting matches with passersby worse off than himself. Drunk or stoned, he would stand in front of our church (Saint Joseph's in Greenwich Village) with his arms outstretched, praying for God to "deliver the world from the clergy." He often fought with the pastor, and he would scream for him to come out so he could "kick his Irish backside" (though he was never so daring when he knew the pastor was home). One Sunday, to get even with the ushers who had barred him from Mass, he turned in a false fire alarm that brought the engines clanging in the middle of the homily.

Still, he was sensitive enough to be a teacher or scholar. "I've had half an education," he once told me. "And I once was in jail, with time on my hands, so I read books. I memorized poetry. I would think of poems when I fell asleep in prison at night. Poetry when it's good feels like praying."

"What were you in jail for?" I asked.

"Well, I was in the Army, and I wanted to get out. I forget which war it was. My daddy fought in France and he told me, "Peter, all wars are the same.""

He once invited me to join him for coffee in a restaurant. He was charming, like a college professor taking the evening off. I found him sharp as a tack in sizing up human nature; he understood the strange assortment of people around him.

I knew, too, that he was generous. He shared the fairly stable dole of money he collected in his hat with other unfortunates, specializing in the tiresome people no one else had time for. These included one particular bag lady. She should have been in a home; she was always unkempt, and seemed almost incapable of fastening a button. Peter was her part-time nurse. He fed her, led her on walks like her seeing-eye dog, and put her to bed at night in a friendly doorway.

Some time after our shared coffee break, I heard that Peter was taking Communion wafers out of the church. On receiving the Host he would break it and put one half in his mouth, the other in his pocket. I didn't like him being so free and casual with the sacramental bread.

When I told Peter he had been observed, he explained that he had been taking Communion to a sick friend.

"I would be happy to take Communion to anyone who wants it," I said.

"You couldn't go there," Peter replied. "It's dangerous. The floorboards are rotted; the rats are bigger than alley cats. The building is condemned—it could crash down on your head."

"The church wants to know where its Eucharist is going," I protested.

"A bunch of them live together," he explained. "They wouldn't be nice to you. They're taking care of an old guy with no place to go. If you show up, you'll spoil it. They'd expect you to bring the police; they'd take off."

Peter then assumed a half-grin, as though preparing an argument that he knew would floor me. "The main reason he wouldn't want to see you is that he used to wear one of those." He pointed at my neck.

"A Roman collar?" I chortled. "You've been taking Communion to a priest?"

"Priest, brother, religious nut—something like that," he said. "He used to be a taxi driver. He keeps an eye on the losers living at the mission. He fixes them up when they're drifting off with the tide, holding their hands, helping them to pray with contrition, notifying their next of kin. He lets on he's a broken-down holy man. You'd be surprised how many people are doing the priests' work for them."

Every city has its stories about the ex-priests who drive taxis. I never knew if Peter's story was true. Later, he let a rumor spread that he gives the holy bread to the pigeons in the park. Now at Mass we put the Host on his tongue and watch until we're sure he's swallowed it.

We're not always sure, of course; sometimes he must get away with his prize. Maybe, when he's alone at night, terrified by indignities like death and madness, he likes to feel Christ is near him: Christ, wrapped in a napkin, in the inside pocket of his coat. Peter sleeping, as he likes to think of it, with his arms around God.

HOW HE PLAYS THE GAME

I'm not much of a jock, and I'm certainly not a sportswriter. I'm not close to Gerry Faust. But I live in his world, and I hear the comments and the stories. They've put ideas in my head that won't go away. I've decided to write about them because I think they hold lessons for me as a Christian.

In his seasons at Notre Dame, Coach Faust has had his ups and downs. He has flashed a smile after a hard win that would bring a song from the heart of a stone. And he has left the field more than once arm in arm with his wife, both of them weeping at a loss. He has won more games than he has lost, but he has not won enough, because he is the head football coach at a school spoiled by a tradition of winning.

Notre Dame takes football seriously. For decades, beginning in 1918 with Rockne, winning football games looked like part of the blessing God gave to us Catholics. The ability of the Fighting Irish to manipulate victories over teams from bigger and richer schools was celebrated across the country as one of the glorious mysteries of Mary. Our own greatest guru, Father John O'Hara, the thirteenth president of Notre Dame, used to urge the students to go to Communion on football Saturdays in support of the team. Wins or losses, he plainly said, were a consequence of whether the daily Communion count was high or low. In 1949, a championship year, our master of novices assured us that there was something supernatural about Notre Dame's luck, that God himself made our quarterbacks wonderful.

Coach Faust takes this tradition seriously. He really wants to win one for the Gipper. He believes in the Notre Dame mystique like a subway alumnus. He goes to the Grotto to ask for miracles in the stadium. Like the rest of us who were told all the old stories, he probably believes that anything is still possible in Notre Dame Stadium. He is still trying to find his own place in the myth.

When he came here four years ago from Moeller High School he looked euphoric. He saw himself as one called to be the heir of the immortals. With his obvious piety, he seemed to come to us from a different, simpler era of Catholicism, from the great years before Vatican II. Most of us wanted to believe in his dream; we cheered him on.

This past season, he gave us some miracles, some additions to a history that is full of surprises. It may not be enough to keep him in his job as long as he wants it, which is a long time indeed.

Whatever happens, it has been good to have Gerry here. In a time when nearly every success story includes at least a chapter of shame, he has displayed dedication and practiced honesty, in victory and defeat. An underdog, even a loser, can still have the last word. That word is "character."

Christianity is a religion in which apparent losers turn out to be winners. Its tradition asks not whether a man has gained the whole world but whether he working toward saving his own soul. Gerry Faust is a Christian gentleman. That may sound irrelevant even to him; he wants to be famous for winning ball games. But he has done many things right in his time here, for which he will be gratefully remembered.

More than any Hemingway hero, he has shown us the kind of grace under pressure that keeps a man fighting, though the odds be great or small. Life should be more fair to a guy who is fighting so hard. His caring for this tradition of ours is of mythic proportions, big enough to fill the stadium. He incarnates the yearning of generations of fans for Notre Dame football. Any time his team loses, he shoulders the general disappointment; he eats, sleeps, and drinks with a personal letdown. But he continues his uphill climb. And off the field, he does generous, thoughtful things for people, which seem like the prayer of his life.

You can debunk the tradition that Faust upholds. You can say it's just a game. You can snicker at the excitement of old men as they remember the big wins; you can tell the little boys that nothing truly epic takes place on autumn Saturdays in the stadium built on Rock. But you can't do all that without a sacrifice. The world will be much less fun when we have lost our awareness of the demiurges that bless our events with magic. When that happens all our places will look ordinary; all undertakings will seem commonplace, or dependent on media hype for their importance.

In the meantime, our tradition endures. Notre Dame football still is played on the Saturdays of an impossible dream. We can't win them all, but we can dream that we can.

This coach keeps our dream and honors our tradition. He wouldn't shine so much when he wins, or suffer so much when he loses, if he thought it was only a game and not an act of homage, in which the team is upstaged while offering up their play to the glory of their patroness, Notre Dame.

FACING LIFE WITHOUT FATHER

In *The Passing of Arthur,* Lord Tennyson wrote:

> The old order changeth, yielding place to new,
> And God fulfills himself in many ways,
> Lest one good custom should corrupt the world.

The old order at Notre Dame has stayed in place for a long time, wonderful in its stability. Since 1952, two years before I was ordained, the university has had the same father figure. The country has gone through seven presidents and the church five popes since the summer day thirty-three years ago when Theodore M. Hesburgh, C.S.C., took over at Notre Dame. Soon, however, the days of transition will be at hand: As many on campus have known for months, Father Hesburgh will retire in the spring of 1987.

To a Holy Cross priest getting older, that is exciting and a little scary. The gifted younger clerics (a religious community never speaks of them as Yuppies, although some of them may belong to the generation of the Yuppies) are efficient and energetic. Unlike nervous senior members of secular corporations, we are more trusting of younger talent; we respect and care for one another and we share a love for Notre Dame and the mutual family of Holy Cross. I do not fear the ascendency of the new order. I have known its members for a long time.

No matter who takes his place, however, Father Hesburgh's going will make a difference. Especially for his fellows in the Congregation of Holy Cross, he has been an essential friend, and such people are irreplaceable. In the trying years since Vatican II, he has been a leader whom his junior colleagues could trust to show his common sense while we all went through the changes. In the church of the late '60s, there seemed to be as many crises of identity as there were vocations, but Holy Cross had the example of this special leader who said Mass every day as though the charism of his ordination kept his priesthood forever young, who stood tall among us with an endurance that no amount of weariness could defeat.

He did something else for his fellow priests: He served as a symbol of our community's greatness in building the University of Notre Dame. Hesburgh had the courage to act on his wonderful dream of a great Catholic university. While he worked to enhance its academic reputation, he strove mightily to insure that Notre Dame would never lose its Catholic soul. For all of us, he set an example by ending his workdays here unfailingly with a visit to the Grotto.

One of my advantages as a campus minister at Hesburgh's Notre Dame is that I am perfectly at home within the old-fashioned Catholic Church in which Hesburgh grew up. He is a worldly man, but he favors the traditional proprieties. He likes the priests who represent the university to be dressed like priests. In the residence halls, he insists on a discipline that favors purity, on rules that encourage order and discourage permissiveness. He feels as strongly as a strict Irish pastor that the campus should have a high moral tone.

But Hesburgh does not encourage today's students to become a new generation of ghetto Catholics. He wants them to follow him out into the world. He believes that the purpose of a Catholic university is not to isolate students so that they will never hear heresies but to arrange things so that when they do hear them, they will also hear truth's eloquent defenders.

He tells students: "If you want to save your souls, be as decent as your parents, stay loyal to Christ and his mother, and make your lives count as servants of the world's underdogs and as peacemakers in a nuclear age." And he does more than tell them; he shows them his own life's work as an example of what it means to be a Catholic citizen of the world.

Students can be unfair in their criticisms. They imagine conspiracies coming out of Corby Hall aimed at denying their rights and ignoring their needs for the sake of pleasing rich alumni. The truth is different: Through his words and his example, Father Hesburgh regularly reminds those of us who work with him that we exist chiefly to love and take care of the students, to help them grow in truth and in grace. In the hall staffs, he recommends the kind of attentiveness that one of his predecessors, Father O'Hara, used to practice when he worked to remember the names and hometowns of all the students. Father Hesburgh considers this practice a part of the tradition handed down from the elders. If your memory is poor and you can't practice it, you live in pastoral guilt.

The Hesburgh style rubs off on you. You can't help but be affected by the fact that one of the busiest men in America is your boss. On this campus, no priest is ever entirely off duty, and often when we want to go to bed, we realize that the light in Hesburgh's office is still on. He is the pastoral president, making himself available. The rest of us feel compelled to be at least half as generous.

The old order changes. The mice in the walls under the Golden Dome can hear the ground shifting. Soon the time will come for nostalgia, for the backward glance.

I will remember notes from him with a sentence or two of praise. I will remember seeing him during the days of Vietnam standing grim-faced in the crowds demanding peace. I will remember the many occasions when we concelebrated Mass, when he gave us the word of life as we buried the dead, when he challenged us anew to Christian greatness. It has been exciting to be inspired by his zeal, to have his ministry overlap one's own, his shadow extend the length of one's lesser shadow. It has been an honor to be here with the famous priest.

"I HAVE CHOSEN YOU"

On the Saturday after Easter, five deacons were ordained as Holy Cross priests in Sacred Heart Church. As they lay prostrate before the altar, I wondered what they were looking forward to.

At my own ordination thirty-one years ago, I was overwhelmed with emotion, so honored was I to become a priest. I wondered how many years of usefulness the Lord would give me. Would I live to be forty, fifty, eighty? Would I be a good priest? I sensed how presumptuous it was to wish to be ordained, to be the agent of transubstantiation, to stand in place of Christ forgiving sins.

I was ordained in a church still steeped in medieval myth and magic. In those waning days of Joe McCarthy, priests came to ordination filled with memories of seminary myths about making the supreme sacrifice. You were warned that the Communists might be hanging priests from the lampposts of New York by the end of the decade. You were told that God in his infinite wisdom might send you behind the Iron Curtain where, if you were caught saying Mass, you would be martyred. Some myths did without the Commies. Sick calls, for instance, could be dangerous: You might have to be lowered down a well to anoint the dying— or be tortured by a jealous husband trying to learn the sins his wife had brought to the confessional. The symbolism of vocation promoted in those days forced you to feel responsible. You could commit mortal sin by inattentiveness in saying Mass.

The folklore made me shiver, but I was delighted to be ordained. When I stood up after the Litany of the Saints was sung, I could see that the stone floor in front of me was wet with my tears.

Ordinations still are bittersweet affairs for me. I get scared by the speed with which the torch is being passed to a new generation; I am reminded of the ways in which the parade is passing me by. Some of the youngsters treat the old days as a joke, and I don't enjoy their brashness. I try to do the homework that keeps me current, and I hope the younger priests will maintain some sympathy for the venerable traditions.

One of the major ceremonies of ordination is the laying of hands on the new priests' heads, the traditional way of handing on power in the church. The bishop imposes his hands first, followed by all the priests present. In Sacred Heart it is an impressive sight, with more than a hundred shepherds confirming the younger ones as caretakers of the fold. I've always felt that I was sharing something painful and sacred.

I thought on that day last April that if I had it to do over, I would still be a priest, but at my age I don't take anything for granted. Would I have chosen to kneel with these five men, to begin my ministry in these uncertain years? In my time, any pious kid who could read Latin was accepted into the seminary if he were not an obvious misfit; I'm not sure I have the strength they are looking for today. The priesthood isn't as protected as it used to be.

Still, I love being a priest. I cling to the shipwreck of the old mythology. I am at home with priests as traditional as myself; they have been my companions for forty years. I would disappoint them if I left; I would disappoint myself.

I was a convert to Catholicism, and the church I joined forty years ago was without equal, a church that was arrogant, uncompromising, dogmatic, mysterious. At Mass the priest stood at the altar with his back turned, whispering to God in a dead language. The sacraments were hocus-pocus with the clout of miracles. Creeds came in a catechism a believer was supposed to learn by heart. The priest was a medicine man; even Catholics got to talk to him mostly in the confessional. The local Catholic church, with its closed windows and guarded ghetto gates, was exotic, the haunted house at the end of the lane, one of the world's supernatural wonders. The church of forty years ago had a public grimness like that of the French Foreign Legion. Its emblem was the cross to which Jesus was nailed, inviting you to thirst with him. You could develop a love-hate relationship with an outfit so much like the theater of the absurd. All the memberships were lifetime memberships, and you needed guts to stay around that long.

Today's Sunday-morning breakfast clubs, with their Rotarian handclasps of friendship, are a far cry from the cold introduction to God you got at Mass back in 1945. In those days the faithful kept their distance from one another as they bobbed up and down in the movements of worship. In these days, old Mother Church has given up the look of a medieval passion play. The poetry left town with the Latin rite. The liturgy lapses into triteness. But I have to acknowledge that the converts still come to be born again at Easter; they still see the magic that I've somehow lost sight of.

I take comfort, though, in the knowledge that my decision to become a priest seems as fixed as birth; it would be pointless to reconsider it. For me, the grace of vocation was irresistible. The Lord said it best: "You have not chosen me; I have chosen you." In saying *yes* to God so willingly, I consented to all that came after. The church goes on as a network of redemption. If God finds the church tired, he will update it; he will keep it young.

As a priest, I am one of the pinpoints of light in a sky filled with stars. I have an infinitesimal share of the glory in belonging to the firmament. It is an honor to flash across the sky. I could have been a glowworm flashing semaphores over swampland.

The newly ordained priests last Easter week looked very dear as they gave their first blessing. I saw them not as strangers to be feared or as invaders stealing the treasure from God's house. The bells in the tower rang joyfully that day. My bitterness was gone; only the sweetness remained.

UNDER THE DOME,
MOST OF IT SEEMS TRUE

Patrick had just come back from a year with the Holy Cross Associates, and he surprised me by talking about his spirituality—an old-fashioned word with a bad reputation as something phony.

I admire and respect Patrick; he is young, confident, vital, and beautiful. Like any seminarian, he knows the jargon of the vocations that take God seriously. He has struggled with temptation and doubt.

But hearing him speak with great innocence of his spiritual life, I suspected his Catholic faith has never been tested. He has never had his back to the wall, or seriously failed, or had the cards stacked against him. He has never felt like a lamb led to slaughter, or spent time alone, fearing the cosmic indifference. He hasn't survived those crises when he will wonder if his religion is harmful, like an addiction to opium.

Vietnam veterans, trying to describe jungle warfare, pile up obscenities not found in the dictionary. Christians, having their faces shoved in bitterness from arm-wrestling with the Devil, would feel naive, like apprentice nuns, using textbook words to describe their ordeal in darkness. Patrick, pleased to have a spiritual life to tell me about, is still in boot camp, far from the foxholes of battle. He's proud of himself as a young Christian, and I want him to stay on as a member of the Catholic team. He would be discouraged if I told him he was still wet behind the ears.

Patrick represents a lot of the old grads who come back to talk. I meet them after a game or at the reunion in June. Or I meet them on summer nights, when the moon cruises the sky over Manhattan, as those of us who have spent time in the Emerald City gather for a cookout. As Domers, many have had all the Catholic advantages.

I'm too old to be shy about asking them if they still go to Mass, or if they were married before a priest, or how soon they intend to have children. Nor are they shy about telling me they're bored with institutional religion, or they think the pope is out of touch. A number of them say they hang onto the Faith because they hope it's true; but they are waiting for something convincing to happen.

I don't lay burdens on them if I can help it. I offer them my help if I think they need it. The church can show them unforgettable kindness, like relieving them of guilt in confession. Sometimes they don't have the courage to ask a priest for the church's grace. I try to let them see I'll be kind, because I know from experience how hard it is to admit sin.

Patrick said he was having a misunderstanding with his father, who felt the year with the Holy Cross Associates wasn't as worthwhile as a real job would have been.

I asked, "Is he religious?" Patrick said, "He is very religious, in his own way. But he doesn't go along with all the doctrines of the church." I thought: he would be lucky if he *knows* all the doctrines of the church.

I said: "In Greenwich Village I say Mass every day in a parish church on Sixth Avenue. In summer the windows are always open wide, and I have to compete against the street noises: police sirens, the heavy traffic of trucks and buses, ambulances with honking horns, fire engines, sidewalk brawls, pedestrians with loud radios, children playing games, the outcries from the human jungle.

"Some days I wonder if the Gospel is only true in the context of the Mass, which tells losers there's a chance of salvation. Outside, in the zoo, maybe you need something more practical than a doctrine of love. On Sixth Avenue, maybe you need a code of survival. Christianity says that in God's country love is the ethic of a code of survival. There are some doctrines that you have to be a saint to believe. It takes a lot of grace to believe the wisdom of the Gospel."

I gave Patrick a copy of *The Great Gatsby* to add to his reading on the spiritual life. "I love *Gatsby* because it begins so well," I told him. At my suggestion, he read the opening paragraph aloud.

In my younger and more vulnerable years my father gave me some advice that I've been turning over in my mind ever since.

"Whenever you feel like criticizing anyone," he told me, "just remember that all the people in this world haven't had the advantages that you've had."

Gatsby, I explained, is a novel of the Lost Generation, which turned out not to be lost, merely disillusioned. Every generation since then, in times of trouble, has examined itself to see if it can describe itself as lost. The Jazz Age, as Nick described it, was a night scene of distortion by El Greco, and its people were careless and confused: *They smashed up things and creatures and then retreated back into their money or their vast carelessness, or whatever it was that kept them together, and let other people clean up the mess they made.*

I said to Patrick, "You worked for a year on a youth program in the inner city. How do your juveniles stack up as a lost generation?"

He said, "Notre Dame students don't have a clue what the ghettos are up to. The self-destruction, the crime, the pregnancies, and abortions. The students here live in an ivory tower. You priests never see the teenagers who don't go to college."

Sometimes I meet them in the drug store; they wear tee shirts saying "Born to Lose." Other times I meet them in restaurants; they are going to the prom and will not be so dressed up again until their weddings. I feel sorry, knowing they will have to work twice as hard to get half as far. Hard work will make them look too old, too soon. They don't even have a grotto to walk to at night.

I asked, "What's happening to them?" Patrick answered, "In the city where I worked the pastor told us, 'We have five ministers of the Eucharist at the Sunday Masses. In twenty years we won't need any of them because everyone who comes here is over fifty. We have lost the young people.'"

I have many impressions of youngsters who spend their evenings cruising West Eighth Street, off Sixth Avenue. They look like models for

Rolling Stone—weirdoes who smoke too much dope. The guys go home to middle-class neighborhoods in Jersey wearing earrings, to keep their parents worried about whether they're gay. It's hard to tell, if you've heard them singing *Where the Boys Are* to give the tourists something to gape at. Ambiguity seems to be part of the plan.

Some make themselves ugly in the punk style: Mohican haircuts, orange hair, painted eyelids, black and white lips, leg-hugging pants with a matching vest in black leather, high heel boots, chains to the navel. In their uniforms of the counter-culture, they look like freaks, apparently because they need to go a step or two beyond anything they think their permissive parents will tolerate. It's tough being cooler than your father and mother, especially if they thought they were very cool growing up.

Seeing Patrick giving me his close attention, I thought how spoiled one gets as a priest at Notre Dame. We think we give them faith; the truth is, they give it to us. They show us the courtesy of letting us see that they take us seriously. Under the Dome, most of it seems true, because we are set up like a theater where they are entertained.

Corruption doesn't touch them very much on Our Lady's campus. They are helped over the losses of innocence by padres eager to make them feel special, like prodigal sons and daughters at home in their Father's arms. They allow us the last word, especially if it's in their favor. They're not saints, and we're not wise like scholars; but mutual affection and respect make our perjuries feel harmless. In the real world, we find we're not very real at all. Who, in the real world, ever talked from the pulpit about the Velveteen Rabbit?

"WE HAVE MET THE ENEMY
AND HE IS US"

In front of the North Dining Hall, some Gideons hand out small, green-backed copies of the New Testament. The middle-aged men smile pleasantly when I ask, "How's it going?" and accept a Bible as a sign I like Gideons. Half the students accept the little books out of politeness; they leave them later on shelves and tables all over campus.

A week later, a team of evangelists shows up on campus, uninvited, to preach the Gospel. Sadly for the Gospel, they have more zeal than brains. The students size them up as Jesus freaks, and the arguments begin.

A rabble-rouser arrives to urge us to divest in South Africa. On the steps of the Main Building, under administrative noses, she advises: "Don't listen to the Big Man on this campus. His fire's gone out." She's bad mannered and the students see it.

The rock stars come, bringing the power and light company with them. They fret and strut on stage, then are gone. Their groupies don't leave with them. This house is safe from Pied Pipers.

The Pied Piper is a story of the Devil, out of the crusades, told to punish parents. Robert Burton wrote in the *Anatomy of Melancholy:* "At Hamelin in Saxony, on the 20th of June 1484, the devil, in the likeness of a Pied Piper, carried away 130 children, that were never seen after." Even the whimsy of Robert Browning's version can't hide the horror of an archetypal theme: the thief who stole children, enticing them with tunes that once tickled rats' ears.

Hamelin was desolate after the junior citizens left it forever. Parents, feeling their hearts torn out, scrambled up and down the sides of the mountain looking for the portal through which the enchanted army passed. If they could split the mountain, the children would be free. Their dishonesty in cheating the Piper of his wage set the everlasting hills against them. Eventually, they did not weep; they were turned to stone inside.

The Pied Piper's story offers a universal paradigm, but it doesn't explain why the children of the church are gone. Fifteen million baptized Catholics, they say, are presently dropouts.

What happened? You'd like to fault someone for all this alienation, yet we have no scapegoat, no Pied Piper out of hell to blame. It would be pastoral nonsense to pretend that disenchanted Catholics left the church in droves during the '60s and '70s because the Devil made them do it. The dropouts didn't leave because they were forced out of the pews by black magic. I doubt that God dragged them out as though, in a divine judgment, he were visiting the sins of the parents onto the children from whom he hides his face. We can't point to the stranger in motley, reeking of brimstone, who teased unwilling feet down the primrose path to a witches' Sabbath from which erstwhile Christians tell themselves they can't go home again.

In looking for scapegoats, I suspect, we are following a circular trail: as Pogo would say, "We have met the enemy, and he is us." The birth control issue may have caused many to doubt the pope. Next to birth control, perhaps, the thing that hurt us—I guess this by taking a head count of bored teenagers at Mass—is that the Greatest Show on Earth forgot the value of entertainment. Dullness is not a low card the Devil dealt to defeat us. We demythologized the church into dullness. We domesticated the sharp sense of cosmic drama, and became as colorless as pigeons. After that, nobody mistook us for birds of Paradise.

Robert Penn Warren wrote a novel called *All the King's Men;* the bishops should read it to see how the game is played. Willie Stark was a politician who got elected governor of Louisiana because he could make the voters feel alive. Good ol' country boys brought their faded wives to hear Willie. They loved him because he stirred them up. Their false teeth didn't fit; half of them were so dried up they couldn't spit a wet streak. Willie talked to them in the plain language of a field hand. He made simple things—indoor plumbing and new pants or a dress—sound like the biggest deal since free salvation. He left them with their eyes bugging out, and they were sure of two things: They were going to make love that night, and they were going to vote for Willie. The most exciting preacher on television today is a crowd-pleaser out of Willie Stark country. He gets those Pentecostalists handclapping, talking in tongues, and crying out to Jesus for Holy Ghost revival. All of them go home swearing they've been born again.

Twenty years ago, we Catholics clipped our own wings. We held a Vatican Council in which priests changed the things that priests wanted to change. When we finished listening to the Holy Spirit, we were an updated church, as much a part of the twentieth century as Big Macs. It took courage to replace the Mass—praised even by our detractors as one of the great art forms of Western civilization—with a vernacular version deprived of grandeur. The new Mass texts weren't bad, but they did nothing to nourish you on a dull day. At that point, the absolutes got fuzzy, symbolism got ambiguous.

Meanwhile, liturgies of excitement were being staged in the streets. Selma, on television, looked like the set of a passion play. Protesters marched hand in hand with Martin Luther King, singing "We Shall Overcome." They seemed transfigured, as nuns used to seem transfigured, beatific at the bishop's Mass. The great songs of the '60s were protest songs; the great issues had to do with saving the country.

On college campuses, the popular priests borrowed the tactics that made the folk singers and social prophets unforgettable. To be relevant at Mass, you passed out flowers and sang "Blowin' in the Wind." "Where have all the flowers gone?" we asked, "Where have all the good men gone?" They had gone to Vietnam. We were so sure that if we hated napalm bombings and Pentagon sins, we were on God's side; unquestionably we were. We weren't as sure about the wisdom of the church as we were of the righteousness of our causes.

The good men whom the flower children sang about marched back from their war. Others are beginning to return from different battlefields. Yet fifteen million Catholics are still missing in action. Getting them back five or six at a time on Saturday afternoons will take forever. The church wants them back. Half of them, they say, are ready to come. The priest asks: "How long have you been away?" The answers vary: ten years, twelve years, fifteen years. "Why were you away so long?" "It didn't seem to matter." "Why have you come back?" "I hated going it alone."

I know only one reason for any human being to be a practicing Catholic: Christ is the Way, the Truth, and the Life. The church, as a grace-bearing institution, is the channel of his peace. True, the church has a human element from which all of us have suffered, and this human element backs the wrong horse more often than we like to think about. The human element is not the rock on which the church was built, Christ is.

Catholics are most at ease, I think, when they are at peace with that dear old Establishment whose *raison d'etre* is to offer them the symbols of salvation. Christ is always the church's Christ, just as Prince Hamlet is always Shakespeare's Hamlet. As soon as you take Christ out of the context of the church, you begin to make him into your own image. He shrinks in size until he is unrecognizable as anybody's idea of God, or anybody's idea of man. All the thousand names of God don't describe him; however, he's considerably diminished if you treat him—in the mistaken idea that one opinion is as good as another—as a "reg'la fella," like the Catholic chaplain who buys you a drink at the Elks. The church keeps us honest about Christ.

As a Holy Cross priest at Notre Dame, I wonder how many Domers continue to fight the good fight. I used to hesitate to ask: "Do you still go to Mass?" Now I ask it freely; the question doesn't seem to cause embarrassment. Some grads didn't go as students. Some gave up the church as soon as they got their degrees: "I tried it for a while. I got nothing out of it." Some have marriage problems. Some have doubts or questions about authority. Some are angry and hate the Catholic system. Some say religion is a delusion they rejected as children. Some blame their teachers for crippling them religiously. Some think religion is a racket run by priests hungry for money or power. Some believe everything except confession. A large number are faithful to the tradition.

It would be interesting to know the whole picture. Notre Dame was built on the faith that human beings have souls to save. Graduates once left here convinced of the worth of receiving Holy Communion every day. How does a campus grade itself on how well nearly ninety thousand graduates have learned the lesson, "God was man in Palestine / And lives today in Bread and Wine"? If fifteen million Catholics live without sacramental identity with the Mystical Body, a number of them must be Domers. Where have we gone wrong? What have we done right?

On a personal level, what mistakes has this servant of the church made, one trusted as another Christ? Which were the idle words for which he will be held liable in the judgment? Did he help or hurt by acting as a morale officer to the counterculture in the years of protest?

Ivan Meštrović's genius gave us the statue of the compassionate father receiving home the prodigal. Notre Dame has children scattered over the face of the earth. How does a campus export compassion to the prodigals too far away for a homecoming? Grace is everywhere; everything is grace. Sin itself can be turned into an occasion of grace. Any ground that you kneel on is as holy as the Grotto when you're asking for grace. One church is as good as another as a house of God and gate of heaven, when you're receiving a sacrament.

The church would die if it stopped forgiving; such a church would be of no use to Christ. The question is: Can fifteen million Catholics forgive the church? So many mistakes were made, so much pain was inflicted, so many church members have suffered injustices in the name of Christ. Our greatest parable tells of a boy prostrate before his father saying: "I'm sorry." What answer would love make in return other than to say: "I'm sorry, too, for the harm I did you." The church has a sacrament in which homecomings are negotiated one-on-one with the shepherd of one's choice. Where does the church go to be reconciled with those more sinned against than sinning? The church has its penance to do for the misuse of grace. This is not heresy. Ask the Jews throughout history. Ask the Separated Brethren. Ask the fifteen million unchurched Catholics.

Holy Cross priests at Notre Dame are in business to attend to the faithful and to welcome the strays. The doors are open.

"I PRAYED LIKE HELL
EVERY DAMN NIGHT"

The massive stone columns are in place. Notre Dame's memorial to her war dead has been compared, not necessarily as a compliment, to Stonehenge and the Wailing Wall. So far, seen from a distance in the moonlight, it looks like a sacrificial altar that pagan priests might have used. It's strange, impressive, disturbing: a dramatic symbol, appropriately stark to remind a nation of the awful price it pays when her soldiers make the supreme sacrifice.

Many blessings will be needed to domesticate this massive limestone heap. Old soldiers' ghosts should come here to haunt the spot created as a holy of holies in honor of the dead. A temple of remembrance shouldn't seem so anonymous; maybe an eternal flame could be lighted as a sign of solidarity with older memorials. In Russia, these arches would be the chief emblems of a memory garden, with a brooding sculpture of Mother Russia on one side, and a helmeted defender of Stalingrad on the other, to make the visitors shiver with fear at seeing the soul of a revolutionary nation made so visible.

We can't very easily recapture the past with art forms that understate the truth. Yet the survivors of the death camps keep reminding us that we can't afford to forget the past. Otherwise, we are doomed to repeat it.

Every landmark needs the myths that explain it. The Grotto was important to the Notre Dame tradition as soon as it was built, because of the stories from France about God's mother appearing in a rocky niche near a hillside cave. Grantland Rice preserved the legend of the Four Horsemen as the new figures of an apocalypse in the football stadium. Our war memorial is presently in need of the myths that will make it endearing. Who were the chroniclers who saved the legends of our war heroes for us?

During World War II, the *Religious Bulletin*—that mimeographed sheet put out several times a week by the university chaplains—kept the campus informed of the daily tragedies and victories of the war. From the *Bulletin,* students and faculty got a picture of the war in progress: a limited picture, telling them things that would help them save their souls.

It is instructive to read the *Bulletin* chronologically as a meditation on the twelfth station of the cross now standing alone on the field house mall. Who are the fallen dead? They have names and dates; they are not unknown soldiers. They are the Fighting Irish, the sons of Notre Dame.

June 12, 1942: Last Tuesday, two Navy blimps collided over the Atlantic while engaged in a hazardous experimental mission. The lone survivor was Ensign Howie Fahey, a Notre Dame man and classmate of the present seniors. He was in the first group of men to leave the campus to join the fighting forces. Before the group left, each man received a special blessing invoking God's protection. No doubt it was instrumental in saving Howie's life.

September 1, 1943: The soldier was tired. He heard the sound of a car behind him and waited. The driver, a Jewish businessman, saw the khaki figure up ahead. The soldier looked thin and worn. The driver picked him up, found he had been near death in the Pacific, and was on his way home for a rest. The soldier told of many things, then he spoke of religion. This is what the Protestant boy told the Jewish merchant:

"It was pretty bad out there in those hellholes. The Japs kept us on edge all the time, sniping and killing. My buddies kept going one by one. But there is one person I'll never forget as long as I live. It was that Catholic chaplain. He'd run out when a man fell, bend over him, and drag him back. We never saw any other chaplains around where the bullets were hitting. Just that Catholic priest standing up real straight, or bent over listening. I don't know what he said to those dying men; all I know is that he didn't seem to realize that he could be cut down like the others.

"Then I got it in the side. When I awoke, he was there. I can't forget that look in his eyes. His lips were moving, but I couldn't hear him. . . . He did something to me inside. When I saw him working hard under fire giving his religion, I decided his must be worth getting. And that's what I'm going to do when I get back home."

September 17, 1943: Killed in Sicily: Lt. Arthur Chedwick '36, Notre Dame's 60th Gold Star. A Catholic chaplain tells the story of an air raid on the battlefield. The attack came suddenly. The chaplain dug a hole in the ground and hid the Blessed Sacrament to prevent desecration during the battle. A furious fight took place. Later, the chaplain returned the consecrated hosts to the tabernacle. Soldiers were on their knees before the Real Presence in the heart of the earth.

September 27, 1943: The number of the Notre Dame war dead is now 62.

October 8, 1943: From Sgt. John Beer '38: "Almost a year has elapsed since our departure from the States, and in that time I have been on two different islands in the southwest Pacific. The thing I miss most in the evening is not being able to slip down to the Grotto and speak to Our Blessed Mother for guidance, assistance, and blessing on everything I do."

October 15, 1943: Prayer *a la* U.S. Marines: "I prayed like hell every damn night," said a Marine returning from months of jungle warfare on Guadalcanal.

October 20, 1943: A Christian soldier's prayer: "Keep me, in the heat of battle, from all blind and unreasoning bravery."

October 25, 1943: A letter from the chaplain. "Dear Men: Sunday morning when I made the announcement about the death of Private Vit Capello, a number of men in the congregation turned in astonishment to their pals beside them. Vit left them only last year, and his memory was still fresh in their minds.

"Just a word to the men who are transferring to other stations. The first persons and things to see at the new station are the chaplain and his chapel and the Notre Dame men on the lot. Post a notice somewhere that you are on board ship and that you want to meet the Notre Damers. Have some information ready for these you meet. They are hungry for campus news."

November 12, 1943: Ray Eichelaub missing in action again. More details in Monday's *Bulletin.*

November 17, 1943: Capt. Herschel G. Horton died a tragic death in New Guinea. Just before he died, he wrote a farewell letter home. The letter bears the date December 11, 1942:

"I came out on a mercy patrol to pick up dog tags of our dead. This was the morning of December 1, 1942. I was trying to turn the body of Capt. Keast, a friend of mine, when I was shot two or three times in my right leg and hip.

"Two days of semideleriousness. . . . Finally Lt. Gibbs and one of his men from the antitank company came for me. Their medic gave me my first drink of water in three days, but he had no food to offer. The medic bandaged me temporarily. . . . He came back and gave me water, but a man helping him got shot there, and that scared him away. Life from then on was a terrible nightmare. The hot burning sun, the delirious nights. . . .

"A Jap shot me in the shoulder and neck as I weakly sat there. I lie here now in this terrible place, wondering why God is making me suffer this terrible end. I am not afraid to die, although I have nearly lost my faith after a couple of days here. I have a pistol here but I could not kill myself. I still have faith in the Lord. I think He must be giving me the supreme test. I know now how Christ felt on the Cross."

November 19, 1943: Lt. Richard J. Coad, our 69th Gold Star.

November 26, 1943: V-mail about the Battle of Salerno: "Dear Father O'Donnell: The Navy men who are coming out of Notre Dame are bringing Notre Dame along with them. Wherever these 'war alumni' meet, Notre Dame is part of their conversation, part of their life—and, yes, part of their death. Their enthusiasm is infectious and British Navy personnel, particularly the young officers, can sing the *Victory March* with the same ardor as the Conleys, the Schwartzes, and the Carideos. In the landings at Salerno in which both British and Americans participated, someone started to sing, and the song was picked up all along the line. . . [it] wasn't the *Star Spangled Banner.* It wasn't *God Save the King.* It was *Cheer, Cheer for Old Notre Dame.*"

December 7, 1943: The price paid by Americans since December 7, 1941: 94,918 dead, wounded, missing, or imprisoned.

December 17, 1943: Excerpts from a letter written on December 25, 1942, by a soldier on Guadalcanal: "The Mass last night sounded grand. The altar was simply beautiful; all around the chancel were native flowers. We shined up the shell cases, and the six candelabra stood at either side of the crucifix, their brass casings shining in the flickering candlelight like pure gold.

"We couldn't beg, borrow, or steal a monstrance for Benediction, so I made one out of a corned beef can, the coppered inside of the can giving a beautiful ray effect."

January 7, 1944: A Notre Dame man, Lt. Fred Wolff '40, carried with him into the service a record of ten years of unbroken First Friday Communions. On one First Friday, he was en route to a new mission. Determined to continue this devotion toward the Sacred Heart, he fasted all day in the hope that the opportunity to receive Communion would come. It came. In the late afternoon, he stepped on the shores of the Aleutians and met a Catholic chaplain who gave him Communion.

January 19, 1944: A passenger on the exchange ship *Gripshol* brought news of the death of Lt. Jacob Paul Sevcik '33. Sevcik and his two-year-old son died in a Japanese prison camp in the Philippines. Sevcik was a mining engineer with a private firm in the islands when the war in the Pacific opened. He enlisted in the engineers and was with General MacArthur's forces on Bataan.

January 21, 1944: Our 81st Gold Star, Capt. John J. McCloskey '36, sacrificed his life to save two fellow officers in a plane crash near Guadalcanal. He was a fighter pilot, returning from a mission, when his motors failed. He knew he could not make his home base, so he nose-dived the plane into the water in such a way that he, and not the other two occupants of the plane, suffered the strongest impact.

February 15, 1944: "I carried my rosary in my hand every moment of that day we invaded Italy," confessed a Catholic ensign.

May 23, 1944: They died for you; 55 Notre Dame men in World War I and 96 in World War II.

July 12, 1944: Lt. Austin Nearns '36 wrote: "When we passed St. Peter's, I took off alone to see the Pope. I contacted a bishop who could speak English. I told him I was a Notre Dame graduate, showed him my Notre Dame ring, told him I met His Holiness when he was at Notre Dame in 1936, and asked for an audience.

"I made quite a contrast with His Holiness—my trousers torn, unshaven, mud on my shoes, and what not. People come from all over the world just to see, not talk with, the Pope and along comes a dirty, unshaven lieutenant who talks with him for seven minutes."

July 26, 1944: The Germans were only a few hundred yards from the Allies. At dawn the American attack was to begin. The Catholics in the outfit wanted Mass. It was a clear night, the moon so bright that if a priest stood in white vestments, the Germans could see him a mile away. The soldiers gathered for Mass would make a compact target. A single shell would bring them doom.

An inspiration struck someone. The boys dug a hole six feet long, four deep, and four wide. They spread a blanket on the bottom, and there the chaplain set up his altar. The congregation could see the priest as he went through the Mass, for his shoulders projected slightly above the pit. C-ration cans covered the candles and were slit so that the candles glimmered only toward the congregation and not in the direction of the Germans.

May 3, 1945: Notre Dame men dead in service: 223 reported to date. Missing in action: 36. Captured: 31. From a letter: "We received a letter this morning from Lt. Ray T. Reed, a boy from Notre Dame, telling us our Bob had been liberated and was in good condition. . . . He said Bob is awaiting the time he can get back to school and play that last year of football.

"Father, we turned to you and Notre Dame when Bob was missing. Your words of encouragement helped us. Your Masses and prayers have been answered, and we know you and all Notre Dame will join us in thanksgiving."

————

Allen Seeger's poetry was in vogue during World War II as it has not been in vogue during any war since. Servicemen used to quote it in their letters home: "I have a rendezvous with Death / At some disputed barricade, / When Spring comes back with rustling shade / And apple-blossoms fill the air." Did war ever look so pretty to a soldier?

Who today thinks it is sweet and seemly to die for one's country? Maybe those limestone columns are an anachronism. Who would believe that a world war could have the clubbiness of a varsity sport at which Notre Dame Catholics excelled?

IN DEFENSE OF THOSE WHO CARE

Again and again the anger surfaces. Students claim the university does not care about them. We are indifferent, they say, and treat them like children.

It's an ongoing argument, one I'd like to avoid. Yet as a member of a religious community that cares very much, I grow defensive against young Catholics rushing to judgment. Only in America, perhaps, does it seem outrageous for the elders of the tribe to claim wisdom based on experience. We are not infallible; the most senior among us could learn lessons from a changing world. But it is possible to care about students even if you're a stick-in-the-mud, bogged down in the morality that was here before the Yuppies.

I want to say as a priest how I feel about the campus controversy of the spring. Every unsolicited line I write could sound to some like an installment of *Father Knows Best*. If I say it well enough, though, others may tell me I have spoken the truth as they believe it to be. I will begin by being as tedious as Polonius.

––––––––––

Moby Dick is Melville's masterpiece. Among other things it is an attack on God as the source of human suffering: God is either actively malicious or indifferent. Twenty years later Melville wrote *Billy Budd*, a smaller masterpiece that is sometimes called his "testament of acceptance." Billy Budd, the handsome sailor, is a Christ-figure destroyed by the evil he meets in Claggart, the jealous first mate who falsely accuses Billy of mutiny. In a reflex action defending himself against the lie, Billy strikes Claggart dead.

The laws of the sea say Billy must be hanged as punishment for murder. The ship's crew views Billy as an innocent victim, guilty only of self-defense. Yet the law must be enforced, and Billy dies like a sacrificial lamb. God's ways are not man's ways, the story says, and man's ways are not godlike. Heaven will judge Billy by laws that are merciful and fair.

Notre Dame is one of the flawed human structures run by rules. How fair the structure is when it punishes students, only the administrators and the angels know for sure—the rest of us are not privy to the facts of a case. According to the letters to *The Observer,* students who offend the system always end up victims of injustice. Billy Budd gets nailed, again and again.

One of the most criticized rules, for which the innocent are crucified, prohibits dorm visitation by members of the opposite sex after midnight, or after 2 a.m. on weekends. It must be irksome to send home a date when you're in the middle of *David Letterman.* It surely is a pain to interrupt the conversations over wine where dreams are shared and fears are quieted. Yet dorms have routines maintained for the common good, just as homes do. The roommate who was told to get lost probably enjoys reclaiming the room he rents. I ask the student who hates parietals, "Would your date be allowed to spend the night in your home?"

The answer comes: "I thought it would be different here. I came to college to live as an adult."

I counter: "Students should bring notes from their parents saying they approve of young men and women sharing beds. If enough parents did so, maybe then we could change the rule. In the meantime, why should a rector be more permissive about what goes on in his dorm than parents are about what goes on under the family roof?"

"*In loco parentis,*" the student chortles, as if he were using a Latin phrase for an infringement of human rights practiced among Catholics.

Parietals complaints are usually the preamble to a discussion of human sexuality. After years at Notre Dame, I know every argument that advances premarital intimacy as a necessary pleasure that young flesh is entitled to. But sex, when you're still wet behind the ears, can turn life into tragedy before you know it. "A thing of beauty is a joy . . . until sunrise," they say. "It's not the stork that brings the baby, but a lark in the night."

This priest's talk is boring: the chattering of a celibate prejudiced against the celebrations of flesh and blood, according to nature's great plan. I tire of repeating the party line, but how else can I say that sex needs a context of commitment confirmed by vows, as in marriage? Jove blushes to hear the perjuries that lovers exchange in the moonlight, according to Shakespeare. The student says, "We promised each other we were married in everything except name, so sex was okay. Now it's over, and I feel dirty." This is an admission men and women make as part of their sacramental confessions. Passion seems as cheap as lust when the breakup comes and you've gotten nothing in writing.

Dr. Ruth can't tell me my business in discouraging sex before marriage. For thirty-two years, I've heard the stories of betrayal, frustration, anguish. I've watched tears trickle down young faces because of unwanted pregnancies, or unwanted abortions, or unwanted adoptions of the babies mothers would be happy to keep "if it weren't so unfair to the child." Looking at the heads hung in shame, I think how happily and innocently two hopeful kids became glib with emotion unsupervised by common sense.

How do you persuade students that the rules in *du Lac* are half a blueprint for taking care of themselves in college?

———

No one wants to be talked down to. I apologize to gay students if I sound condescending. I saw long ago that I couldn't tell them which stars to steer by in the deep waters of an uncharted sea.

It's no surprise that homosexuals are members of the church. Some of the most brilliant Catholics, enriching the church with their genius, have been homosexuals. They have fought lonely battles and been misunderstood. They've been denied the sacraments of mercy they were entitled to as Christians; rigorous confessors didn't make their lives easy.

Not many years ago a gay rights movement started in the Greenwich Village parish where I spend my summers. Tired of the brutality and intolerance shown them, homosexuals wanted to promote gay liberation, gay rights, gay pride. Their battle cry was, "Gay is good." The world needs to hear that gay is good. For centuries gays grew up fearing their homosexuality as a sickness.

The general climate is not heartless in offering fair weather to homosexuals. Everyone living in America has heard by now that gay is good. The pastoral concern for gays has never been so high. Many people I see at Mass in New York make no secret of their sexual preference. Gay Catholics are out in the open if they want to be. None of them acts like an outlaw stealing grace from Christ; nobody asks a gay for his sexual identity card when he goes to Communion. The confessional keeps its own secrets, and most confessors make an effort to temper the wind to the shorn lamb.

About fifteen years ago a group of gay students made their presence known to Campus Ministry. The students wanted to talk about themselves as members of the church. They talked about organizing a club to promote gay awareness. A couple of them suggested holding a gay dance in the student center. The idea was discouraged because fistfights might be started by the hecklers showing up to watch the homosexuals dance. Nobody in Campus Ministry was liberal enough to favor a prom.

In a year or two, the students went underground again. They would soon graduate, they said, and didn't want their gay activism to be prejudicial to them in the job market.

This is the way it has been ever since: Students acknowledge their homosexuality, look for coverage in the media as a support group to gays going it alone, and then, after a time, go back into the closet. The group, whenever I have heard of it, stayed small. Gays who want to talk to a priest show up alone, wanting nothing to do with a club.

Notre Dame is still struggling to understand whether gay is good. The administration recently banned the student radio station from reading an announcement from a gay rights group. The hollering that began missed the point: No Catholic worth his salt should need to hear the pleadings for gay students to be treated as the children of God. Gay students bear scars that make you want to offer them love and respect to help make them whole.

They know in Greenwich Village that gay is good, but in the Indiana boondocks gay is still apt to mean you're the odd man out. A club that says everything gay is good or tolerable seems like a nonnegotiable idea here, at least until Halley's Comet comes 'round again. Blame it on the intolerance of the church, which still gets nervous when Catholics get abortions or practice birth control. Blame it on our famous macho mentality. Blame it on the conservatism of Our Lady's school—a pro-choice group or Planned Parenthood wouldn't be allowed a plug on the student station either. There's no need to whitewash the truth: Prejudice has a home under the Golden Dome. Gays know they are an embarrassment when they become active at a school featuring jocks.

Some students accuse the leaders of being hypocrites who pretend the dark realities of the human condition don't exist on these sacred green acres. But they do, and struggles for sexual identity are still going on. I hear the cries for help from students in despair: "Am I, or am I not? Help me to decide!" Understanding that, and accepting it for oneself, is a matter of soul searching, not support groups.

Being gay in America is no blessing. "Gay is good," the boys in the band told us, "but hetero is happier." They'll be battling prejudice all their lives, in spots more cherished or famous than Notre Dame. No need to hurry a student into a role that fits like a suit he'll outgrow next year; whatever will be, will be. There are private decisions having to do with growing up that should be made offstage, where nothing imprudent can happen to cause regrets tomorrow. During Vietnam students were encouraged to burn their draft cards at giant peace rallies while crowds cheered them on. A day or two later you met some of them, gray with the fear of having made a mistake they would pay for dearly.

"Happiness is gay life in college," undergraduates have declared. Then they went to the big city to live life in the fast lane. Gay life can be tough for the new boys in town, and they were sorry, I think, that they ever left the closet. The real world doesn't promise gays, or anyone else, a rose garden.

———

I'm getting to be an old-timer. A coed complained in *The Observer*: "The administration doesn't respect the students. Father Hesburgh keeps our investments in South Africa, and we told him not to."

Honey lamb, I thought, after working a few months at IBM would you tell the president how to run his company? Would you get close enough to honor him with your advice? Our students are such very dear people. Sometimes, though, they sound spoiled.

I hope these words from me in support of the status quo don't generate more anger. In a quieter time, maybe, the students will remember being told they are much loved.

A RABBI HEARS CONFESSION

My nephew Christopher is marrying a Jewish woman. The wedding will take place in a catering hall on Long Island. As part of the package deal, the caterer will supply the services of the presiding rabbi. I'll be at his side, looking like a stage-priest out of *Abie's Irish Rose.*

Chris said he and Bonnie wanted a reading from Ruth: "Where you go, I will go, and where you lodge, I will lodge. Your people shall be my people, and your God, my God." The rabbi turned them down, "This is something a Jew could never tell a Christian," he said. Chris would express something just as powerful, I suggested, if he honored his bride by crushing a glass, the Jewish custom symbolizing the destruction of the temple in Jerusalem.

My nephew expects his marriage to survive on tolerance; to him, that means being good-natured about the dietary laws at his mother-in-law's house. But the new kosher cousins who eat with their hats on may surprise him. New York rabbis are not pleased with mixed marriages. The catered rabbi could ask him to promise that his male children be educated in Hebrew schools for their bar mitzvahs. Maybe Chris's children, on their own initiative, will choose Judaism as their way to God. That would be fine with me.

Before Chris was born, I read myself into the membership of the Catholic Church. The great Catholic writers were my teachers before I ever met a priest. Lately, I'm trying to imagine what it is like to be a Jew, and I'm embarrassed to admit that I'm investigating a new religion.

Chris is too young to remember *Exodus*. His acquaintance with Judaism is at the level of *Yentl* and *Fiddler on the Roof*. When I tell him that Jews put their trust in the Talmud and the Torah, he thinks I'm arguing with him. "The Torah," I explain, "belongs to Christians as well as the Jews. The Talmud is as exclusively Jewish as the Temple was."

Chris listens patiently, hoping I will soon make sense. He feels it's an uncle's job to talk over the heads of his family. He doesn't know I'm pushing a Jewish catechesis on him because I have my own ax to grind.

I said: "Hitler's dream of a master race died quickly. Yahweh never promised Hitler the German Reich would last a thousand years. But he swore an oath to the Jews he would love them like a bridegroom until the stars fell from the sky. Hitler's viciousness had no limits; but Christians, too, some of them popes and archbishops, have blood on their hands."

Chris tried to get off the subject. "Bonnie and I may see the pope on our honeymoon. As airline employees, we can fly to Rome free." I tried not to notice that he had heard enough already.

"Every generation of Jews has had its share of persecution in Christian lands," I pressed on. "Christians have justified their cruelty and greed with a hateful theology hanging guilt on the Jews."

"Have you ever met the pope, Father Bob? What do you think of him?"

I would have preferred to tell him that I once shook hands with Golda Meir. James Joyce said Rome reminded him of a family that made a living from exhibiting the body of their dead grandmother. Seeing the pope at a general audience in St. Peter's Square recently was one of my greatest disappointments. We stood in Italian sun, facing a heaving wall of backs as fifty thousand other tourists waited for a glimpse. Trying to see the pope was like trying to spot Halley's Comet with the naked eye.

Going to Rome, they say, you either increase your faith, or lose it. The old Romans had the right idea of crowd control: Throw the Christians to the lions before they start taking advantage of a good thing. But why should I tell my nephew that St. Peter's is another three-ring circus?

Rabbi Aaron, supplied by the caterer, was an older man, bearded and fatherly. He agreed the two of us should sit down with Bonnie and Chris to help them understand each other's religious traditions, and so we gathered one night at the marriage chapel.

"What do you think we should tell our children?" asked Rabbi Aaron.

I felt as though I were going to confession. I had a lot on my mind, and the rabbi was a good listener. Bonnie and Chris sat there like eavesdroppers.

I began: "Christianity doesn't have a miracle that's as fair a show as Judaism's miracle." The rabbi wagged his head as though to say: That's a matter of opinion.

"Judaism's faith is important for its insights because of the Jewish experience of suffering," I said. "Suffering is the argument atheists use to prove there is no God. But Jews knew sooner than Christians that in man's suffering, God suffers. The great Christian philosophers rejected the idea of God in pain. He would stop being God, they argued, if pain could touch him. In Belsen, a prisoner was being hanged. A man kept crying, 'Where is God? Where is He?' The answer came, 'He is there on the rope.'"

The rabbi shrugged. "It's a tough world. You could sign up workers for the kibbutzim in Israel with that toughness."

"Rabbi," I said, "the Christians owe the Jews."

"Ah, as I suspected, it was Gentile guilt talking," he replied with a groan.

"The pope failed to protect the Jews," I said. "The German bishops failed to stop Hitler."

Again he shrugged. "So? You want me to say there's a few rotten apples in every crowd? You want me to forgive them? I forgive them. That changes nothing; not one dead Jew comes back. Forgive them yourself. That changes you. Still, the dead stay dead. The world kills Jews. What has this to do with a wedding?"

Bonnie and Chris, I noticed, were asleep with their heads together.

"Chris faces so much he will not understand," I said. "He doesn't know what the pope is talking about when he says the church is sorry for its treatment of Jews."

"No!" he shouted. "Do not say you are sorry! 'Sorry' does not ask Jewish girls to have Irish babies. 'Sorry' forgets that the Master of the Universe writes the names of Abraham's children in the Book of Life."

"I see your point," I said, feeling overpowered. Later, when I was less naive, I did see his point. The catered rabbi was warning me not to rain on his parade. The tough cookie from Queens was telling me that the handwringing over deaths that happened in another country a generation ago was not required from me as a bystander. He was asking me not to unbury pain. As another rabbi told us, "Sufficient for the day is the evil thereof." I was inviting ghosts onstage unnecessarily. I was burdening a new marriage with ancient horrors, turning the wedding party into a Holocaust committee.

He said, "Do not forget the Holocaust, but do not sentimentalize Jews. Do not sentimentalize Hell. Do not tell us if God was with us in the pit of damnation. How would you know about death camps? Were you there when the fool said in his heart: 'There is no God. There can never be a God again. God is dead, and gone to the grave!'"

The words are terrible to hear, a blasphemy against faith. You want to say a prayer to save God.

"Don't tell us, we'll tell you if God is dead," said Rabbi Aaron. "Our theologians will tell your theologians. Do not write us passion plays of God's sons agnostic with pain, or epic poems of Isaiah's seraphim, surly and sullen with rage, refusing to sing 'Holy, Holy' in protest of Treblinka. Such a favor from the Gentiles to the Jews—to tell Jews the Hebrew God is treating them like *schlemiels.*"

God calls attention to himself as an absence or a presence whenever the unpredictable or disastrous happens. Rabbi Aaron believed a smart Jew could figure out, without help, that they are part of the same *being there.*

Bonnie and Chris were awake now—kids in love, wanting to be married, wondering whether they should elope or ask the caterer for a justice of the peace since the clergymen of their choice were acting like the odd couple. Earlier, Chris had worried that I would show up dressed in rented phylacteries, and by now had probably decided that an interfaith wedding would be more peaceful without the help of a foolish uncle. Still, we kept at it.

"Terrible things happened to Jesus," said the rabbi. "Yet you Christians cheapen the death. Sentimentality cheapens his death. The preachers make it a carnival; it turns into a slogan stuck on car windows. He was a Jew, as we well know. You tell us, with tears on your face, that you know about the death of Jews, the lambs of sacrifice, other Christs led to the ovens. Leave the Jewish deaths alone! Their darkness is our business. The mystery of their loss is part of God's will that is more personal to us than to you.

"Soon, love from a bleeding heart will make six million dead Jews symbols of the counter-culture. It will become a holy act of religion to identify yourself as a sentimentalist who honks twice in memory of children who ended their lives as soap and ashes."

The catered rabbi stopped me cold in my tracks. The monks used to call boredom the noonday devil. Spiritual boredom is the priests' complaint. I've become a little bored with my church. Few surprises are coming out of dear, dull Rome.

And where are the Catholic novels worthy of taking their places with the classics: *Brideshead Revisited* and *The Power and the Glory*. We domesticated the drama of heaven and hell when we translated the Mass. Recent Catholic fiction has become naughty, nostalgic, wishful reminiscing about altar boys looking up schoolgirls' dresses.

Jewish writing, sooner or later, turns your eyes toward the Holocaust. All those deaths finally broke the silence of centuries about Jewish life. Catholics, writing novels of growing up, burn their bridges behind them. Our lives were based on fear, they say, which went away when we became Catholic dropouts. Jews, coming of age, turn their backgrounds into literature. The patriarchs in caftans, the marriage brokers, and the Sabbath peace are always part of the ambience in the *shtetls* or on Hester Street on the lower East Side. The tragedies are never far away; there are always foreshadowings, or echoes, of the knocks on doors by policemen who shatter homes.

Jewish writing makes me sorry I'm not Jewish. Yet the Jews have it hard, and the rabbi nailed me as a romantic meddling in Judaism. It is tempting, when I write, to translate things I'm ignorant of into a Christian parallel. The sacrifice of Isaac starts to look like the death on the cross; the barbed wire of Belsen seems like a newer edition of the crown of thorns. In the eyes of the beholder, I may be reducing them in rank or tampering with their special symbolism. One shouldn't try to explain the millions of dead as though he were reading a text in Milton, asserting Eternal Providence and justifying the ways of God to man.

Israel has a jealous God. A jealous rabbi tells me it's not my job to push my nephew into crushing the wine glass. I've picked out the *mezuzah* they will nail on the doorpost as a sign of their faith. I bought it in Brooklyn as a wedding gift, a metal case enclosing a parchment scroll with Hebrew letters: Hasidic magic, efficacious like holy water. As a priest, bored with his church, I'm ecumenical, available to the caterer as a token Gentile holy man, willing to practice Judaism without a license.

Mazel tov to Rabbi Aaron. *L'Chaim* to Chris and Bonnie. *Shalom* to the Holy Father—we were only having a lovers' quarrel. He recently visited a synagogue in Rome, and it was an historic event. He must have been bored by the show his monsignors put on. I hope he talked to a caterer's rabbi.

AS AMERICAN AS GOD, SIN,
AND JIMMY SWAGGART

Christ is the same yesterday, today, and forever, the Bible says. Yet any handbook will show you that the Byzantine Christ was more cosmic and political than the Christ of St. Francis, celebrating the redemption of nature in the Canticle of the Sun. Is there a difference, then, between the British Christ and the Christ of Billy Graham? Between Christ of the Established Church with its ties to the monarchy, and the grassroots Christ preached at the camp meetings of a young democracy?

Could it be said, without offensiveness, that an American has to work harder at his redemption if his soul is being nourished on English sacraments than if he's making his Communions at familiar altars at home? After a summer as a parish priest in London, how could I tell you? I do know that a relationship with God seems to change after you start saying Mass on English turf. Being a Catholic in England means belonging to a tradition with a calendar of saints hundreds of years old. America has but a handful of saints, most of them immigrants or missionaries.

In two months in London, one scarcely gets over the culture shock. The difference is more than the side of the street you drive on, or whether you shop with dollars or pounds. London is not New York: Canterbury is far from Rome.

Englishmen since the time of Henry VIII, wanting to be free of the yoke of Rome, have claimed that they owe their religious allegiance to the successors of Augustine of Canterbury, sent in the sixth century by Pope Gregory I to teach the Angles the Faith. The term "Anglo-Catholic" may still be applied to members of the Church of England, the state religion which claims to be an English branch of the Catholic Church. But it more specifically describes Anglicans persistently concerned with church unity.

I'm neither an historian nor a theologian. I'm just a plain American, taught to believe in fair play. I am embarrassed by Renaissance popes who divided continents they'd never seen among the Catholic superpowers. So I have no problem being sympathetic to the English version of history, which exempts Canterbury from Rome's control. Henry VIII was a blot on the escutcheon, but in the air warmed by the English sun I easily revise my prejudices against the Reformation in England, which translated the Bible into the Elizabethan language Shakespeare used.

Popes who tried to maintain their ascendancy through interdicts and excommunications in countries where they were not welcome make me angry with their abuse of power. By contrast, George Herbert, the Metaphysical poet who established himself in the seventeenth century as a country parson representing the essence of Anglicanism, seems as wholesome as a psalm of David praising the Lord as his shepherd.

Spanish Catholics at about that time were lugging statues of the Madonna into the New World as consolation to the Indians they had raped of gold. Spanish nuns were having visions of the Savior, who kept them busy with devotions that contradicted simple promises written in the New Testament.

Protestants, of course, were inventing their own errors, but they were aggressive enough with the truth to help make the Catholics honest. Since the pope's was no longer the only game in town, Catholics faced the possibility of their own damnation for sins for which they were personally accountable—once they gave up bondage to the superstition and fear encouraged by priests who made a business of selling God's good will and favor.

In other words, the Reformation did what it was supposed to do. It opened the books on institutional corruption by opening the greatest of all Books, the one by which the church itself will be judged on its fidelity to God's will. The Reformation forcefully reminded the sinner that he had an intellect, a will, and a conscience. These faculties, assisted by the Holy Spirit, could lead him to the vision of God. All the balms in Gilead—all the holy water, blessed oils, rituals, symbols, papal bulls, and encyclicals—couldn't lead him to heaven as surely as the Blood of the Lamb could. Once this good news started making the rounds of the Protestant grapevine, nothing Christendom (even in the heart of the Vatican) would ever again be the same.

In England, where John and Charles Wesley preached the simplicities, where Protestants and Catholics made martyrs of each other, and where the Puritans began their journey to the Bay Colony, I'm not sure which side I'm on. And I'm not sure it matters, since both sides are part of the same holy thing. We waited for centuries—until the time of Pope John XXIII—for that late, great insight. Then all of them—those who began the housecleaning and those who held title to the house—were members of the one and only household of faith.

Only the Irish, who came to England as imports, and maybe the Old Catholics, who didn't change horses at the Reformation, are pure enough in their Catholicity to look askance at the Archbishop of Canterbury. I never met any Old Catholics in London that I know of, though I met Anglican vicars who were tilted toward Rome and Roman Catholic laity sliding toward Canterbury.

American Catholics don't have strong feelings about the validity of Anglican orders (which means: Are these vicars real priests saying honest-to-God Mass or are they only preachers without sacramental power?). American Catholics are busy deciding if they're for or against Father Curran, if it's permissible to read Father Greeley's novels, if they could in good conscience have supported Geraldine Ferraro in the presidential election. And America's fundamentalist Protestants are still fighting the theory of evolution.

But over one hundred years ago John Henry Newman and Frederick William Faber, both Anglican vicars out of Oxford, had most of the vicars in England asking themselves if they were priests of the Catholic

Church as it is represented in the Anglican branch of the Mystical Body. This crisis among the Anglican clergy was the beginning of the Oxford Movement; nothing is more British than the Oxford Movement.

Newman, Faber, and the others didn't want to submit to the pope. Their churches and liturgy, tasteful and restrained, were dear to them. Their piety felt manly, and it encouraged them to show good form and a touch of class. Everything best in life was represented by practicing the religion established by law as the official worship of Oxford, Cambridge, and the realm ruled by Victoria—the British Empire. It would be unpatriotic for an Englishman to go to Rome and kiss the hem of the robe of the pope, that upstart Italian prince ruling the Vatican States who, in a few decades, would declare himself infallible in matters of faith and morals.

So those goodhearted vicars, anxious to keep their vocations from crumbling into ruin, studied the history of dogma to see if the Anglican Church had a Catholic leg to stand on. Newman, the religious genius of his century (comparable to the saints Augustine and Aquinas), studied deeper and harder than anyone. Finally, realizing that the jig was up for him as an Anglican, he quietly resigned his benefice and joined the Church of Rome. The country could not have been more disturbed if the queen had started reciting the rosary.

Faber, who had a flair for the dramatic, went to Rome to ask the pope if he should become a Roman. The pope (what else was he supposed to say?) told Faber to stop dillydallying as an Anglican or he would lose his soul. Faber went home to sweat it out. Finally, at Sunday vespers, he rushed into his pulpit weeping, then rushed down the steps of the pulpit, tearing off his vestment and throwing it on the ground as he fled. When the congregation went to the rectory to comfort him, he begged them to promise that the next morning they would take him to the Catholic bishop (roped and tied, if necessary) to make his application to Rome.

So Faber rejected everything that he formerly believed in, implicitly admitting that all of it was worthless for salvation—so worthless that he had to hurry away from it (without even hanging up his Anglican robes) before he went to hell.

Since Pope John XXIII told us every Christian denomination bears the mark of Christ on its forehead, no vicar will ever again have to be in such a hurry to reject his birthright so unconditionally. But a century passed between the Oxford Movement and Pope John's pontificate, and many tears were shed by dozens of departing vicars. Some still ponder the validity of Anglican orders; the question is not resolved in Rome.

Here at Notre Dame I know the Church of England doesn't hold a candle to the Church of Rome. There in London I wasn't so sure. At Westminster Abbey it all fits together—love of country going hand-in-glove with love of God: the playing fields of Eton, the battle of Trafalgar, the World War I poetry from Picardy, Mrs. Miniver, Dunkirk, the London Blitz.

America does not have an established church. But we have a national religion centered on a nondenominational God who attends the Congregational church on those Sundays when he goes. We praise him at Thanksgiving and ask favors on the Fourth of July. We invite him along when we bury the dead at Arlington or when we mourn the loss of a president. He is a God of blessings, large and generous. He is at home in the redwood forests and has shoulders as big as the Rocky Mountains, and he watches over us from sea to shining sea. He is a God of creation and new beginnings, a God of plantings and harvests. He presides over our freedom with his power, which is as sleepless as the waters crashing down at Niagara.

Last summer in London, I missed Jimmy Swaggart denouncing sin. America is big and successful. We may not have invented sin, but we've made it more of an industry than anyone else has. The winning of the West was violent with shootouts between cowboys and Indians, with Tom Mix and Hopalong Cassidy shooting the hombres who stole water rights from the ranchers. We had the Barbary Coast and Dodge City. We had Chicago in the '20s. We still have Reno, Vegas, and Atlantic City, and notorious neighborhoods in dozens of cities, and statistics that prove we lead the world in violence and sin.

We knew from our Bible that sooner or later, when we were up to our necks in mischief, a preacher would come along and set us straight. So we waited for Jimmy Swaggart to show up and get us ready for the trampling of the vintage where the grapes of wrath are stored. I never miss Jimmy on television. He tells me about Jesus, the fairest of ten thousand, the Rose of Sharon, the morning and evening star, the Ever-lasting Counselor, the Prince of Peace.

Jimmy threatens me with the judgment to come and Armageddon: "The mercy door is almost shut. The ark is ready to sail. The trumpet shall sound. One with the countenance of the Son of Man will arrive on a chariot of the clouds and the two-edge sword will be in his mouth. Then, ungodly America, thy doom will be at hand. You will cry out with weeping and the gnashing of teeth—'Brother Swaggart, why didn't you warn us?'

"'I tried to warn you, but you wouldn't listen.'"

What does Jimmy Swaggart know that the rest of us need to hear? Nothing that Billy Sunday didn't know fifty years ago. Nothing that the circuit riders from the Methodist Conference didn't know a hundred years ago. Nothing that Jonathan Edwards in the Connecticut River Valley didn't know two hundred years ago. Nothing that Cotton Mather, condemning witches in Boston, didn't know three hundred years ago.

Jimmy Swaggart is as American as apple pie. He has the hype we love, a vulgarity to match the country's. He is the confidence man selling snake oil, the riverboat gambler. He's updated and electronic, but he's the slick, sweet-talking pitch artist who sold Bibles to dirt farmers who couldn't even read. Above all, his show is as big as a circus tent. His bigness is worthy of the bigness of America.

I'm not sure I can be saved without Jimmy's kind of theology. He convinces me that the Lord, when he comes, will have the hard hands of a working man, that his eyes will be blue and his face tanned. He will say, "Hello, neighbor," and perhaps his accent will be Southern, like the preacher's. And he'll know about cotton as though he had chopped it.

In which pulpit of the jeweled churches in London will you find the vicar, the dean, or the canon who makes you see the face of the Jewish Messiah as perfectly as Jimmy does?

I now know how the Oxford Movement was possible. Newman was a star, a scholar, and a saint. A number of stars, all more knowledgeable about God than I, came to the rectory I inhabited in London. They were reading the mystics; I was reading the moralists and the apologists who wrote "Why I became a Catholic." For them Christ was more than a cockney or a ploughman, though they never told me who he was or where I could find him. They thought I already knew, which I probably did, but not in London. I was often lonesome for his company; if they were lonesome for his company, they never admitted it. They just read the mystics as though the mystics wrote maps to holy hiding places. Beside them in the church, I felt like a beginner.

I was happy in London, but I had to come home before I began to like the tea, which is watery. Tea is not a man's drink anyway. I can't imagine Jesus drinking tea. Neither the tea nor the theology in England could make me feel born again. I had to come home to hear Jimmy to find out if I was.

CONFESSIONS OF A BIBLIOMANIAC

To use the formula of the A. A.'s: My name is Bob. I'm a bibliomaniac. I've been addicted to book-buying all my life. Lately it's been getting out of control.

I'm in love with the Notre Dame Bookstore. That's because I shop better than I pray or preach. The bookstore is the equivalent of the old-time village well—a place where you catch up on the news. I leave looking like a bricklayer staggering under his load. I haven't read all the books yet. They say you can't take it with you; but if you could, I'd have crates following me to the grave.

I do grow disgusted with myself when I find unread, still-boxed books gathering dust in the corner. "What do you think you're doing with your expensive hobby?" I ask myself.

The answer to myself is: "Oh, well now, you never can tell. If the bombs fall, civilization may be grateful that I have kept all the master-pieces here. Imagine a barge-keeper in ancient Egypt dredging a strangely marked boulder out of the Red Sea, a war relic from the time of Exodus. An Egyptian probably threw it at a Jew and missed. The barge-keeper sold it to an embalmer and the embalmer hauled it home to his library. His wife objected: 'It's a language chart from the Berlitz School transposing pluperfect verb forms from cuneiform and hieroglyphics to Greek. Are you planning a trip to Athens? Why do you need it here?'

"'Honey,' he answered, 'haven't you heard of the papyrus revolution? Boulder teaching aids in the classroom have had their day. Someday this granite hunk will be famous as a collector's item. When it is, they'll call it the *Rosetta stone.*'"

You can't argue with history.

But I don't buy books for the sake of looking at them, though the sight of them is a consolation. I hope the truth in them is sacramental, like the meaning of the Eucharist. Visiting a church, you can make a spiritual communion from which grace is forthcoming. Perhaps something analogous happens when you touch Shakespeare or the Bible.

Last year the first of twelve volumes of Yeats' letters showed up in the bookstore. It was a handsome, expensive book. That same week a collection of Dylan Thomas' letters became available; the price was $40. I have them both; the letters survive as a living legacy from the dead. Each letter began as a spark in the soul of a poet, a movement among the chemicals in the brain of a genius. The idea resulting from this psychosomatic energy now lies as words scrawled on a page.

What would it mean if we now had Shakespeare's love letters or a note in the handwriting of St. Paul? Emily Dickinson's letters tend to be as exquisitely terse as her poems are. In one that announces that she is dying, she captures it in two words: "Called back!"

Must I read all twelve volumes of Yeats' letters (if I live to see them published) as a condition of owning them, as proof I haven't wasted my money? I'd be embarrassed to accumulate treasure that could be called an estate. But I'm honored to be the caretaker of a deposit of truth in viable form.

Every day in the summer when I'm in New York I scout the bookstores. Starting at Central Park and walking south on Fifth Avenue, I stop at Doubleday West, which is the main store, then Doubleday East, which is a branch. Then I come to Dalton's, Brentano's (now closed), Harper and Row, over a sidestreet to Laurel on Sixth Avenue; then back to Scribner's and Barnes & Noble on Fifth. Then, perhaps, I will take a bus to the bookstores on Astor Place.

The Strand bookstore in Greenwich Village, at the corner of Broadway and 11th, has eight or ten miles of bookshelves loaded with secondhand books. The tourists enjoy looking for rare editions, unaware the professionals have been much ahead of them. The older books are, the more Americans tend to canonize them; it's a symptom of how young we feel as a country.

Scribner's is my favorite. It has the elegant air of a fashionable Episcopal church. It has a corner where the books by Scribner's own authors are kept. It's the nearest thing America has to the poets' corner in Westminster Abbey. Hemingway, Wolfe, and Fitzgerald are available in hardback as on the first day of sale. Scribner's leaves you hopeful about the rebirth of religion with literature as the revealed will of God.

I'm appalled at the amount of junk now on the market in the malls. When you're a veteran, you can smell the minor league reading—Stephen King, Jane Fonda exercise manuals, Garfield the Cat, diet books, manuals on the power of positive thinking, *Real Men Don't Eat Quiche.* The paper hasn't been invented that will refuse the ink detailing the sorrows of Marilyn Monroe, and I'm angered and bitter at the hirelings of an industry that keeps telling you more than you need to know about Papa, Scott and Zelda, Thomas Merton. But I don't rain on anybody's parade; nobody reads *Moby Dick* all the time.

I enjoy John le Carré, P. D. James, and Dorothy Sayers. I'm not too tight to buy best-sellers in hardback, choosing selectively among authors I admire: Iris Murdoch, John Updike, Peter De Vries, Graham Greene. Then I pass them along, hoping their circulation will be continuous and long-lived. Nobody wants to throw away a book. It's part of the Puritan ethic to be reverent before books, as though they had been lugged onto the *Mayflower* in place of food.

As a confessed bibliomaniac, I offer myself this word of encouragement: It's nice to be snobbish about things that matter. Your bookcase makes a statement about you; most people like statements about themselves to be complimentary . . . and credible. I'd be a phony if I had an eye-catching lineup of Dante in medieval Latin, the *Odyssey* in Greek, and *The Remembrance of Things Past* in French. I like my books to be a classy act, for another simple reason: I used to be an English teacher. Part of my trade was to respect books that had value—*War and Peace, Crime and Punishment,* everything by Dickens.

As a priest, I have a limited amount of money; but at sixty-one, I have more money than I have time. The time comes in small intervals between the dusk and the daylight. And life comes like a roll of paper towels which I see one sheet at a time as it comes off the dispenser. But even if I were issued a blank check I could fill in for life and time as well as money, what about the eyesight? How soon before the warranty on eyesight expires? I'm in a race against the darkness to get the essential books read before I'm as blind as Homer or Milton.

Divinity students argue whether we are more saved by works than by grace and faith; but that is not the problem. The amount of salvation we're allowed is related to how smart we grew, and how much we took advantage of our intellects (although in heaven the pint-size and the quart-size are filled with grace all the way to the top).

Our vocation is to become saints and scholars. Man's highest faculties are his will and intellect. The object of the will is love; the object of the intellect is truth. The highest love is the love of God, and of your neighbor as yourself; the highest truth is the truth of God and of one's neighbor as himself. To be perfect in loving and knowing God is to become a saint and a scholar. *Quod erat demonstrandum*. Which, if you'll pardon my metaphysics, is what I set out to prove.

In a world divided by light and darkness, religion began as stories of the gods. Our greatest stories have godliness in them, in heroes tragically flawed and outlaws heroic in their love of villainy. Ahab the sailor and Satan the doomed archangel match each other in the grandeur of their rebellion against enthroned power.

Divine revelation comes in words on a page. If we didn't have words like mercy, compassion, forgiveness, love, sacrifice, and grace, not only would our vocabulary be poorer, but we'd also be spiritually impoverished, as though the word gives birth to the idea which brings forth the possibility.

Or to put it another way: To know God is to know him revealed in his Son—the Word made flesh. Christ is the Word written by the Father, the perfect idea from the divine mind, the mental image God has of himself. All of which means you can begin theology if you understand what the poet and writer do.

APOLOGIA PRO VITA MEA

I've been aware of God for as long as I've been aware of anything. A vivid childhood memory is my mother telling me there's a God in heaven who could send for me anytime. Dying is nothing to be afraid of, she insisted. When you woke up in the morning, you couldn't be sure if your heart would stop beating during the day or if you would be in God's house by suppertime. She didn't mention sin or anything to make me fear God, except for this warning that death is natural—and it's not wise to make plans without adding, "If God spares me."

The God who could keep a child on his toes like that must be moody, I decided, and the human heart sounded about as dependable as a cheap flashlight battery. This Irish brand of fatalism was instilled in me very young. I was suspicious of the allegedly kind Creator who could ruin the family picnic, interrupt the games a boy plays, or otherwise screw up my personal timetable with his decision to promote me to wearing wings.

So I've been listening for God for a very long time. I was baptized into three churches before I was twenty and confirmed in two of them. I don't take great pride in this track record, but it shows how I've tried.

The Catholic Church sounded irresistible from the time I heard that priests could prove the existence of God. But I found they weren't very helpful unless you believed in God already. I can't prove the existence of God and don't even try. God is more obvious to me than common sense. What do you hang existence (or love or hope) on if there isn't a God? A world without God would be as awkward to me as a door without hinges to attach it to the rest of the house.

Lately I've been reading Cardinal Newman's spiritual autobiography, *Apologia pro Vita Sua*. Newman had been attacked by a Protestant doctor of divinity who accused him of publicly admitting that priests don't place great value on telling the truth. Newman published a protest, and his assailant continued the altercation with a question that became as enduring as a code word: "What, then, does Dr. Newman mean?" In the *Apologia* John Henry Newman told what he meant in no uncertain terms. It's a masterpiece.

Lately I've been getting mail asking, "What, then, does Father Griffin mean by his tolerance of homosexuals, his love of Judaism, his excitement over Jimmy Swaggart's message?" What I mean is, if you're listening for God you don't hesitate to walk a mile in your brother's moccasins. What else could "gay is good" mean except that nothing God makes is bad? Homosexuals need to know that before they turn suicidal from self-hatred. I wouldn't help them if I said anything less, or anything more.

Did the Jews meet the God of the covenant in the death camps? Are the Pentecostals to whom Swaggart preaches born again in the Spirit? How can I tell unless I keep listening? A former teacher whom I have loved for years recently asked, "What, then, does Father Griffin mean?" It hurts when a mentor describes you as a *poseur*—one who pretends to be what he is really not. If I'm not a faithful priest, I don't know what I am, though I'm conscious of being a careful listener. Listening is what you must do if you want to be faithful to grace. The great scholars, I believe, keep listening. What they hear is combined with scholarship and becomes truth the church can cherish. An unlicensed lightweight like me, without scholarly credentials or the pretensions of being a Newman, has to hear *something* in a lifetime of listening. The result may not be serious, like truth, but at least it is charming, like joy.

At year's end, on a night flight out of Newark to South Bend, I was reading a critical essay on *The Great Gatsby*, that perfect novel with the sadness of an Irving Berlin love-lament. The critic argued that the novel embodies the myth of the American dream. What, I wondered, did he mean by myth, that encyclopedic term that covers everything from the birth and death of gods to the illusions or disillusions young bachelors have about marriage? The Gatsby story is mythical, I gathered, because it helps explain the Lost Generation in the way the Genesis story explains the fall of man.

Huck Finn, Captain Ahab, Natty Bumppo, and Hester Prynne stand for archetypal hunks of truth about America. Our writers didn't have the primitive legends to draw upon that would have given us an *Iliad* or an *Odyssey*, so they created myths about a boy following a great river and a Nantucket whaling captain in pursuit of a biblical leviathan. Jay Gatsby is one of the minor deities in that pantheon of immortals who are serviceable as metaphors for the national character—a poor boy who climbed from rags to riches, a Midwesterner who made a religion out of *Poor Richard's Almanac*. What could be more American?

Where are the Catholics, I wondered as the plane took off, in this national gallery of the imagination? How did Catholics shape the American dream? For an enchanted moment I could see Manhattan, once described as a "jeweled iceberg," lit up for New Year's Eve. Catholic memories of New York conjure Irish working girls who built St. Patrick's Cathedral with their nickels and dimes; five thousand cops marching down Fifth Avenue on the 17th of March; the Rainbow Division of the Fighting 69th, singing "Give my regards to Broadway" as they slogged through the mud of France in World War I.

Catholics did their share to build the country. The Jesuits explored the wilderness, discovering the geography of "a promised land." Spanish missions, built before the Puritans left England, are still standing in California and Texas. The Irish laid tracks for the railroads to the West. Every war in history has its stories of brave chaplains and self-sacrificing Catholic patriots. What else could I think of that's Catholic and could be raised to the level of an archetype? The song-and-dance man, George M. Cohan? The parish churches, Italian and Irish? Most of them, I suspect, are throwbacks to the old country. The immigrants who built them wanted to be reminded of home, so the ecclesiastical landmarks on the banks of the Liffey were duplicated on the banks of the Hudson, complete with the Virgin's altars and Sacred Heart statues. The Irish wanted to preserve their faith in the New World, and their churches guaranteed the preservation.

When the changes came after Vatican II, the buildings were stripped bare. Pastors still haven't figured out how to fill the empty spaces. There's nothing about any of them that's worth writing home about. Thinking of the naked churches makes you wonder where they all disappeared to—the fifteen million who gave up the religion, the new recruits who were supposed to fill up the convents and seminaries (built so hopefully in the '50s, looking like luxury hotels on the outside—now white elephants).

Eating the airline's potted beef, I reflected: Where can you find the American equivalent of a Catholic masterpiece like *Brideshead Revisited*? Although England, with its Established Church, is a Protestant country, Waugh is as elegiac in his recall of the glory that was Roman as Fitzgerald is about the passing of the Jazz Age. Gatsby's house on Long Island, standing empty, reminds the next-door neighbor of the distortions in an El Greco night scene, but the lovely house at Brideshead waits like the church for the exiles' return as though they were being pulled back on a thread by the grace of God.

Waugh's novel ends on an up note: As a result of the fortunes of war, Mass is once again being said in the chapel at Brideshead, so long unused, as sad as the desolate City of the Lamentations. The lamp has been lighted before the bronze doors of the tabernacle to signify the presence of the Eucharist familiar to the Crusaders.

I'm not at my scholarly best at night, thirty thousand feet in the air, but as I made a list in my head of the American Catholic masterpieces or who could have written them, I realized that Protestants seem to have provided us with the richest part of our literary heritage.

As a minority group, we Catholics huddled together in a ghetto church, on the defensive. When we finally opened the windows at the *aggiornamento*, the fresh winds blowing in were more secular than holy. We had invented no domestic myths for ourselves, only imported myths, which we found foreign, like something worn in Paris. We were like a conquered people adopting the local gods, mixing their religion with our own. This is what Vatican II means for us.

I'm trying to figure out: Where have all the flowers gone, fifteen million of them, whose departure closed the seminaries? Now you have seen the *poseur* in full plumage, usurping the role of Andrew Greeley as sociologist.

————

I'm a down-easter from Maine. Other Yankees live much farther down on that rugged coast than I did. I'm familiar with the seashore where Winslow Homer painted; his seafarers were my relatives. As a boy I attended the white-steepled churches, as eloquent in their simplicity as cathedrals are in their ornateness. My hometown was Longfellow's home town. At heart I'm still part WASP.

Growing up, I was proud that my relatives were not Johnny-come-latelies in New England like the Catholics in my town, who were a mere generation or two away from being greenhorns. They couldn't be expected to know much, and they stole jobs from their betters because they were willing to work cheap. The priests I saw never spoke to the Protestant children. The Catholics bragged how smart the priests were. Most had been educated in French Canadian seminaries, which meant they had suffered a lot from the discipline and were undernourished because the food was poor. Part of their mystique was that they had never gotten over their early privations; half of them had ulcers, which was probably why they were so quiet.

In 1943, the Jesuits came to staff the boys' high school. They lived in dark rooms in an old house. Though they were rumored to be bright, they all talked as though they were from South Boston. It is hard to credit an Irishman as a genius if he sounds as though he shipped in from Liverpool with the Beatles to do imitations of Tip O'Neill. Everyone made noises like that on City Point, lace curtain or not. I compared the Jesuits with the Protestant pastors, graduates of Amherst, Bowdoin, Williams, and other rich colleges that trained preppies in the Protestant ethic. The priests knew everything about basketball and Greek, and they always referred to the Savior as "Our Blessed Lord." The ministers knew more about cookie-pushing, Tennyson, and delivering homilies on the discipleship of Jesus; none of them had the chastened, ascetic look of the Jesuits.

As a teen-ager who kept score, I wasn't any different from other kids who sign up with the Leathernecks because they like the uniform, or join the Dominicans because they admire the white habit. Most youngsters tend to be superficial in examining the outward marks of inward grace.

The Jesuit priest who instructed me as a Catholic didn't fool around. He made me learn the Act of Contrition, then the Acts of Faith, Hope, and Love. "The Act of Contrition could come in handy in case of an emergency," he said. He meant that if I were dying without a priest, the Act of Contrition could save my soul. He was Irish, like my mother, warning me that death could be sudden.

He made no bones about it: "You will not find much Catholic religion in the Bible. It's the book Protestants use." I loved the honesty. He must have known the religion was there as an embryo, since he made me learn the verses that confirmed the Creed. "A good Catholic boy always enjoys a sermon on the Blessed Mother," he said. That was the test by which I could measure myself, and it still is.

As a convert under instruction, I read Chesterton, Waugh, Graham Greene, Cardinal Newman, and Ronald Knox, English converts all. I can't remember whether I appreciated them then, or whether I found them mystifying and boring. I asked if I could join the Jesuits. "Go to a good Catholic college for three or four years. Then, if you want to, come back and talk to me." I ended up at Notre Dame, where in my senior year I read the biography that served my generation as a contemporary document matching St. Augustine's *Confessions*. It was Thomas Merton's *Seven-Storey Mountain*. The book assured me I could be, and should be, a priest. I've never been so sure of anything. The book was an answer to my prayers to Our Lady at the Grotto.

During the summer when I was being instructed, I looked back only once: on a day when I had lunch with the minister who had preached the sermon at which I was "saved." That evening, going to see my Jesuit, I intended to tell him I couldn't join his church, but I was unable to expose my doubts. I lived with the doubts until they went away, and I've never again looked back. Rome is the only direction for a well-informed Christian.

I didn't join the Jesuits. My father had died and I couldn't tell my mother I would be away from home in a Jesuit seminary for thirteen years. It's just as well. I would have been very obscure as a Jesuit; the Society of Jesus is the size of an army. I don't have the humility to be happy in obscurity while the superstars are out front taking their bows as saints and scholars.

In the seminary of the Holy Cross community, and for the first ten years after ordination, I was a happy ghetto-Catholic: observing the fasts, celebrating the feasts, avoiding the condemned movies and the books on the Index. As a young priest I taught English at Stonehill College near Boston, where I took classes at Harvard (so I could relish the New England Mind).

In 1965, my life fell apart at the same time the church started (so it seemed) to fall apart, as though God had decided that my troubles shouldn't come in single file. For two years before that, I had been trying to take care of my mother, who became sick, and then my brother and sister, both at home, when they became sick. It would have been a lot to manage even if the doctor hadn't given me diet pills to lose weight and sedatives to offset the amphetamines.

I was ignorant then of the harm drugs do; I used them to keep going through a time of great stress. Then one day I couldn't function; most especially, I couldn't slow down. I was addicted to pills that made me sleep; I was addicted to pills that energized me in the morning. Scared and feeling guilty about cheating to get extra prescriptions, I went to another doctor to tell him the trouble I was in. He prescribed Librium. It weakened me so much I was afraid to walk.

I'm not proud of all this. Coriolanus, in Shakespeare's tragedy, hated the political necessity of showing his war wounds to the crowd so they could applaud him as their general. Everyone hates making a spectacle of himself; that's why I'm understating the terrors of the nightmare in which our family was caught. But I was dealing with family breakdowns, mental illness, and hospitalizations that humiliated my loved ones. I dreaded to hear the phone ring at night. Finally, I began slipping close to the edge myself. Alone in the Damariscotta rectory, not far from the sea that summer, I had my own lost weekend. You survive the lost weekend, but the battle scars are nothing you want to talk about later.

I spent six months healing in a community infirmary on St. Joseph's Lake. Getting off the pills was no problem, but I spent a couple of years recovering from the numbness that replaced the pain of all I thought I had lost. I abstained from saying Mass until the marrow in my bones could unfreeze. This doesn't mean that my mind wasn't working or that I lost touch with reality. But I had to leave those stricken people at home to the care of others. The guilt of it was like the great boulder that Sisyphus had to push to the hilltop every day so it could rush down on him every night.

In 1966, I went to Holy Cross Seminary to teach for a year. The next September I moved into Keenan Hall as the assistant rector. The friendships in those two places showed me that my life wasn't even half over, that I still had work to do.

In 1970, I began writing the articles for *The Observer* that eventually were called "Letters to a Lonely God." All the letters are exploratory, ideas in search of meaning; nothing in them is so dogmatic that it needs to be put down in stone, or even in print.

Is God lonely? Perhaps it is reckless to predicate a loneliness of the Trinity, as though the Father, Son, and Holy Spirit could need anyone. Yet the Son on the cross must have been terrified of his loneliness—else why that great cry, "My God, my God, why hast thou forsaken me?" The Father who tore open the sky above the cross must have had something in mind, like seeing the son in whom he was well pleased free of pain and hugged into everlasting arms. The Holy Ghost, the spirit of love, must have been partner to their emotions.

Yet it's comforting to think of the God of the lonely people, those you meet in the lonely places, the unwanted and unloved, as "a man of sorrows, acquainted with grief." "He came not to take away our sufferings, but to fill them with his presence." That's what a great theologian wrote. Do you have to be a great theologian to write of Jesus? It seems to me that what was so humanly done when he revealed himself as the great high priest who would represent us in heaven, could be humanly spoken of, not reserved to some special treatment in metaphysics.

Theologians today are more ready to write a theology of the cross than they were when I was a student, although the crucifixion has always been the showpiece of sacrificial love (which the resurrection completed). After the death camps, the wars, the famines, the diseases, who wants to hear of the "Divine Complacency" or the "Impassibility of

God"? Faith wants to know, "Does he understand what I am going through? How does he know? Why does he let it happen?" If we didn't have a theology of the cross, we might have to invent one.

I didn't invent the idea that he's there, on the hangman's rope at Dachau. If the Jews of the Holocaust couldn't have hoped that God was with them in their suffering—and not just as an observer—their sorrow might have left them atheists. The God who stays well hidden above the story isn't much help to a brutalized world. In the crucifixion he meets suffering head on. After that, the so-called meaningless deaths don't seem so much like evidence that He has abandoned us. The cry, "My God, my God, why hast thou abandoned me?" prompts the answer: "My child, I was never *closer* to you."

I don't mind being wrong. My ideas are personal, like the answers to prayers which surprise me when they come. They may be trite, sentimental, shallow, silly, but please don't tell me they're not honestly searched for or that I mustn't trust what love and pain have taught me. Guides who should have been there had nothing to say to me when I was ready to throw in the sponge; they knew I was in trouble. Now, at this late hour, after I've found answers that work for me as a hypothesis, I feel hurt and ashamed of myself as a fool when I'm told my answers are dishonest, that I shouldn't trust my conclusions, that I am pretentious.

I would like to be more than a laureate of loneliness, God's or anyone's. I'm half Celtic, half Yankee—good blood lines for a writer. The language in the pubs of Dublin, they say, is richer than that used for speeches in the House of Parliament. Yankees have a talent for "seeing New Englandly." You can understand what Emily Dickinson meant by that if you page through Thoreau's *Walden*. I spend time with craftsmen who knew how to turn words into magic: Yeats, Shakespeare, Dylan Thomas, Joyce; they are like Druids casting spells. I sit down with them like a curious novice going to school to be a priest and listen to the divinity coming out of them. Before I die, I would like to write a piece for the world to admire as it admires a sonnet by Hopkins.

I'm sixty-one now; I haven't many more hostages for death to take from me. I'm at peace with the dead; I did nearly as much for them as I could. In the time left before sunset and the evening star, I want to write love songs that will show them I'm not all gloom and fuss, a curmudgeon measuring out his years in coffee spoons. I want to speak beautifully of the joys, to show that I have not lived in vain. Here is part of the cataloging of blessings freely given: the books; the friends; the children friends have shared; the meals; the days of wine and roses; the laughter and the refreshment of peaceful sleep; the mornings when I wake to music; the afternoons free of dullness, when there wasn't enough time for the words. And love. God. Being his priest.

If I keep in fine health, will I be wise enough at seventy-five to achieve immortality through a single piece of writing that breathes so perfectly it couldn't die? I want to delay the final goodbyes until after I have written a *gloria* that a Metaphysical would not be embarrassed by, to explain what an honor it has been to be allowed to eavesdrop on the universe like a spy who moves between countries telling secrets with God's name on them.

Flying home at the end of last year I had to change planes in Dayton. In the airport bookstore I saw a large poster of Humpty Dumpty. "All the king's horses, All the king's men / Couldn't put Humpty together again." They couldn't put him together for an obvious reason: He was an egg, a silly, proud egg.

The prophets of doom are saying that the Catholic Church, after Vatican II, met Humpty Dumpty's fate: It was an arrogant political structure with divine pretensions; trying to update itself, casting off the medievalisms that made it interesting, it smashed into pieces. It had a thin shell (even Baptists know they have to be hard-shelled) with a soft center, like an egg. Now all the pope's horses and all of his men can't put the church together again.

It's unfair to ask, "Where are the Catholic heroes? Where are the myths? Where are the masterpieces that your tradition has created in the land of the pilgrims' pride?" Old-timers had a myth of institutional infallibility they were proud of, but they wouldn't have given two cents for those pagan transcendentalists, Emerson and Thoreau. What makes me suspicious that a number of our members have sold out to the dominant culture is their willingness to see the church run like a democracy. The Catholic Church has lost its identity as a power structure; many seem happy to behave like Protestants—free to believe anything. Every time Rome clears its throat to bring the meeting to order and conduct business, liberated nuns and priests claim their right to dissent.

A more delicate image than Humpty Dumpty is the light-catching unicorn, a traditional image of Christ as the "horn of salvation" promised by Zechariah. In *The Glass Menagerie*, the Gentleman Caller, bumping the table, knocks the unicorn on the floor. Picking it up, he apologizes, "The horn broke off. It looks like a little horse." Laura reassures the Caller: "That's all right. Now it's like the others." The church, after its fall, is like the others. Now Catholics are like everybody else in the country, with nothing to distinguish them—as free of the magic, miracles, and hocus-pocus as they wanted to be. Unless of course, the pope puts Humpty Dumpty together again.

Personally, I don't *need* to belong to an infallible church. I've been a member of denominations in which the preacher enforces the doctrine with his personal authority and a verse from the Bible. That was the kind of liberal establishment that the Unitarians had in New England when Emerson resigned from the ministry because he no longer believed in the Lord's Supper. New England now has churches in which *clergymen* reject the celebration of the Eucharist as a cannibalistic rite.

How, in a democratic faith structure, do you control the heresies? Having found a church with an infallible pope, I wouldn't be happy to lose him to the levelers.

––––––

Nick Carraway's final judgment of Gatsby was that this *poseur*, wearing his ridiculous pink suits—this self-conceived son of God, dreaming his immaculate dream of touching the stars to gulp down the milk of Paradise—was worth more than all the rest of them in the book put together.

I was thinking the same thing about the Catholic Church as I boarded the plane in Dayton for the half-hour flight home. I respect any person's way to God: church, synagogue, or the great temple of nature with stars for a roof. But the church ruled by Pope John Paul II in collegiality with the bishops and the theologians as part of the magisterium, with the documents of Vatican II as part of its teaching, is worth more than the other two hundred Christian denominations put together. The myth of the infallible church is infinitely more valuable than all the stars-and-stripes-forever hoopla and Fourth-of-July jingoism that have ever gone into the making of the American dream.

ONE POPE AT A TIME

Richard McBrien is a soft-spoken priest whom you like on sight. I tell him: "Your name comes up frequently in the mail I get. Is my name ever mentioned in yours?" The head of Notre Dame's theology department looks amused at the idea. He's too innocent to suspect what I'm hinting at: In the hate mail I get as a columnist, Dick McBrien receives his share of abuse.

Dick works hard at being smart. I'm reading his new book, *Caesar's Coin.* I've never finished his two-volume work *Catholicism* because I keep giving away my copies to converts. His essay on the pope in last Spring's *Notre Dame Magazine* troubled me, as it troubled others who consider themselves folk Catholics. I can tell this from my mail, most of which is from sincere church members. His article assessing the tensions between the pope and the American church left me wondering what's happening in the church. Is it unnecessarily and dangerously polarizing itself?

If Dick's essay had been kinder to John Paul II, he would have saved a number of believers pain that they don't deserve. Since the beginning of the world, human beings have had symbols for use in their contact with the Infinite. Prophets in every clime and time have been inspired to write bibles, set up altars, create liturgies, offer worship, and invent commandments in the name of a deity who revealed his will to them. Supporters of one deity used to make their livings by going to war with those of a rival deity. Perhaps it is true that nearly every war is part political and part religious.

Eventually, the great gurus started pointing out the good you can find in any faith. Americans especially, proud of their country as a melting pot, try as a matter of principle to give a fair shake to every creed, provided it isn't brutal or stupid. Ashrams of the Hindu sages are found in South Bend. Buddha's birthday has been celebrated on the Notre Dame campus. Thomas Merton died while on pilgrimage to the Dalai Lama of Tibet.

Ecumenism is no longer a local display of good will in the neighborhood; it looks forward to the union of the world's great religions in a celebration of Christ, Mohammed, Buddha, and Confucius as the sons of God, bringing enlightenment from heaven. Even Vatican II, while insisting on the name of Jesus as the only name under heaven by which men can be saved, acknowledged the spiritual kinship of the great teachers and admitted that the symbolism of these traditions can be productive of grace.

The pope, however, continues to be controversial as a symbolic figure of faith. The fundamentalists consign him to the outer darkness. Bigotry has created a literature out of the theme of the Italian prince seeking to enslave the world in ignorance and fear. He's a tyrant worse than Stalin or Hitler; *they* never claimed the power to send souls to hell. The Catholic Church is his evil empire; the Jesuits, with their general known as the "black pope," are his army.

With the new freedom in the church, the Sisters are currently taking turns at verbally tweaking the pope's nose, sometimes in his presence, for the benefit of the gallery. Some of them, seen on Donahue, wave to the retirees at the Motherhouse as they identify themselves as U.S. nuns with chips on their shoulders. B'nai B'rith gets fairer handling in the enlightened Catholic press than John Paul II does. It seems ironic when a liberal who would prefer dying to attacking a Jew, a black, a gay, or a feminist makes an art form out of treating the pope as a buffoon.

I'm not a conservative with an ax to grind or a stake in the status quo before Vatican II. But Catholics who grew up praying for the intentions of the pope after every Mass feel violated when he's treated with insolence rather than kid gloves. They cringe at seeing the visible symbols of faith tampered with, especially the pope or the Eucharist. Of the two, the symbolism of the Eucharist is more up for grabs, since the Eucharist has already been divested of part of its magic. As long as popes who understand the tradition stay in charge, they figure, you can trust them to keep Transubstantiation from being eased out of the Mass altogether. The disappointment in the English Mass canons was so great that even liturgists were questioning whether the texts were really what the church had in mind for its memorial sacrifice. This wasn't abortion, on which you might feel entitled to a free choice you could make by yourself. Only the pontiff could examine the ritual that serves the church as a heartbeat, checking it for vital signs. He's the chosen servant of the servants of God, on whom, *ex officio*, God's favor rests. This is a folk Catholic's version of ecclesiology.

The pope's job is to keep the bishops honest. The bishops and the theologians keep each other honest. The *sensus fidelium* at the grassroots level keeps the church honest. The Holy Spirit keeps the magisterium honest. Whether the grace flows from the bottom up, with lateral interventions, or from the top down in a horizontal diffusion from the center, all the elements mesh together into the collegiality of a mystical body to which all the baptized, Roman or not, belong.

I became a Catholic before the silly seasons started. Pius XII was pope then—an intellectual, an aristocrat, the final pope to remain a prisoner in the Vatican. After his death, they cut him down to size, but for us, in our hearts, he was the Holy Father whose symbol was a dove, since he worked for peace in the time of war. When he died, he had been pope so long we felt as though we had lost a father. The papers carried wonderful stories of Pius XII laid out for his funeral. The Harlem Globetrotters, strutting their stuff before him, had set his feet to dancing with "Sweet Georgia Brown." The Chief Rabbi of Rome became a Catholic after World War II out of love for Pius, for his work in saving the Jews from the Holocaust. Golda Meir honored him. David Ben-Gurion planted a tree in Jerusalem to honor him in a garden of Jewish remembrance. Eight hundred thousand Jews were saved from the camps by the church, which hid or furnished them with baptismal certificates to help them escape. Eyewitnesses with firsthand knowledge report the pope's anguish over the fate of the Jews, afraid to make a grandstand play for fear of bringing immediate reprisals on the Jews themselves. Why, then, are Catholics so uncritical of Hockhuth's play *The Deputy*, which alleges that the pontiff was more interested in protecting church property than in offering a hand to displaced persons?

In John XXIII, we had a pope who made us laugh. As patriarch of Venice, Roncalli was seated as a dinner guest next to a woman who was flimsily attired. When the fruit bowl was passed, she declined a serving. The patriarch, watching her, said, "Oh, please help yourself. Eve didn't know that she was naked until she ate the apple." He told Catholics new things about Protestants that they had needed to hear since the Reformation. His death was as holy as though he were dying for us on a cross under which we were standing.

Pope Paul VI in his lifetime was an unsung hero. But at the beginning, in the last session of Vatican II, the Protestant observers said he showed them what the pope is for. He saved the "Declaration of Religious Liberty," so dear to Americans, from curial diplomats who would have blocked it. As time wore on, he was clearly the suffering servant who bore in his own person the signs of a church in trouble. His encyclical *Humanae Vitae*, a disappointing statement on birth control, cost him the affection of millions. He was punished for being right on the ills that would accompany contraception universally practiced. His tragedy ended with the victory of his death. Our tragedy is still unfolding.

John Paul I was the happy pope who kept the *Imitation of Christ* on his night stand. His brief appearance was like the serving of sherbet that cleanses the palate between the courses of a meal.

We were heady with amazement at the election of a non-Italian Holy Father. How proud we were of him as a linguist, at home with twelve or fifteen languages, so that he would not be at a loss for words in any nation. As a Pole, he knows the ways of communism. Is this a handicap? Hasn't he learned anything else from his experience of Russians than possibly the politics of push and shove? Did he have to be shoved into an appreciation of the Jesuits or of liberation theology? Couldn't he be persuaded in a reasonable way by the theologians of liberation or the Jesuit provincials when he talked to them face-to-face? Does he push around national councils of bishops, treating them the way Stan, the Polack brother-in-law in *A Streetcar Named Desire*, pushed around Blanche DuBois?

Maybe he's the most reactionary pope since Pio Nono published the *Syllabus of Errors*. Do you suppose he feels the Prince of Darkness breathing down his back? What would I do if I had to walk a mile in his moccasins? What would I say to nuns and priests acting giddy? Would I sponsor "pluralism," that omnium-gatherum catch-all cover-up that liberalism resorts to when it wants you to agree that a condemned Arian notion of Christ is orthodox? Or that the only Real Presence in the Eucharist is the one you imagine is there?

What does John Paul have on his mind when he hunkers down in his PJs at night under a piece of needlework from the bell-ringer at Poznan to remind him: "You are Peter, and upon this rock I will build my Church"? A leading Catholic theologian keeps wanting to tell the seminarians of his diocese that an Easter faith doesn't mean that they couldn't have found the body. A Catholic exegete wants to tell them that calling Mary a virgin was a New Testament way of writing theology that doesn't exclude the possibility of Jesus having a human father. Nuns sign ads in *The New York Times* taken out by Catholics for a Free Choice. A scholarly writer advises Catholic women to abstain from Communion in a church that will not ordain them. Warring factions of the Catholic press race to publish stories of priests dying of AIDS, priests coming out of the closet, priests who are child molesters. (Here the pontiff might pop out of bed onto his knees to pray for priests in pain, sin, or other trouble.)

If the pontiff fell asleep to dream of America, would he feel attacked by nightmares? America is having trouble electing a president whose feet of clay will stay hidden until the ink is dry on the ballots. Twenty million fetuses have been left behind in American abortion clinics. Unmarried American teen-agers are yearly faced with a million unwanted pregnancies. We now have sexuality without procreation; procreation without sexuality. We have transsexuality and pathetic neutered males stuffing themselves with female hormones. We have sexual identity problems out of Sodom and Gomorrha, and surrogate motherhood, or rent-a-womb. We have a surgeon general who condemns smoking in restaurants but wants condoms passed out like after-dinner mints. We have sexual epidemics so horrifying that they make herpes look like acne. We have a drug problem that doubles with every dollar spent to control it. Our cities have turned thousands of the mentally ill onto the streets to freeze to death on the doorsteps of luxury apartment buildings. We're in an arms race, and the pastoral letter that the hierarchy took two years to write hasn't made a dent in it. We have a shortage of vocations that has reached epidemic proportions, and fifteen million dropouts whom pastors approaching their dotage are not apt to win back.

With all this bad news awaiting the pope when he came to America in September, should the bishops have challenged the pontiff, or bullied him as some of them bullied Geraldine Ferraro in 1984? Instead, maybe the bishops should have asked for directions.

Before he died, Karl Rahner said he had hoped at the end of Vatican II that the church was on the threshold of a second spring, but the conservatives in Rome made him feel that the winter of our discontent was back. What would a second springtime mean? Should a pope start acting *primus inter pares* with the bishops, divesting himself of the prerogatives that were legally defined for him in the infallibility doctrine a century ago? Is this a point the bishops should challenge the pontiff on, telling him to demote himself? The pontiff could survive that; could the bishops?

What was the church's view of itself at the end of that very hopeful council? Didn't it regard itself then, as now, as the servant of the world but not its copycat? What else could a church in the image of Christ be but a servant? Isn't Mary, conspicuous for her obedience to the will of God, the model for all Christians? What does obedience mean to a bishop who is persuaded that the way to treat his boss is with push and shove?

Father McBrien's article had a strong political flavor. Is that what made me find it unsatisfactory? The tone was one a *Times* columnist would use in an assessment of the president. Didn't priests writing in newspapers used to be polite, even ingratiating, in discussing a living Holy Father?

I'm a lightweight, in over my head, but millions of us are out here, like star differing from star in glory. The professionals entrusted with the word of life have the training to separate the wheat from the chaff, the blade from the ear. Are they helping women gain their rights (can you imagine that there were only fifteen women observers covering the sessions of Vatican II? It's not surprising they're ticked off at a chauvinist outfit) by encouraging them to ask for ordination as though it were an option now? An ecumenical council might have a high time pulling off a change like that without splitting the church. Is abortion a topic on which we need to dialogue? Are there now optional theologies? Is pluralism truth?

John Paul II may not be everyone's cup of tea, but when nuns and priests dismiss him as though he were bad news, they should see that what they are doing is poisoning the well. They say he should spend more time as a pastor in Rome and less time in traveling across continents like a rock star. The dissidents may not be wrong; maybe, like Galileo, they're ahead of their time. But as lone rangers or Davids against Goliath, in love with the romance of their solitary splendor, they could cut themselves off from too much. They could end as embittered dropouts, their talents wasted, their theories set aside, their admirers confused, all because they did not have the humility and patience to wait their turns in an institution that allows only one pope at a time. Giants from this century, as Father McBrien knows better than I do, have remained in obscurity, officially regarded with suspicion, in order to stay in the communion of faith with leaders who can only see the data of revelation with their own kind of brilliance.

The sheep are not being fed. Many of them are resentful toward the second-stringers, as careless as hirelings, who threaten to get in the way of the shepherd who could offer them food for thought and imperishable bread. They want their faith strengthened, their hope renewed. They're tired of liturgies that don't lift their hearts up to God, of priests who whimper, of cranky nuns.

They are folk Catholics who were taught from their mothers' knees the danger of losing the state of grace. They know the burdens of an authoritarian religion, but the more the burdens have been lifted off their backs the more they have felt robbed of mystery and privilege. Freedom, to them, is a half-Protestant word. If you try to untie a few knots for them in the confessional, they may not want to hear you. They like their sins; the commission of sin for which they can be held accountable at the judgment is a proof that God is watching.

This article is not as good-natured as I hoped it would be, though I have not written in bad will. Dick McBrien's essay took my breath away. He was touching truths that men live by: If the pope is a *poseur*, then the Catholic sun is setting. Any Catholic who fought against King Billy at the battle of the Boyne could tell you that the Catholic sun rises and sets on the pope. Telling Catholics that the pope is a stumbling block is like telling them that the Blessed Lord came down from the Cross when his enemies mocked him. If the pope, under Christ, isn't the true shepherd of the flock, they might just as well tear down the church, after cleaning out the poor box.

LOVE ON TRIAL

Contemporary folk wisdom sends a message to priests: "You don't play the game. Why should you make the rules?" But marriage, like baseball, can be a spectator sport. You don't have to dress like a Cubbie to see how well the game is played.

Any celibate I know is made of common clay. He may not know what's going on behind the scenes in a particular marriage, but he knows what happens generally in marriages. A priest who has kept his ear to the ground may have views as valid as those of a husband who is a specialist about what goes on in his bedroom, but not about what's going on in every bedroom on the block.

A celibate keeping his vows faithfully is not transported to some ex-alted plain where he is immune to suffering from thorns in the flesh. Sexual energy is not prepackaged for a priest by the Vatican. He knows what desire is and how it cools and why. He knows about fidelity, curiosity, and the temptation to wander. He's been lonely and bored; he can guess how difficult loneliness and boredom must be if they seem structured into a marriage.

A priest is ordained to live unmarried, free of romantic involvement, in order to single-heartedly serve God's people. Yet a priest can, and sometimes does, fall in love. The church never promised him immunity from a woman's charms. Falling in love doesn't hurt him, and the bittersweetness may do him good if he keeps in mind that he has promises to keep.

What is being tested today is people's willingness to make and keep promises. As Christians with vows, we're obligated in honor not to wander off the reservation. But our steadfastness is tempted in a dishonorable world where presidents lie to the country and high-placed prelates are connected to scandal.

Lovers, too, perjure themselves seriously in making commitments, especially if the weather is good or the stars are bright. As a presider at weddings, you are asked to bless their perjuries in the name of the church. You have to decide whether the love between them is enduring enough for them to become husband and wife. Watching them come down the aisle, you're wondering if you've done them a favor. If the marriage fails, you curse yourself for taking chances, for being incapable of telling the difference between true love and its many counterfeits. You swear it will be a cold day in hell before you let another pair of charming kids, beguiled by puppy love, talk you into receiving their marriage vows.

Christian marriage is in deep, deep trouble; that's why an amateur like me wants to put in his two-cents worth. Every time I hear of a marriage being annulled after the birth of two or three children, I grow more cynical about the sacrament of matrimony. An annulment means that a marriage which was supposed to endure until death never got off the ground.

The ceremony, the honeymoon, the wedding gifts were expensive and beautiful. The first apartment was in the high-rent district. Hundreds of physical consummations confirming the alleged spiritual union took place; from the consummations came children. Two people lived together, paying bills, having children, celebrating birthdays, growing older, raising a dog. "What God has joined, no man may divide."

Suddenly, the couple announces that the social chemistry of their togetherness isn't working, and the experiment in intimacy is over.

The church looks over the shambles of a relationship, *ratum et consummantum* as a *fait accompli*, and declares: "This was never, from its inception, a marriage in Christ." Why? Because one or both of these beautiful people didn't have their heads screwed on straight? Why couldn't the priest doing the honors see that this pair was never hedged in by divinity? The church tells them, "Better luck next time."

Or a couple marries; each is twenty-three and sexually uninitiated. With the help of God's grace, each will be faithful and chaste in their marriage. But is either of them ever attracted to somebody else? Is either one curious about what it would be like to box the compass with another partner? God knows, sometimes men and women sin in their imaginations. A husband once admitted that when he sins in his imagination with Greta Garbo, he congratulates himself later on his impeccable good taste.

Old lovers are beautiful when they're still treating each other as sweethearts at ninety. But the world according to Judith Krantz is a soap opera with heavy breathing. Love, or *its parody* (which she measures by describing the panting), is either an ego trip or the symptom of a disease. Women's magazines feature cosmetics ads promising an impossible dream and rituals for keeping romance alive as though it depended on artificial respiration. Leaving a daily love letter for your spouse under the commode lid sounds as phony as an aid to romance as mandating a handshake at Mass would be in spreading peace. Isn't romance trivialized when you subject it to hand-clapping as though it needed encouragement like a Pentecostal preacher?

The *New Yorker* once published a cartoon showing an overweight woman wrapped in a kimono, her hair in curlers, cold cream on her face. She's seated at the breakfast table across from a beer-bellied guy shaped like an ice man; he's wearing an undershirt and his hair is gone. She asks, "When did the romance go out of our marriage?" The caption is poignant, like a cry from the heart. "When did we start treating each other like this?"

How do you pull yourself back from going to seed when weariness with life makes you indifferent to shaving before noon? It was to get the attention of the household frumps, they say, that Liberace used to dress in near-drag and set his piano with candelabra, in the decades before *Dallas* and *I'll Take Manhattan* spread the magic carpet to fantasy land. Now skinflicks on the VCR and love poetry from Yeats on a Hallmark card are on sale as home cures for the imagination from which eroticism has faded.

What is the reasonableness of continuing a marriage when one partner has grown tired of the other, not just sexually but in every other way as well? He is a clod, a bore, a bully, and a drunkard, a lecher, an idiot. She is a nag, a gossip; she always has a headache. Why should they go on together, in the name of a religious ideal, if this punishment is all that is left of the marriage?

Why should one tolerate dragging around a ball and chain? Why should one get stuck with a mate who's bad news, and as tiresome as an albatross hanging around one's neck, once love has died? The sounds of the marching feet of Catholic liberation are heard everywhere.

The only jewelry my mother ever wore was her wedding ring. She never took it off, and it was buried with her, as though to identify her as a wife when she met God. She was faithful to my father, and that ring was a sign of her fidelity. But I'm not sure if she loved my father, though as a child I tried to make her say so. I would ask, "Do you love Papa?" She would shake her head. "Does Papa love you?" She would reply with a nod, positive that the answer was yes. I would persist, "Do you love Papa?" But she gave me no answer I wanted to hear.

When he died, the earth disappeared from under her feet; she was sick with grief for a year. By then, I was too old to question her about her love for her husband. She remained a widow until her death more than forty years later, but I never heard her admit that she was in love with my old man. Perhaps she had some model lovers in mind and felt her marriage didn't fit the paradigm. But she did the things a faithful wife does. Her actions showed the sentiments she refused to talk about.

When I was a child, grown-ups used the word "love" mostly with their children. The word was almost as sacred as the Jewish name for God. These days the word "love," though it is considered holy, is the most overused word in our language. A generation that has cheapened the word makes the entire tradition of marriage depend on love, even in the church.

Why is love always on trial as the scapegoat when marriages fail? Hasn't love always been a moveable feast? The love light usually shines in a newlywed's eyes. Love, as the angel's glow that lights a star, doesn't always have the toughness of the love which St. Paul describes for the Corinthians. Love, in the best or worst of times, continuously undergoes a metamorphosis. As a radiance that brightens your beloved's face from within, it is irresistible; because of it, all the world is in love with a lover.

"Does John love Mary?" He thinks he does. "Does Mary love John?" She's sure she's in love. Who is smart enough to second-guess them? But is love all that needs to be tested when you're deciding whether a young man or woman should make a match? Is this all the catechism a priest requires of the candidates?

Sunken cheeks, too, are part of the poetry of love in old age when beauty has gone past its prime. What radiant bride ever pictures a future in which her own true love wears ill-fitting dentures? Other changes will precede the loss of teeth—changes that will make the sight of empty gums a small thing. How, without getting gross or physical, can a priest prepare lovers for the future contingencies of growing up and growing old? Marriage, for better and for worse, in sickness and in health, can be long-lived, with the help of God's grace taking the initiative—although talk-show therapists say, "Wise up. Marriage until-death-do-us-part is an anachronism."

Love is essential to a marriage only if it is generous. Selfish love could drag down a dynasty, unless God breathes on it everlastingly. Love alone can't be the glue in a marriage, unless it's godlike; but then it isn't love alone, but love as the hub of the wheel on which other kinds of strength—truthfulness, patience, hopefulness, trust—depend as a center.

Actually, when you speak of love, you must define your terms. Love, as pale as green cheese, is too anemic to serve a marriage as its life's blood. But love from the heart of a tiger isn't enough if two people are still in all other ways wet behind the ears.

And so the priest asks, "Are they grown up enough to remain steadfast in love's off season? Is there loyalty here, like that between friends ready to stand by each other through thick and thin? Are they willing to be responsible for each other, even in the interims of doubt when they are undergoing disappointments as they discover each other's flaws? Do they show each other kindness and respect? Will they punish each other when their married life subjects them to trials? Do they have a sense of duty which will keep them going through the tough times?

Positive qualities have God's good grace in them; they do love's work well enough to keep a marriage going. Love without romance, in its working clothes, is responsible, kind, respectful, and dutiful. You could raise a family, even if love has grown cold, if partners could give each other this kind of support. But love, which you are only aware of because it keeps the pulses racing, isn't enough to start a family.

Perhaps marriage, Christian or otherwise, is doomed unless we reconsider it as a cultural landmark which shouldn't be compromised. Perhaps the church itself has to send marriage back to the drawing board, to examine it again as a sacrament of Christ. Such theorizing is the work of scholars. I'm a simple priest troubled by a world indifferent to traditions the church offers as aids to salvation.

It's harder to prepare young people for marriage. How can you help them internalize a belief in sacrificial love, exemplified by Christ, as grace upon which their union depends? If the idea of sacrificial love means anything, it means that they may not be spared the stab of nails. They have to die a little if they want to be his disciples. The Lord showed us a love that was openhanded and tireless and forgiving.

A husband doesn't live to please himself, nor a wife to please herself; but one lives to please the other. Whoever marries in Christ undertakes a union so selfless that it will be in the image of his love for the world. None of this can happen without suffering, since self-sacrifice is required to join souls together, as the Lord sacrificed himself to enter our lives. But spouses are there to fill the other's suffering with their presence just as the joy of his nearness is in us.

Here is the ideal which faith puts before us on the day of marriage. It seems to be more of heaven than it is of earth; but nothing is simple for a Christian accepting a supernatural religion handed down from the God who became our servant. A theology has to be powerful if it is going to overcome our attraction to the world. In very plain language, one Christian marries another because each needs a partner to help the other save his or her soul. Since Christ is the redeemer upon whom salvation depends, semimystical language is needed to describe our mortal struggle to escape from sin and to grow in grace as God's children. But then the purpose for our existence is not to buy limousines, build mansions, or scale the corporate ladder.

Christianity is a relationship with the Son of God. Perhaps it is less traumatic to love or to doubt the Savior you don't see than it is to carry on a love-hate relationship with a spouse who can't shut up and won't leave town. If you stare long enough into the void of doubt, you could turn agnostic. If you brood incessantly on the disappointments of a passion that has melted, you could start divorce proceedings.

Is this too grim? Is it more frightening than truthful? How do you temper the wind to the shorn lambs? How do you explain that, despite every love song, marriage was never planned as a bed of roses? How does Christian marriage compare with anything that's taught in the MBA program at Harvard? Does every promise end ". . . and they live happily ever after"? Does taking up a cross and following Jesus sound like a downer if you've grown up building castles in Spain?

I do believe that Christian marriage is still possible. To doubt its efficacy would be the same as doubting the efficacy of remaining or-dained. A priest's mission is to chase away the shadows with light; that's what he tries to do in every confession he hears. Marriage also is a voca-tion in the service of Christ. Every bridal couple lights a fresh candle of hope on their wedding day. Where love is, if the love is holy—and not some wimpish, sentimental facsimile—there, as a breath of that holi-ness, is God.

Christian marriage can and does work. A couple with three strikes against them—perhaps they are young, poor, and with a baby—can prosper in all the ways that the nuptial blessing asks. Contrast them with the couple who has everything except the intention to persevere in marriage; they may need an annulment before the honeymoon is over.

Marriages are unpredictable because the intentions of a bride and groom stay hidden in a private place they don't always share with you. You can't predict the miracles that God will send to exalt the humble-hearted, and you don't promise to make miracles happen. A man and woman make miracles happen by themselves; or perhaps their miracle is that they prosper without a miracle.

An old man told me, "I was married for twenty-nine years before I realized that my wife was happiest when I told her I loved her." He was married for fifty-nine years before his wife died. By the end of her life, she was confused in her mind so much that she was unable to take care of herself. He used to dress her, feed her, and bring her to Mass every day. It didn't matter to him that she was years older than he was, or that the other women liked him and enjoyed his company, and he liked them back. He could have become a lady's man. He loved his Mary as though she were still his young, pretty bride. Because he loved her so much, everyone else loved them both. Is this kind of fidelity a miracle?

Are the days of such spiritual miracles over? Not as long as human goodness is left in the world. God is generous in allowing miracles as signs to the times in which he is rumored to be dead. You should have no fear of miracles not happening: only that the skeptics will be too blind to see them.

MORTAL FRIENDS

Jesus
he was a handsome man
*   and what i want to know is*
how do you like your blue-eyed boy
Mister Death

—e.e. cummings

You are awakened by an early morning phone call. Thad, one of your dearest friends, was just found in his living room, dead. A heart attack. He was a firefighter, age forty-one. He is survived by Muriel, his widow, and four sons; the youngest, not yet a year old, is named after you.

For the next three days you're called into service as a comforter. You can't let the survivors see your grief. You have to hide your rage at God, or at least your disappointment and displeasure with Him. As a priest, you are his public relations man; you have to accept his will and defend it as though you were convinced it is always wise and wonderful. In your heart, though, you're questioning whether God's will has anything to do with the absurdities of our existence on this darkling plain. Maybe God is powerless to put restraints on death, through which his own Son had to pass.

You remember driving with Thad to towns on Cape Cod or heading off to Boston to see *My Fair Lady* and *South Pacific*. You were, for the last time in your lives, being boys together, having a night on the town, carefree, and feeling good. You and Thad will never again joke about the girls' college in the foothills of the Wasatch Mountains (Thad had read about it in *Time*) where, he said, he would like to be the night watchman in a dorm and stage fire drills at three in the morning.

If Thad's boys asked, you could tell them jokes their father invented. You could tell them how he wanted to get well after his first heart attack so he could be strong for them, and strong for their mother, all the years they were growing up. Thad was allowed two years after the first attack; was he afraid to die? Not so that you could notice it. He wanted to see his sons grow up. He didn't want his wife left struggling by herself; is it a mystery why he left her with leftover life to live?

The frustration about death is that you can bless it or curse it, but you can't put God on the witness stand to explain or defend himself. He is as untouchable as though he never existed. As a result, in the middle of the funeral, you're trying to protect yourself from the temptation to become agnostic. You ask God for a sign that will help you be more trusting of him. Then you stay on the alert, watching for thunderbolts, afraid he will overwhelm you with an answer as he overwhelmed Job. You wonder whether you will ever understand.

You know a hundred evasive things to tell Catholics curious about death. Through all your years as a priest, you've tried to figure out what life and death and dying are all about. Why are we sentenced to live in a vale of tears, praising God for the good times, pleading with him to spare us the bad times, waiting for the shoe to drop as a signal that our time is about to end? You never admit the truth that would leave them saddened and scandalized: at times the fear of death can leave you, a holy priest, witless with fright.

Death's hideous face, warts and all with none of the terror painted out, stares up at you from the bottom of every cup. You try not to look at it, but the impression registers—"You're going to die!"—before you can turn your head. The fatal ticket may not be drawn today, tomorrow, this year, perhaps for thirty years. But the numbered balls bounce continuously on a jet of air, and every second the Eternal Footman picks one at random. How soon before yours is called? "Better not to think about it." That's what Hemingway's heroes told themselves: "Thinking could drive you crazy."

As a child, you shivered yourself to sleep on nights when you were afraid of dying. Feeling your heart pound with fear, you were positive it was self-destructing. Your folks didn't understand the waking nightmares that arrived at bedtime, nor your need for the nightlight. The bedside lamp left burning till sunrise annoyed your father, who complained you were singlehandedly keeping the power company in clover. You would defend yourself with the pretense that you had fallen asleep reading, until finally you were forbidden to read in bed at all. With that comfort taken away, you made friends with the street lamp outside your window.

Even now you don't sleep easily if there is not a light, a least a dim one, visible from another room or shining through a window to relieve the chance of waking up in the pitch darkness in which ancient terrors might lurk. Is this neurosis? You're not proud of it; but it is a neurosis shared with those wounded war heroes in Hemingway, who could not sleep without a light for the night to keep *nada*, or nothingness, at a distance.

When did the fear of death begin? You remember, as a boy of six or seven, waiting in a car outside a hospital. Your parents were inside at the sick bed of a great-aunt dying of cancer. "She was in great pain today," they said, returning to the car parked along a dark side street with trees tall enough to hide the stars. "Soon they'll put her on morphine, but they don't want to start the morphine too soon. Its effectiveness as a pain-killer diminishes quickly. Then there's nothing left to help her through the pain."

The earlier lies they told you—that death is falling asleep and waking in God's house—dissolve in horror at the picture of an old person struggling against naked, undisguised, and unalleviated suffering, suffering that plunges the victim closer to the darkness from which there is no exit.

Children exposed to grief are no different than their elders. They start to think about God. A shaken child with God on his mind starts to look for proof. Perhaps you have spent your life as a priest because years ago you rode home from the hospital with adults who startled you into wanting to know how involved with us God is. In aggressive pursuit of him, you have followed his trail over hill and dale, and still the trail goes ahead of you. You will not know until you die how close you've gotten to catching up with him and his teasing ways.

Like the undertaker, you are a professional in dealing with death, keeping it at a distance even when you enter into grief or share it with mourners. Hallmark has written the consolatory notes that one bereaved Christian sends another, on cards cheerful with the message of the flower that still blooms beyond the wall. The American way of death makes earth's last farewell look almost pleasant—after the cosmetologists have finished their work and set the castoff human shell on taffeta cushions in a mahogany showcase guaranteed to remain waterproof and worm-proof, and so to rob the grave of its victory, death of its sting. The liturgy promises that we shall see Thad again when the dead in Christ have their great getting-up morning.

The undertaker has other tricks with which we are willing to let him deceive us. The dead one sleeps in a quiet room full of flowers. At the cemetery the earth that will cover him is hidden by a blanket of artificial grass. Wining and dining our senses on the beauty of the stage effects which the tradespeople of funerals supply us, we send the dead to eternity as though we were launching a funeral barge carrying Arthur to Avalon, as though death were not dusty and full of dry rot.

Only in monasteries of the strict observance is Christian burial kept simple these days, free of the pagan additives. The body is laid in the ground unprotected so it can return to the mothering dust as quickly as possible. A grain of wheat is thrown into the ground to rot, in the devout hope that from the death of the one body, the incorruptible body will rise as from a seed.

A priest burying his family dead is as quick as a Hibernian to offer the Irish blessing: "May the wind be always at your back . . . may the rain fall soft upon your fields . . . may the road rise to greet you." Nature makes the planted corpse no such happy promises. Any Christian, saying goodbye to the dead, must (if he wishes to resolve grief in a religious way) make a separate peace with God, without lying to himself about the undiscovered country from which no traveler returns. Death—no matter how prettily we dress it—is a punishment that is permitted to catch up with us from our first parents, with God's consent. That is why the thought of death can send a tingle running up and down a Christian spine.

There is also grief, so sharp and poignant, that later you can't remember when it started to turn you numb. A huddling together follows as people comfort each other. In hugging, they are also hugging the one who died. These moods are ritualized at the offering of the memorial service. At Mass you're doing something appropriate, paying your respects, just by being there. Before that, the most you could find to do was to volunteer to drive a car to the airport, answer the doorbell, make some coffee.

"After great pain," wrote Emily Dickinson, "a formal feeling comes." The nerves sit ceremoniously, rigid with mourning, like tombstones. You have to let the nerves unfreeze, then thaw out. You tell them, like a drill sergeant, "At ease!" When the nerves finally let go their hold on the emotions, peace starts to descend as comfort from the Holy Ghost. How is peace possible? Because love is stronger than death. Is death the enemy? Sometimes; at other times it's a friend. But even when it's an enemy, death is also a teacher.

You have warm memories of the times you spent with Thad's and Muriel's boys. Sometimes, waiting dinner, within earshot of their parents, you would tell them stories—sometimes even stories of God. Only with the help of stories, you explained, could you say anything about God. Christmas is a story. Good Friday and Easter are part of the same story. Some of the God-stories are called allegories; others are called myths. The gospel of God's sending his only Son has been called the greatest love story ever told. The Last Supper and the death on the cross depend on that love story to give them a context.

Is religion a system of myths that mankind has arranged as a nightlight? The famous argument, recorded in Bede, for adopting Christianity in England put this before the king: "Your majesty, when we compare the present life of man on earth with that time of which we have no knowledge, it seems to me like the swift flight of a single sparrow through the banqueting hall where you are sitting at dinner on a winter's day. In the midst there is a comforting fire to warm the hall; outside, the storms of winter snow or rain are raging. This sparrow flies swiftly in through one door of the hall, and out through another. While he is inside, he is safe from the winter storms; but after a few moments of comfort, he vanishes from sight into the wintry world from which he came. Even so, man appears on earth for a little while; but of what went before this life, or of what follows, we know nothing. Therefore, if this new teaching has brought any more certain knowledge, it seems only right that we should follow it."

Christianity is not just a snug harbor for ships to hide in until the bad weather passes. It is considerably more complicated than the folk tales invented to explain the seasons. Christianity has a sublimity of teaching whose source must be the God of love. Brotherly love is not an instinctive idea that could have sprung up with the grass roots of human experience. Man, struggling to evolve through the survival of the fittest and observing Nature red in tooth and claw, was shown the idea of loving his neighbor as himself. When concern for one's neighbor shows up as a religious duty, it has the air of a moral practice that came into religion from outside, as from a Teacher whose sensibilities are higher than those of the nomads adopting revealed truth.

More wonderful still is the ideal at Christianity's heart—sacrificial love: the love than which none can be greater, that a man should lay down his life for his friend. The Friend of the Friendless gave love a new definition when, as the Lamb of God, he did something for creatures that creatures cannot do for one another—bore on his back the punishment and consequences of their sins. Through Christ the word began to experience the mystical love which is the ambience in which God lives.

From the religion that Christ taught came our awareness of the love that is stronger than death—a love which drove the Son of God naked into the jaws of death to show us love's power to endure the horror that threatens us with extinction and to emerge from the grave triumphant with grace.

When Jesus was taken down from the cross, who could have understood from his appearance that He was God? Only the eyes of faith could see his holiness; only the eyes of faith can see the holiness of life. Sometimes you are not on that plateau of faith; sometimes you're afraid that what appears is all there is, and that any idea of underlying holiness is entirely imaginary. Still, you try to face the tough questions as though you expect to find answers that will keep the mind quiet and the heart from pounding—on nights when you must sleep without the light that holds the dread of *nada* at a distance.

Over the years the nightmares subsided as you learned to understand and appreciate the darkness at the end of the lighted tunnel, as a place of rest you'd go to when rest would be welcomed, since eternal rest would not be troubled by vermin that gnaw the mind.

These answers have validity, of course, unless you can prove that physical matter is everything and that spirit counts for nothing. And this is plainly not true. If matter were all, could one hope so much and try to love what he cannot see? Your faith tells you that the grace of Christ is for everyone—just as the sun is for everyone, even the blind man who does not know how much he owes the sun. Jesus is the model of all who will be judged on love. He was dragged as a criminal to the tree of shame, yet died asking the Father's absolution for his enemies.

So the boy from Maine, with the help of God, worked his way through the fear that began when he saw the light from the hospital window, to the light that helped him sleep, to the light that shines in the darkness on which the Christian mythology centers. A Christian, reflecting on death and trying to decide if there is a better world to come that will welcome him, has, as his only light, the promises the saints made: that in the evening of life, he will be judged on love.

You're sixty-two now, too old to kid yourself. You've seen a lot of people die and met death once yourself, suffering from congestive heart failure, on an ambulance ride to St. Vincent's Hospital. Death, met face-to-face, had the look of a good-natured though somewhat reserved cab driver who wanted you to see you had nothing to fear when he comes for you with the meter running.

We think that a lifespan should be three score years and ten. Yet geniuses manage to finish their essential life's work at a precocious age. It was so with Einstein discovering relativity, with Keats and Shelley writing deathless verse. So, too, with Jesus as a great religious teacher. And so it was with Thad saving his grace-filled soul.

Thad's lads have souls of their own to save and trials of their own to face and masterpieces of love to work at. They are lucky to have a memory of their father as a good man, lucky to have a mother and siblings to lean on after their father's death. Perhaps God allowed them to become fatherless so they could try their wings early.

Are there lessons to be learned from the untimely death of a friend? Is there any escape from the caprice of the Maker? Could you contract with God for him to leave you alone until you've finished the work that he should allow you to do? Wasn't it cruel of God to take Thad, the father of four, instead of calling home the old and tired?

Gloucester's great complaint was: "As flies to wanton boys, are we to the gods, / They kill us for their sport." When you lose a friend, you wonder if your turn is next. You did not despair when Thad died, but you were in the mood to ask yourself if this mysterious will of God's doesn't bear watching.

THE FLAME KEEPERS

Daniel Berrigan describes the elder priests of the Society of Jesus as "mandarin Jesuits," and I can picture them: wise, imperial, aloof, with high cheek bones and all-seeing eyes. Sometimes I think all older priests are in the mandarin class: venerable and untouchable, gifted, gentle, humble men, scholarly or pastoral. In time of trouble they light up the sky around them with flashes of faith, reminding me they still believe in poverty, chastity, and obedience—and in the Mother of God, the Real Presence, and the beautiful hands of a priest.

These are the trailblazers against whom I measure myself. Many have been crucified. Suffering and dying spiritually, they have risen from humiliations that could turn souls gray overnight. Now their battle wounds have healed, and their scars authenticate them as genuine Christ-figures, like a signature handed down from the cross. Yet when I meet them as charming incorrigibles, happier to play the devil's advocate than to be treated like a ghostly father, all the elaborate imagery based on the Passion seems as inappropriate as calling them mandarins. What counts is that they've clearly been to the wall and back, and are now at peace as humble servants of the church—unpretentious, often witty, and embarrassed when I try to canonize them without due process.

Some of the best old men I have ever met are priests who have been endowed by nature with class and by their Maker with grace. In them, grace and nature have cooperated to make their lives as beautiful as a moral miracle useful in arguing the existence of God. The Catholic priesthood has thousands of human faces, but these mandarins are the prototypes from whom my generation derived its myths of *alter Christus*. That's why I look to them as models and find myself lacking.

In the seminary we read a lot of fiction, because fiction can be more truthful than the lives of the saints; the fictional priests were the kind of saints we could pray to become. Yet no matter how much I loved Bernanos's country priest (for whom, at death, "everything is grace"), it was no ideal of mine to remain as humble as he was when the upper class felt free to bully him. I would never be a Dom Camillo competing against a communist mayor for the loyalty of Italian peasants. I could, if I were weak, be as sinful as Graham Greene's whiskey priest, but would I have the courage to become a martyr for taking the sacraments to poor Mexicans whom the government wanted to be officially godless? Could I realistically envision myself hiding in a priest's hole to escape being executed on the hanging tree at Tyburn, then being drawn and quartered, like the Jesuits who were impertinent enough to say Mass in Merrie England in the time of Elizabeth I? Did I expect to become a pastor in Ireland, ruling a parish like a fiefdom? We didn't have Father Greeley in my seminary days, holding up his portraits of the Chicago clergy like a mirror, but the novelist J. F. Powers showed us the faults we were heir to, and we were warned by his satire.

I don't ever remember a priest for his sins, if he had any, because it is not my business to judge him. I may remember him for the sadness in his life; and if his sadness made him look shabby, he is beautiful to me for the Masses he said, and I'm sorry for him for the Masses he couldn't say. I remember him for battles lost and won, or for the tragedy that destroyed him. I trust that mercy awaited him in heaven, that he found peace in eternal life. He is entitled to all the blessings mentioned in the myths of the eternal priesthood.

If I weep at his funeral, I weep for myself. I know a hillside where hundreds of priests are asleep in the Lord, and not one of them was buried as a Judas, for the Lord said to them: "My grace is sufficient for thee." If he had not said it, I believe the priests would ask God to take the grace that's available and spread it around until each of their confreres has enough. For good priests are like good soldiers who lay down their lives for their friends.

The mystique I rely on includes all this, even if it's wishful thinking. Loyalty isn't just a form of clubbiness practiced by boys being boys; it is a gentlemanly virtue which priests open to charity have conferred on them as a charismatic gift.

Does all this seem improbable, like a private mythology? Why shouldn't I believe in the priesthood as a poetic myth? Didn't God himself invent metaphors to describe truth that touches the mind but eludes the fingertips? What else is redemption but a poetic drama in which Christ plays himself and, in some of the scenes, the imagination interprets everything in the light of a cultic tradition, so that Christ is the Lamb and his cross is an altar and thunder and lightning over Calvary represent the Father's grief? How can I be his priest except as a metaphor in conjunction with other metaphors authorized by the church as a visual expression of invisible truth?

I believe in the mystique of a priesthood passed down like the apostolic succession, and that's why I love the mandarin priests. After they're gone it will be up to priests of my age to maintain the mystique as if we were mandarins. Any community that has me as a mandarin has seen better days, because I have a feeling that I was absent when mystique was passed out. Yet on days when I'm happy saying Mass—not bored or distracted—I feel sure that part of the mystique has rubbed off on me; that I am in the image of priests who are in the image of Christ visible in the church when the church is worshipping; that the church uses me as a Christ-like figure able to bless, consecrate, and forgive sins; that my Eucharist is as valid as the bishop's; that my sacraments are as efficacious as any other priest's; and that when I give an absolution, the penitent does not have to take it to another confessor for a second opinion.

Every time I get a flow of energy from recognizing myself as the genuine, Vatican-approved holy man, I swear I'll stop behaving like a maverick and lone-wolf who lives on the doorstep of the church like a beggar surviving on coins from the poor box. In such moments I want to put on all the outward signs of an inner mystique and wear them like a uniform: the black hat, the black suit, the black shoes, the collar. Then I start to respect the breviary tucked under my arm and the rosary in my pocket as symbols of my dignity as a priest instead of as options I don't have time for.

The mystique of the priesthood is as plain and simple as a desire of the human heart in need of bonding, though you could imagine that being in league with the mandarins confers a kind of magic. That mystique is a feeling that as a priest you're so special to God that you must always respect your own worth as a priest. Moreover, you must always respect and cherish the vocations of your fellow priests and let no one demean them. Didn't Christ have priests in mind at the Last Supper when he said, "I pray, Father, that they may be one just as we are one?" How beautiful it is to see priests helping each other through hell and high water. Even in instances where the blind seem to be leading the blind, God's grace furnishes light for them to see by.

The mandarins worth their salt are unreservedly courteous when I'm standing among them, looking shabby; they treat me as one of the apples of God's eye, as though the mystique I share with them elevates me to the mandarin level. They address me in a way that reminds me of the beautiful words which Christ spoke to the apostles at the Last Supper and which the bishop repeats to the priests at their ordination: "I no longer call you servants, but friends."

Conversely, younger colleagues have it in their power to hurt me when they treat me with scant respect bordering on insolence, as though my style of the priesthood is in need of updating, so that I should be sent back to the seminary to be mythologized, body and soul. Sometimes the nuns, back from Fordham with a master's degree in theology after five summers, gently work me over as a proclaimer of truth. If they have truth on their side, how did the church dare to let the working clergy get so out of touch?

Is this why, after thirty-five years of saying Mass, I sometimes stand on the altar waiting to be arrested for practicing religion on an expired license? Is it because in the silly season, when I was in my salad days, green of judgment, I was imprudent at Mass in doing my own thing? Or maybe the church—which once canonized the rubrics as if they were footnotes to the law of God by printing them in Latin until there were enough of them to fill a book sporting an imprimatur from the Holy See—confused me. Maybe it was because suddenly, as we were vesting for Mass, we would get handouts on which were mimeographed the rules of the week for the vernacular liturgy: You could get the idea you were standing on shifting ground, that the rubrics themselves were being written on water.

In 1965 I attended a workshop in scripture held to update the priests. The scholar in charge was asked, "What's going to happen to the very old priests too set in their ways to be comfortable with the changes?" His answer was, "It's too bad that we don't have a place to send them, where we could pull the chain." Good riddance to old rubbish in that diocese. He was speaking of the mandarins who were forerunners of the present mandarins. His words were an early warning that the mystique was in danger.

A priest of my years hasn't very much to do if he can only write critically of the church. What good would the church be if it had to remain frozen in time to keep our myths alive? If you saved up newspaper stories of priests in trouble, you could start a new myth that's so dangerous it has the force of an attack. Maybe the myth of priests swearing loyalty to one another like lodge brothers represents the triumph of hope over ecclesiastical experience. Maybe the myth that good ol' boys understand the uses of love better than the lads is a libel of the young. Old priests *and* young go to the hospital rooms of patients suffering from AIDS. When a young priest dies from AIDS, his classmates don't have to be told by the mandarins not to have long faces as they say goodbye to a close friend who has not gone gentle into that good night. The mandarins could take lessons in class from the way their junior colleagues behave when the chips are down.

It is not the fault of a younger generation that the church was smarter after Vatican II than it was before. A quarter of a century ago, a cold war developed between priests who grew old saying the Latin Mass and those who never said Mass in Latin, who had no affection for the Latin even if they had been trained to use it. There were other bones of contention, but the disappointment that the mandarins and the mandarins-in-waiting felt when the vernacular was introduced is enough to explain the division of the church into liberals and conservatives.

Very quickly pastors began to distrust their young curates, and the priests in their swaddling vestments lost respect for the pastors who wanted to keep the innovations on the back burner. You could tell from the quarrels *and* the silences at the dinner table when tensions were dividing the rectory. It used to be that when certain subjects came up, like the apparitions of Mary, one priest could tell what another priest was thinking. If the boss made a hobby out of pilgrimages to Lourdes, the assistants would hold their tongues as co-conspirators in silent amusement. If the new boy in town joined the charismatics and sat through supper speaking in tongues, his elders would agree, through a meeting of eyes, on the kind of campaign they would wage to deprogram him. But 1965 was like that day in Jerusalem when the veil of the temple was rent; suddenly nobody was sure what the other fellow was thinking, and so the silences turned ominous. The priestly mystique has been in tatters ever since.

But old soldiers never die, and young soldiers grow into old soldiers who tell stories of wars whose battlefields are now peace gardens. Priests my age, who never engaged in any war, tell horror stories of the church when it had the look of a banana republic self-destructing with revolution.

By 1970 the faith structure, which was expected to be the same a hundred thousand years from now as it has always been, had a devastated look, like a tree half-killed by lightning. And for awhile you could wonder if the church had a future worth mentioning. Cynics called it "the graveyard of Christianity." God was dead; his Mystical Body would soon be in need of Christian burial. The church, of course, was sure of its own survival; Vatican II was not its swan-song. Even born-agains can have a battered look, if their delivery has been difficult.

But a curious thing happened on the way to the *aggiornamento*: Thousands of priests and countless nuns and brothers abandoned ship, scuttling vocations that made them feel as doomed as the deck stewards on the *Titanic*. Even the priests, sisters, and brothers who stayed wondered if they were a dying breed—the dead who'd been left to bury the dead.

As a foot soldier in the army of the Lord, I didn't have any maps showing me the big picture; I only knew stories that told me the church was in danger. I have always loved being a priest, though that has not kept me from being inadequate, careless, and too much of a maverick. As a priest looking for fulfillment, you can make some big mistakes. Losing your sense of direction, you can stumble into a minefield. When that happened to me, I was saved from blowing myself up because I had compassionate superiors. Sick at heart over the trouble I was in, I wanted to take my troubles and run—if I could find a place outside my community to run to. My superiors said: "Hold still a minute, until we have walked you off the minefield you're trapped on." In straightening me out, they saved my vocation.

Other priests were not so lucky. Many left ministries in which they had reached an impasse, in search of work that would save them from a sense of futility, in search of grace that would help them save their souls. Priests have often felt trapped by the stupidity with which the system is flawed. Caught between a notorious pastor and a chancery that was not listening, what could they do but become saints, if bitterness didn't destroy them first? How much injustice could be done by a monsignor of the old school who had the manners of a mandarin and the mind of a tyrant as he chewed through the hides of two hundred curates in ten years?

In some of the worst hardship cases, priests, cantankerous from twenty years in apostolates they hated, became *personae non gratae* to the superiors to whom they brought their complaints. The superiors, who took advantage of the new freedom in their own way, unlovingly left them to shift for themselves as middle-aged men nobody wanted. They became like wandering Jews to whom nobody would give houseroom. Who could blame them for going AWOL?

How many priests left because they perceived the church is long on rules, short on justice? A bishop would ask, when a priest was missing, was it Punch or Judy? Did any bishop ask if the priest felt loved enough, or if he left because he could no longer stand to be treated as a flunky who lacked a soul?

Does it matter who's to blame if the church has the look of a bare, ruined choir that is getting barer because of the lack of priests? A recent newspaper had a story about a midwestern diocese where twenty-nine parish churches are being closed. Once the exodus of the alleged expendables began, the church was left with real estate—seminaries, convents, schools, hospitals, rectories, and now the parish churches—that litters the Catholic turf like white elephants.

The church doesn't need a war memorial like the wall for the Vietnam veterans, but a ritual of reconciliation that's the equivalent of a wall—a place where young priests can be reconciled with the mandarins who are fighting ghosts from the cold war, not because they're still angry at the changes (which they may partly enjoy) but because they are creatures with stubborn old habits in whom foolish pride burns brightly. Is there a diocese where the Mass is offered, as it used to be, for shepherds missing in action? Has any amnesty been offered to shepherds who want to come back to a church that loves them enough to want them back?

Exegetes teach that the joyful old man in Luke's parable who welcomed the prodigal son home was a God-figure. It is neither possible nor desirable for all the priests, nuns, and brothers to come back. But some would come, and they will tell you so.

Of course, if these exiles were allowed to return from the far country, many priests would have their noses out of joint, like the elder brother in the prodigal's parable, and who would blame them? But the scandal of Christ's teaching is a doctrine of love which reverses all merely human priorities: The needs of the humble and the shopworn, God regards as his own. The wages of the latecomers are the same as those who labored through the heat of the day. Much is forgiven the prostitute who has loved much but not always wisely. Peter, who denied Christ, is given the mandate to feed his lambs. The moral is that you can never go so far that your father's love can't draw you back.

What are mandarins for if not to help us recover our lost ground? If the church has any reason to exist, it shows in their worth as the witnesses of God's will. They have learned from experience the difference between the law and the spirit of the law. If the Eucharist is Christ's bread, its godliness is nothing I can prove with my eyes. If the church is endowed with power from on high, that power can be mismanaged by the frail creatures who exercise authority. If the church has a lion's share of truth, that truth on earth can be diluted by lies, errors, and the intention to deceive. And the truth which will be confirmed in heaven I can only assent to as a matter of faith.

Long ago the first converts trusted the church because they had the word of itinerant preachers who claimed they had seen the Lord. What made the preachers credible and powerful was the grace you could see in them. It came from their conviction about what St. Paul proclaims: "I live now not I, but Christ liveth in me." So it is with the elders and venerables who have a sweetness in them that is as much of Christ as I expect to see on this side of paradise.

To say it simply, the mandarin priests are the feather in the cap of our tainted church. Isn't this what we should expect of them, since God walked beside them every step of the way?

THE AMERICAN DREAM
AS A RELIGIOUS EXPERIENCE

I grew up in the '30s, the decade of the Great Depression when the American Dream temporarily hit the skids. I went to college with the GI-Bill veterans, back from World War II, who were pursuing a piece of the American Dream offered them by a grateful government. I remember the success symbol of the '50s, Elvis Presley, going from rock-'n'-roll to riches, and the lads he influenced, finished with the heartbreak of acne and half sneering the way Elvis did, as though they were fit to be King.

In the '60s and '70s there were Beatles and Rolling Stones and subway prophets on a bridge over troubled waters looking for Lucy in the sky with diamonds. I can't remember if I met a single fellow with a hundred dreams or a hundred fellows with the same dream, but I spent a lot of time listening while somebody sang me songs. Now, in the '80s, I meet finance majors who plan to become Wall Street tycoons or to go into business with papa but strike it richer than he did.

Looking back to 1931, I'm amused to see how Protestant the American Dream is, after all: straight out of Harvard and copyrighted by Jonathan, the Yankee peddler. Does it matter that the Dream comes to us as a uniquely Protestant brainstorm? It matters a lot, because that makes it hard to separate church from state and God from Mammon, or to decide, when you're rendering, which is God's and which is Caesar's. It's hard because if you lapse as a WASP, you feel unpatriotic.

Success may be one of the religions America is best at, but God is nonetheless worshipped in some vague way. The Bible is a religious symbol that works effectively, reminding you of redemption and salvation; of Luther and Calvin, of repressive popes and the intolerance of Catholics. It's a book the Protestants appropriated during the Reformation, and they don't share it as a sign of common faith. When Catholics and the Bible are mentioned in the same breath, nothing will be said that is going to flatter the Catholic Church.

The New England meeting house is a Protestant symbol Catholics respect as patriots. The Boston we celebrate as the "cradle of liberty" is also the cradle of white, steepled churches that are as lovely as an Emily Dickinson metaphor that takes the top of our heads off.

The Civil War would have been a much poorer war without the *Battle Hymn of the Republic.* When Robert Kennedy's body was brought to Arlington, the *Battle Hymn* reminded us that we have paid a heavy price for the American dream, and will continue to pay it. The Passion Play that is repeated many times every year—in wars and assassinations, in street violence, when Marines die defending an embassy in the Middle East—has the efficacy of a Mass at which sacrificial lambs die for our sins.

But these are Catholic figures of speech, and inappropriate in a discussion of the American Dream. The Calvinists of Massachusetts turned their dream of a new Canaan on this side of the Atlantic into a liberation theology which they preached as gospel to the Royalists to make them patriots. The dream of freedom was first of all the dream of WASPs, but Catholics have supported it enthusiastically as Johnny-come-latelies.

There is an eighteenth-century chasteness to the structure of the American Dream, as though the designers who could build dignified, simple, elegant meeting houses had hearts and souls that were pure. They became our best teachers, and by the time the Bill of Rights was framed, with its freedom of religion clause, they were light-years ahead of the Catholic think tank, which couldn't make up its mind whether error had the right to exist until 1965 at Vatican II.

When you think of the part religion has had in shaping the American Dream, you think of Quakers, who legitimated nonviolence as an American tradition; you think of the Methodists holding camp meetings that tamed the West; you think of the Protestant clerics who were zealous to the point of fanaticism in promoting abolition—as much of an embarrassment to their flocks then as some nuns and priests are today.

Emerson resigned from the ministry to preach transcendentalism to the New England conscience, and transcendentalism is the spirit of religion you're left with after outgrowing Unitarianism. The young candidates for ordination at the Harvard Divinity School were ready to believe Emerson when he told them, "Hitch your wagon to a star. If you nourish your souls, which are open to God in a limitless way, with fresh insights instead of that other stale stuff, you can teach truth even better than Jesus did." Transcendentalism taught that if you're in touch with the soul of Nature, you're in the company of royalty even when you're all alone.

None of the fonts of revelation you encounter in tracing the patterns of the American Dream, alas, were Catholics. We do have good Catholic writers in America, but none of them counts as a major mythmaker except F. Scott Fitzgerald, who was a Catholic dropout, and Ernest Hemingway, who had a half-assed Catholic connection that qualified him, when he died, to have a priest say the rosary at his burial.

Catholics have contributed enormously to the growth of America, but many of their contributions never made it to the top drawer of the dresser where the prime myths are locked up. On the documents enshrined in the Library of Congress as the birth certificates of freedom, there is only one Catholic name: John Carroll of Carrollton, signer of the Declaration of Independence.

The greatest Catholic contribution was unquestionably the parochial school, built to keep the children safe in the Irish ghetto. Using the separation of church and state as an excuse, the government always managed to keep those schools at arm's length because they were a luxury, a damned nuisance, and not quite the American cup of tea.

The Irish built the railroads, fought in all the wars and won medals, and then, recruited as gumshoes, kept the world safe for J. Edgar Hoover. Then an Irish lad was elected president and, at his inauguration, startled and pleased us by making the sign of the cross when the cardinal-archbishop of Boston led the prayer. We saw him swear on the Bible when he took the oath; if he had put his hand on a crucifix instead, Jimmy Swaggart's America would have doubted the oath.

John Kennedy's election was a spit in the eye to the Old Guard, who saw him as a parvenu with lace curtains in the window. He probably enjoyed carrying the cross of Catholicism into the White House; it hadn't been done before, and it gave him a chance to watch Yankees from Parnassus eat turkey, not in thanksgiving but as a price for their sins.

Would the American Dream be much different if we could color parts of it Catholic? You wonder what would have happened in the movement for women's liberation and the abortion crisis if the women of the Establishment, so frequently named for the strong women of the Bible, had been taught to respect Mary as a role model and exemplar.

On the hundredth birthday of Knute Rockne, Ronald Reagan came to Notre Dame and told us things I'd forgotten—that Rockne was saying the rosary when the plane went down; that, as Reagan said, "Rock had a great devotion to the mother of God." I was grateful to him for saying that. This was the president telling us about Our Lady because it was important to him, too. I had tears in my eyes as I listened.

Father Sorin's great vision for this campus showed how much faith *he* had in the American Dream. He put a statue on the dome so people could see in whose honor the place was built. At the dedication, he could have used the words of Bishop Latimer: "We shall light such a candle by God's grace . . . as I trust shall never be put out."

Are those who have come to Notre Dame far off the course of the American Dream?

A BRIDGE TOO FAR

Call him Wystan, the first name of the poet Auden, because some of Auden's loveliest verses were on homoerotic love. Wystan, who has spent many years at Notre Dame, serves as *Eminence Grise* to gay students. And he recently gave me a piece of his mind for an article on gays I wrote for *The Observer*, the campus daily. "I'm here to tell you to your face what you don't want Notre Dame students to hear," he said, leading off with a haymaker; "namely, that you are the secret and implacable enemy of gay people while hiding under a certain cloak of naive affability. More and more your articles give you away for all to see just how perverse you are."

Good heavens, I thought, *has he prepared a cup of hemlock for to me drink?* Obviously, I flattered myself. I'm not Socrates. I'm not even remotely a Christ-figure.

He continued, "Once upon a time, I thought perhaps you were just a relatively harmless eccentric with a possible ministry to some of the freaks on campus. No more! You have gone out of your way to say loudly and clearly that you are against gay people, that they had better stay in their closet at all costs, that they are not acceptable to you."

I could have argued, but it seemed more prudent to sit patiently and listen.

"You have trashed them unmercifully," Wystan continued, expressing an anger that apparently has been simmering for years. "If you realized the harm you do by rejecting some of the people who need care the most, you would end your ministering at the first opportunity. Shame on you!"

In his *Harvard Diary*, the psychiatrist Robert Coles pointed out how demeaning it is for homosexuals of "all sorts and conditions" to subsume their daily existence under such a confining rubric as "gays"— just as it is mind-boggling to find heterosexuals, in all their diversity, so narrowly defining themselves as "straights." All of us tend to be tragic. In my book gays tend to be more tragic than most, though it sounds oxymoronic to say so. Maybe the harm I cause gays is in tending to overprotect them.

Wystan had reached a plateau in describing the worthlessness of the University chaplain. His concluding gasp was: "I await your resignation with eager anticipation."

Like all other creatures, great and small, university chaplains outlive their usefulness. Late or soon, the cup of hemlock is shoved near. Resignation, retirement, or being let go does the hemlock's work. Whether you're young or old, somebody's always waiting in line who can do a better job. Anyone can tell you everything it means to be a priest except how to be the particular priest God has called you to be, with your lights, your faith, and your accessibility to his storehouse of grace and truth.

At age sixty-three, I have a pretty good idea who I am. I'm no great shakes as a liturgical presider or as a preacher. As a rector, I wasn't efficient, so they removed me and made me the University chaplain. That's a nice title, but it didn't put me in charge of anything. They didn't intend that it should; they were trying to encourage me to be as creative as possible in things I do well. So I dip in my oar here and there, a jack-of-all-trades in ministry, never advancing beyond amateur status, never pretending to be a master of the spiritual life, always embarrassed to see that even when I am successful at something, the professionals could do it better—or at least they tell me they could.

I've kept myself busy ministering to the periphery—to groups outside the mainstream whose special needs are apt to be overlooked in the division of labor that Campus Ministry undertakes. That's why I started

Darby's as a clean, well-lighted place for the night people, and started the Urchins' Mass for the children As a weekly columnist for *The Observer*, I've preached hundreds of sermons to people of all faiths who never go to places where sermons are heard.

I try to show that the religion which has outgrown the Baltimore Catechism can do more for a campus than keep the young natives from getting restless. If that's all it does, then Marx was right: Religion is the opium of the people. In my *Observer* column, "Letters to a Lonely God," I've been dealing for nineteen years, not always glibly, with topics like love, death, marriage, human sexuality, fulfillment, and the American novel, as well as the joys of smoking and the consolations of owning a cocker spaniel. As the University chaplain, I hang out my explorative ideas to twist in the wind. Nobody else on campus airs their laundry quite so publicly, in a place where it can't be overlooked.

When you have a ministry to the periphery, you do your best to speak to students who are listening for a voice in the wilderness. It takes gall to go outside or beyond the tradition, and you can't be sensitive if you're hollered at for doing it. I'm not sure what it means to be a witness, but maybe I could call myself a witness who has tried to keep the losers from feeling lost. What else can you do but witness when you meet life's rejects and see them bleeding?

Witnessing to the good news in God's world—that there's a place in the sun for everybody—is the kind of Gospel I've preached to the periphery. It's an interim truth that's not truthful enough to please everyone, but it looks like God's truth to me.

Now Wystan asks, "What do you think gays think of you for putting them down so sickeningly in *The Observer*?" That, of course, is what I was waiting to find out from this conversation filled with abusiveness that I didn't think I deserved.

A long time ago I went out on a limb for gays. For them more than anyone, I held up interim truth to survive on—until the church said I shouldn't—as they waited for priests to tell them what they wanted most to hear. The brave, new church could only tell them that for gays nothing had changed, and they should continue to go on as they have always gone on—following the way of the cross for the sake of their immortal souls.

Then I tried to point out publicly (as every priest, I hope, points out privately) the ways in which the wind is tempered to the shorn lamb. This is more than just a happy metaphor in a religion that exists for the sake of sinners. It means that on good days and bad days you do the best you can. His mercy is always there hugging you as the waters of a tideless sea hug the shoreline. The greater the struggle, the dearer you are to him.

It was a hell of a package, and I didn't know if I, as a shepherd, could deliver it—or if the shorn lamb could accept it. But that's all right, since the deal was not one we could make between us. Who but God can promise that God's wind will blow through a life? In telling gays as objectively, as simply, and as unsentimentally as I could that God's grace was there for them, every step of the way, how was I hurting them?

I said to Wystan, "In offering gays a ministry of the written word, which they were free to read or not read, I've tried to avoid hurting anybody."

"Ministry?" he exclaimed. "You should be embarrassed to use that self-justifying word. It is people like you who spend your 'ministry' telling gay students they will never be happy, fulfilled, or content. It is only when they believe you and other lying oppressors that your prophecies turn out to be true. I know your kind too well from bitter experience."

I said, "When the first gay students chose to become visible at Notre Dame in 1971, I was one of several priests they turned to for help. They said they wanted to build a bridge between themselves and the church. I helped them set up a series of meetings with members of Campus Ministry. I made the first public mention of the group's existence on campus in the first of a number of columns I wrote promoting gay awareness."

"That is surely news to me," Wystan answered. "You may think you promoted gay awareness, but I am sure your readers could barely discern which side you were on if you were true to your usual style of speaking out of both sides of your mouth at once."

"Nevertheless," I said, "I eventually got into trouble for what I wrote. Father Kenna, the provincial in those days, asked to see me. 'You've been reported to Rome for a recent article you wrote on homosexuals.' Then he gave me a sly verbal poke in the ribs: 'You've become important, you see, like Karl Rahner.' Rome's decision, and its problem with what I'd written, was that a priest having a strong influence on students should not encourage homosexuals to have any false hopes that the church will ever look favorably upon their lifestyle. Those probably weren't Rome's words, but it was clear that gays shouldn't expect to make a separate peace with the church, on the way they expressed their sexuality."

"So now," Wystan said, "you live in fear of ecclesiastical censure."

"Not in the least," I replied, because I don't, and it's a good thing, because it's scary when it happens, especially the first time. There was a wildness in the air in the '70s that led you to believe you were a free spirit obliged to be innovative if you really wanted to be part of the church's renewal.

The conversation had reached a turning point. Wystan was less fiery once he accepted the fact that I had shed a little blood on behalf of gays and had a couple of scars on my memory to prove it. "The situation of gay students at Notre Dame hasn't changed in eighteen years," I said. "The bridge hasn't even been started." He nodded agreement.

Gays are invisible because they live underground. The signs of the gay underground are all around us, says Wystan, as we could see if we knew what to look for. Now the invisible gay world is becoming visible in a way that startles us, especially when we see their anger against the Catholic Church.

A scene described in *Newsweek* a couple of years ago is memorable, like the twelfth station of the Cross. A Jesuit wrote of his hospital ministry to dying AIDS patients. One patient told him, "I don't want you here as 'Father,' but you can stay, if you like, as a friend whom I will call by his first name. The church didn't want me as a gay man in good health; now I don't want the church or any of its comforters bringing me last-minute forgiveness."

The priest said he recognized the justice behind the dying man's rejection, so he befriended this patient, though not as a priest. How terrible it must have been for the Jesuit, deeply ashamed of the church he felt justified in not defending. Isn't it hard to think that the drift of gays away from Christ could begin at Notre Dame, because the cloak of invisibility is all we have to offer the gay student? I'd hate to think that any student who came here would say to a priest later, "I don't want you here as Father."

Life at du Lac was easier when all gays stayed in the closet, out of sight, out of harm's way. Clusters of them have been coming out of the closet since 1971, and I keep hoping that some big-hearted group that befriends the underdog would have a kind word for them or take them in from the cold. A question that should gnaw at our Catholic conscience is: How honest can this university be, priding itself on its openness to truth, if it has nothing to say to a tenth of the students here about the truth of their seemingly ill-fated lives, of which some are already weary before finishing their teens?

Wystan wasn't dragging me kicking and screaming onto a new plane of awareness so that I could continue to feel sorry for gays. Pitying a gay is an act of condescension that could degrade him more than hatred does. How humiliating it must be for an AIDS patient to be sentimentalized. Elie Wiesel resented the pope at Auschwitz saying Mass for dead Jews. "He seemed to be appropriating them for Christianity after the fact," said Wiesel.

Wystan continued to try to raise my level of awareness, saying, "I agree with the Quaker Theological Statement that says, 'Homosexuality is no more to be deplored than left-handedness.' It is a simple natural variant on human sexuality and, indeed, animal sexuality, as any zoologist can tell you." (I didn't argue with him. It surprised me to find Quakers had an opinion on homosexuality.) He added, "Unless you agree with me on that statement, we shall always be at odds on this subject, and you will constantly be maintaining your negative attitudes and remarks about the status of gay people because, radically, you feel they are flawed human beings."

To tell the truth, I feel we're *all* flawed human beings. According to Freud, everyone is neurotic in one fashion or another. Is homosexuality just an alternative lifestyle? How, Robert Coles asks in the *Harvard Diary*, ought that question be asked by someone who tries to be mindful of Jesus as he walked ancient Palestine, attending the world's sinners? How ought his manner of approaching humankind in all its variously flawed conditions persuade us to consider this vexing matter of homosexuality? Coles answers: "I do not see that I have the moral authority to condemn another person for his or her sexual makeup. . . . We all owe each other compassionate understanding . . . but 'understanding' . . . is not meant to include a toleration of violence, cruelty, hatefulness, obscene sexuality, no matter the sex of the participants."

Coles writes further: "I find it sad that a particular aspect of human behavior has become the basis of a political movement, a so-called liberation movement." The absence of restraint, and yes, of guilt and shame (in connection with all kinds of lusts we have, heterosexual and homosexual) means the loss of our distinctive humanity. Man, says Coles, has been inspired by God to tame, not flaunt, the passions, so that we may all live a better life, and wonder and pray about this life's meaning.

Coles concludes: "A number of homosexuals have told me of their dismay at what gets called 'gay liberation'—and their anger that any refusal to go along with it gets immediately denounced as cowardice. . . . The point for these men and women is their privacy, their dignity, their struggle to live on their own an honorably decent life—without being hectored."

Would it be reasonable to rely on Coles' sensible statement as a *via media* between what Wystan describes as "the false and pernicious religious system falsely claiming to be the church of Jesus Christ," and the zealots of the movement whose obsession with sexual freedom in the '70s made slaves to illness, in the form of the AIDS epidemic, of thousands of the gay people it sought to liberate? How could I explain to Wystan my reservations about the Gay Liberation Movement without provoking him again to deep anger?

He began expressing his contempt for the "flimsy arguments of *Humanae Vitae*," which, as far as he was concerned, threw the whole sexual teaching of the church into doubt. One thing became clear to me as a result of *Humanae Vitae* and, once it became clear, I could take that encyclical in stride as a confessor. The insight I had was: An adult Catholic should be made to take charge of his or her own conscience because priests are not godlike enough to take over a conscience. When I'm asked as a confessor to absolve a Catholic from guilt, it's guilt from the sins he has accused himself of, not from sins I have accused him of. If he says, "I've been practicing birth control; is it a sin?" I answer, "You be the judge." There's no wisdom like Solomon's in the work I do as a confessor; but if I met Wystan in the confessional, I wouldn't let *Humanae Vitae* come between us.

I started in on an *apologia pro vita mea* as a bleeding-heart liberal grown long in the tooth. "In my salad days, when I was green in judgment," I said, "I was a pioneer in the promotion of the idea that everybody is entitled to be famous for fifteen minutes, and proved it by writing gay press notices." But I soon outlived my usefulness.

Nobody in Campus Ministry knew what to do for the gays we were meeting with until they asked if they could hold a dance, and we knew we were acting in their best interests, doing them a favor, when we told them no. In the big cities, the liberation movement was growing, and the fifty or so gays that were becoming visible on campus—at least to one another—wanted to be a part of it. As I understand it, the number of gays who attend meetings on campus has remained at about fifty since 1971. Wystan, agreeing on that figure, said he is aware of many Notre Dame gays who never attend meetings.

The gays who came to the surface in 1971 quickly became seniors. Going on job interviews, some were sorry they had become semivisible to the public, or had attached their names to letters and articles appearing in the paper. They felt that being known as liberated gays wouldn't help them find jobs.

Ever since then, gays have made their presence known—as a way of educating Notre Dame in gay awareness and as a plea for acceptance. One year groups of them appeared on a local TV show to talk about themselves; and to tell the truth, they were a little heartbreaking. They tried to be above board and honest, and showed great personal courage; in doing so, they brought static on themselves from students who didn't want them around.

I didn't want to tell Wystan how much time I've spent giving moral support to gay Catholics, for I didn't want him to tell me that I was paternalistic, unctuous, and shallow. All the Notre Dame gays I have ever talked with, or gotten mail from, have wanted to know how they stand with the church. It has never seemed like a great idea to let any of them drift off into a limbo of alienation, regarding themselves as unacceptable in the eyes of the church. I have always offered them hope, no matter what they are up to.

The church was charted to be of use to sinners in constant need of forgiveness who must keep accepting the grace of Christ that is always waiting for them. That grace is everywhere, so why shouldn't I be hopeful? In many ways, as the church's minister, I fly blind, trusting that this is true: It is not the fish who catches Christ the Fisherman. He catches the fish and is skillful at not letting one get away. The priest is like a piece of tackle in the Fisherman's experienced hand.

I'm always pleased when any Catholic, whatever his sin, trusts me and asks me to hear his confession. In helping him lighten his conscience, I try to be kind and make things as painless as possible. Eventually, you may find that you have the name for being a "good" confessor, and one gay tells another and your name may go out over the gay network as a priest the homosexual can talk to. This is what a "ministry" to gays amounts to.

I've found it pays to advertise the forgiveness of sins, letting students know that there are always balms of Gilead available to cure the sin-sick soul. Sometimes it seems risky to say it. You don't want to give people the impression that as a priest in the business of saving souls, you're giving discounts that make grace cheap, or that you're giving it away recklessly to prodigals who aren't properly disposed to receive absolution. Christ authorized the church to declare the forgiveness of sins, but this doesn't mean the priest is free to hand out divine mercy as though it were a candy cane from his personal sack of sweets. But if you believe that the sacraments were given to keep potential losers from becoming lost, you give them whatever help you can from the Catholic pharmacopeia of grace and truth as instinctively as you'd put oil on the wheel that squeaks.

There is a hell, either of time or eternity, that we need to be saved from. The vivid biblical images of fire and the never-dying worm seem to be precise metaphors describing the mind in hell. Hell is a state of mind we create for ourselves. Self-hatred, anger, and despair could put us hopelessly, perhaps eternally, out of touch with the joy of God. The souls we take with us to the grave and beyond could go restlessly around in circles, lost in the darkness that comes from being spiritually blind. If free will means anything, it means we could become so unloving and feel so unloved that we forfeit our chance to find happiness by letting ourselves be possessed by the love of God.

The good news is that God so loved the world that he gave his only-begotten Son. The college chaplain must preach this message, even when it sounds irrelevant and trite, to students who are not really listening, hoping that the meaning of the good news will come home to them at shabby moments in the years ahead when they're feeling so defeated that they're ready to turn on the gas pipe and say good night to the world. The message is no different for the gay student than for the straight, except that a gay student may need it sooner because his cross has an unfairness that makes it especially heavy.

Wystan, of course, didn't hear a word of this interior monologue. But now I said to him, "Can't gay students understand I want them to take care of themselves? Pub-crawling in the gay bars of New York and San Francisco isn't a great way of taking care of themselves. Liberated gays, as far as I can see, have turned out to be their own worst enemies. Gay students can't wait to shake the dust from their feet of repressive, homophobic Notre Dame."

"Neither can straight students," he interjected.

"But gay students are years earlier in getting the hurt look of a wounded animal in their eyes. When you meet them later in the cities, some of them have terrible stories to tell."

Wystan said, "Whether you believe it or not, I have spent my entire career so far in helping gays to the degree I know how, trying to set a good example to students seeking a role model. The Catholic Church lies when it says that gay people are inevitably promiscuous, unfaithful to one another, and unable to maintain lasting relationships. If gays felt at home in the church, they would have much to contribute to its understanding of sexuality and of dedicated relationships. As it is, many leave its hostile and unyielding environment for a riskier and freer existence on their own."

I said, "I was very touched when a gay man told me he had lived as a celibate for thirty years with another gay. He said, 'How could we do otherwise if we wanted to go every day to the Eucharist?'"

"The same thing is true of many gay couples," he said. "So why do you imply that gays always lead one another into mutual self-destruction?"

"Gay liberation has made many strange bedfellows," I said. "A few years ago a creepy little man came to South Bend to start a gay church for Notre Dame students. I found out how much of a religious illiterate he was when he called me on the phone to ask what the priest says when he 'does' Holy Communion."

Wystan explained, "Gay liberation was an answer—a very small one—to the homophobic attacks on gay people. Why don't you spend your energies defending the oppressed against homophobic virulence, since you pose as a friend to the downtrodden?"

The truth is, as Wystan's remark made me realize, though I've spent a lot of time lately trying to protect gays from themselves, it's been years since I tried to defend them against attack. As a matter of fact, except for an occasional letter in *The Observer* that says condescendingly that gays are as good as regular people, the only ones at Notre Dame to defend gays are gays themselves.

I told Wystan, "I've tried to save gays from choosing a lifestyle that would burn them out early. I've tried to save them from participating in the tragic human comedy in which gays march, arm-in-arm with their parents, down Fifth Avenue in the Gay Parade, shouting, 'Gay is good.' Every drag-queen in sight is living proof to the onlookers that gay is sick. I have tried to save freshmen who have just decided they're gay from hanging out in gay neighborhoods in Chicago. Then later, on a day when they're not feeling good, they're panicking until they see a doctor to be tested for AIDS.

"I've tried to save them from the idea that they should become a big campus club, promoting themselves like varsity athletes, which would tempt youngsters in search of their sexual identity, or only passingly, temporarily, tentatively gay, to emerge from the closet, years before they are ready (if they are ever ready, which they may not be if they're not truly gay) to face the brave new world which has liberated gay people in it. Yet in trying to save and protect gays, it has never struck me that I might have a duty to protect them from gay-baiters."

Wystan's reply began, "Can't you see that all your talk of saving gays is negative?" Then, in a reasonable, compelling, and moving way, he gave me the picture of a gay person becoming sexually aware, from the time he feels the first stirrings of sexuality within him. While he's trying to understand what it means to be a sexual animal in need of fulfillment, he's made aware that his sexual orientation is a serious mistake of nature. Everything he hears about his sexuality leaves him convinced that he's sick and perverted, and he'll spend his life being the object of endlessly cruel jokes. He'd better not let the world see his true sexual feelings, for the world has ugly words to describe the homosexual person, whom nobody credits with innocence or as being above suspicion.

This must be hard to take when you're sixteen, forced to remain mute when you're aching all over from puppy love, afraid that you'll be placed under a psychiatrist's care if you admitted having a crush on another sixteen-year-old of the same gender.

Growing up gay, you know that your family, if it knew, would be ashamed of you; that your schoolmates, if they knew, would leave you ostracized; that your teachers, if they knew, would watch you distrustfully; the coaches, the scoutmaster, the parents would discourage your chums from hanging around with you. If you should tell the priests you're gay, they'd tell you that you can always be beautiful in God's sight, as long as you don't go near the table while you're attending the feast of life.

Going to the greatest Catholic university in all the land, the brain-tank where the one true church does its thinking in America, you hear the same doubletalk that you heard from the priests at home. And you're advised to be quiet, stay hidden in the closet, don't rock the boat. If the homophobes don't know who you are, they can't hurt you. If you don't come out of the closet, you can't harm anyone else in matters of faith and morals.

When you're a priest of sixty-three, convinced that there's nothing new under the sun, it's powerful to find out that God hasn't finished with you yet. I thought I knew about gays. I formed opinions about them without paying attention to what they were thinking about themselves. Wystan was the only adult gay who ever told me, in effect, to shut up and listen to a couple of simple facts about gay life I had failed to understand. I became glib in speaking about gays, using honey words that I thought were insightful and compassionate. Gays, hearing me talk down to them in my good-hearted way of wanting what was best for them (which was to save them from the temptation of living as gays) thought I was talking out of both sides of my mouth, as Wystan had said.

I told him, "I finally understand what students have tried to tell me in letters and conversations. They tried hard, God bless them. And when priests and nuns took to the hustings to promote the gay cause, all I could hear was the jargon which made them sound radically chic. This is the first time I've ever talked to an adult gay who said simply the way things are."

"The way things are," Wystan said, "would make your hair curl. Last summer some parents brought their autistic child to Notre Dame for the Special Olympics. Before leaving home, they had things out with their twenty-year-old son who had recently told them he was gay. His mother told him that if she had known he would be a homosexual, she would have had him aborted. Then the couple came to Notre Dame to express their parental pride in their Special Olympian. While they were gone, their beautiful son took his life."

"Oh, Jesus!" I said, feeling sick.

"Gays at Notre Dame could get the idea that Jesus wants nothing to do with them. Gays can't get permission for a priest on campus to say Mass for them or for a chapel to say it in. They've been told that the only room available to them is in the confessional."

I pointed out, "Rome has told the bishops to put an end to the Dignity Masses that have been taking place in many parish churches for that Catholic gay organization."

"How do you think that makes gay people feel?" Wystan asked bitterly. "The churches have been closed to them. Notre Dame can't help them because gay education lies outside its official mission. You, Father Griffin, don't want gays helping each other in an organized way for fear the old will corrupt the young."

"Gay liberation has a way of turning out tacky," I protested.

"That's what happens when you keep people repressed by telling them they're bad," he said. "Once the lid's off anything goes, because they have such a poor self-image they don't care what people, who would look down on them anyway, think."

"'Freedom's just another word for nothing left to lose,'" I thought.

Wystan said, "The pope and his curial enforcers seem determined to sacrifice gay people on the altar of expediency. Gay people have been gratuitously insulted as never before in recent papal pronouncements on sexuality, and most of us have gotten the message loud and clear. Even if Cardinal Ratzinger and company would change their tune, a return to the church is out of the question. We have discerned the true face of the Roman Church and find it to be the antithesis of the Gospel."

I recall that once after Mass, standing on the church steps of a parish in Greenwich Village, one of the Village gays coming out of Mass scolded me for an article I'd written for *Notre Dame Magazine*. I had told the story of a young gay who confessed sinning against the promise he had made to be faithful to the young gay he was living with. Instead of trying to persuade him that the relationship was wrong, I left him in good faith, since I felt that the relationship gave a center to his life that kept him off the streets cruising. The Village gay gave me a piece of his mind. "We've struggled along without priests' approval up to now. At this point, we don't need their help, making them feel good, letting them tell us it's still true that Father knows best."

I don't share Wystan's disaffection for the church. He's right, of course, on what he says about our failure to agree. But after what he taught me, I'll not be quick to sound off about gays.

Whatever problems the church has, Notre Dame has a share in. Don't we pride ourselves on giving the students an education that speaks to their conscience and gives them a sense of their own beauty in the sight of God? If gay students are worth something too, shouldn't we be able to find a way of telling them so, since nobody else manages to do them this favor?

I said—mistakenly, it turned out—as a way of registering my concern, "The Christian army is the only army that shoots its wounded."

Wystan answered, "Sometimes the wounded make it easier for the Christian army—they shoot themselves."

We'd covered that already, so he didn't have to say it. I should have known he would. It wasn't an easy conversation. We had nothing left to say to each other, but we could solve nothing. Maybe he will not be so angry if we talk again. Maybe he will not have reason to be angry if I can be more sensitive tomorrow than I was yesterday.

AND ONE OF THEM WAS MY BROTHER

When George died seven years ago, I chose Robert Louis Stevenson's "Requiem" as his epitaph, as if my brother had been the happy wanderer, worn and weather-beaten from being blown by the wind: "Here he lies where he longed to be; / Home is the sailor, home from the sea, / And the hunter home from the hill." But his life was no child's garden of verses, and my excuse for glossing over his sufferings (for which he deserved a gold medal in the Special Olympics) was that his pain was my pain, too, and I wasn't willing to face the memories that left me heartbroken.

The neatest thing I ever did for him was to unite him in death with Dad in a burial place by the sea, the sailor's snug harbor of a family in which all the men were fishermen. I thought, "Now he's out of harm's way, immune at last from humiliations." Maybe the only decent break he ever got was to be brought there for the long sleep, for he would have been restless buried with strangers, cruelly separated from his loved ones in death as he was in life.

To tell the truth, I don't know which direction to turn for cheerfulness when I remember my brother. I could paper over grief with the customary Christian consolations were it not for the Jimmy Swaggarts warning us of the hellfire that awaits sinners who die without accepting Christ as their personal savior. The Catholic version of doomsday is brought to us by the crepehangers in the church who spend their lives praying for a happy death—to die in the state of sanctifying grace, freshly fortified by the last sacraments.

Once you've buried a brother who's regarded by outsiders as the black sheep of the family, you start looking for schemes of salvation that come, like health insurance, as a package deal for all the family, though it has never troubled me excessively that George, in his lifetime, wasn't conventionally religious. I can't really believe that my brother's life, or any life, should mean so little in the sight of heaven that I should have to defend him from God's trashing him in flames for all eternity.

The restoration of peace in the family begins with the recognition that grace works overtime in an incredible way to bring the mavericks home, though sometimes it's over the road of hard knocks. It's not sentimental to say that nothing is impossible with God—that Christ doesn't give up on anyone.

Our Lord was very fond of telling stories about the father who had two sons, both of them in need of paternal love and wisdom. This is why, if I could write my life as a gospel parable, I would begin it, "A man in Maine had two sons, and one of them was my brother." Is it possible that brothers can lead each other into God's presence, that one can appear as a character witness for the other?

In the parable of the prodigal, don't you suppose that later the younger lad would willingly go to court to testify to the worthiness of his elder brother who stayed at the father's side, working hard all his life, even when the old man gave half of his savings to be wasted by the playboy of the family? In Bible stories the brother who obeys his father's instructions and the brother who flouts them often strike me as being the same son in different moods. In those stories one son can see in his brother his own better, or darker, half. One brother can see the other as his twin in mediocrity or his counterpart in virtue or vice. This homemade insight may be shallow or unimportant, like pop psychology, but in my house I think it was true. How can I sort out what Christ means in my life except to say that, in my family, I got the vocation to be *alter Christus* and my brother George got the vocation to be Simon of Cyrene, helping Christ carry the cross in a way I never did. It must have been Christ's cross that George was struggling under, considering its size and weight. So I became the priest who got spoiled by attention, and he was the ne'er-do-well brother, expected to keep out of sight. Still, he must have gotten the lion's share of grace or he couldn't have been so patient. I never did as much for him by the influence of my good example as he did for me.

George was my handsome and gentle elder (there were nine years between us), whose name must have been on the short list of the Beautiful and the Damned. Even as one of the boys of summer in their ruin, he still had a head like Lord Byron's. I'm not willing to tell you, even now, how often and how cruelly he was wounded. I could say, as many have said to me, that he was his own worst enemy, but it wasn't true. Life was the enemy that kept defeating him, though only by a TKO. He was a plucky lad with style and class, and he never ran out of that courage called grace under pressure. Unfortunately, that's a secular grace that doesn't sanctify you, but perhaps God accepted it in lieu of the sanctifying grace which is the credential you need for entering heaven.

He never married, though he was in love with an Irish girl named Eileen, sister to his teen-age chum, Carl. She may have loved George, though it worried her that he wasn't a Catholic. Then Carl got killed riding piggy-back on a boxcar, his head knocked off by a low-lying bridge, and Eileen gave up dating the young and restless. Soon George had his own injuries to deal with: He fell off the back of a truck and was dragged through the streets until the toes of his shoes were burned off before the driver knew he had a hitchhiker in tow. He was left with a scar on his brain from which he suffered ill effects the rest of his life.

When he was in his late forties, he started to have anxiety attacks that left him so manic he would have to be hospitalized. Once, when he felt an attack coming on, he tried to take his own life by slicing his throat. After that my mother kept the razor blades out of sight. When he finally died in a nursing home, crippled by a stroke and confined to a wheel chair, this helpless man was a prisoner in a locked room—though he was as peaceable as a nun breathless with adoration—to keep him out of harm's way in case he had a mood swing.

The saddest scene of his life must have taken place on the day he went in a wheelchair from his nursing home to see my old, blind mother in her nursing home where she was confined to a room on the second floor. The home didn't have an elevator—only stairs he couldn't climb up and she couldn't walk down. George, stunningly disappointed, never got to visit the mother he adored and hadn't seen in several years. Because of their illnesses, he never saw her again.

He shouldn't have died at sixty-six from a stomach aneurism that started to hemorrhage. When the bleeding began, the doctors couldn't figure out where the blood was coming from; no mention had been made on his medical record of the aneurism he had had repaired ten years before. By this time in his life, he may have felt that his soul was being stretched over a wheel of fire, but I have no way of telling whether he felt ready and willing to die. All you can say, in the words of Thomas Hardy, is that the President of the Immortals had finished using George for his sport.

Years before I opened Darby's as "a clean, well-lighted place" for the night people of Notre Dame, George was trying to open a social club for people who needed a light for the night. It would cater especially to dried-out drinkers who sought something happier or more swinging than an AA meeting as a barrier against feeling empty inside.

George started to drink when he was very young. As a boy, he got into the sneaky habit of sampling the home brew that my uncle made in my grandfather's cellar. My first awareness of what the repeal of Prohibition could mean was when George, at seventeen, was brought home pissed to the gills and passed out in the back seat of a police car. That's the only time I ever saw him under the influence, for he never drank at home and I never was with him when he took a drink.

After the age of forty-five or so, he never touched a drop. Another hail-fellow-well-met had smashed George's leg to pieces by breaking a two-by-four across it, and from then on George was afraid to drink for fear of getting hurt again. The pain from his shattered limb must have bled into the pain circulating through his head. Even if he'd wanted to find the amnesia that lies at the bottom of a cup, the sobriety forced on him when he was hospitalized for months deprived him of the chance to use liquor as a crutch. You'd have to be a shrink to understand the damage so much trauma can cause. All I can tell you is that after that, his mental health gave him a run for the money.

The first time we noticed that our boy was in deep trouble was when he told us about the "Blackbird Club" he was trying to find premises for. The name came to him from a song: "Make my bed, and light the light / I'll be home, late tonight. Blackbird, bye-bye." From then on, whenever he mentioned the Blackbird Club we knew his mood was switching from depressive to manic, and neither hell nor high water could have kept him from trying to go into business as Toots Shor.

When he was a practicing alcoholic, George didn't like to lush unseen, wasting his sweetness on the desert air. When he started to practice sobriety as a lifestyle, he would stand outside bars—as he once told me—looking through the window, watching the folks inside who were laughing and having a good time. That's when he started to want his version of Hemingway's clean, well-lighted place, where wallflowers committed to total abstinence could meet to dance.

The older I got, the harder I tried to let him see how fond I was of him, partly as a penance, I suspect, for trying to play him as a fool when I was still a college student. Once I wore, without his knowing it, the good-looking new suit he had shopped for to wear at my father's funeral. It was blue, double-breasted, and Brooks Brothers—the most expensive set of threads either of the Griffin boys had ever had on his back. I wanted it and was jealous of George's having it, though on me the pants were too short, the sleeves not long enough.

Unfortunately, I fell down while I had it on and ripped a hole in one knee. I hung the suit back in the closet without saying a word. When George discovered the damage, I tried to convince him that he, while drunk, must have torn the pants without knowing it. The look he gave me would have wrung tears out of the eye of a turnip, as he realized I was treating him like a dummy. And he probably wondered why I would want to humiliate him, since he wasn't about to get in a fight with me over a suit I could have had for the asking. God love him, he wouldn't have seemed half so tragic in his lifetime if he hadn't been so transparently sensitive. When he was sixty-years old, wobbling like a wino with a wet brain because of his injuries, he still looked elegant in the peajacket and corduroys of a longshoreman.

He was always kind to me and infinitely courteous, full of love and charm for the baby brother. If he was ever unhappy with self-pity or bitterness, he never let me see it. He would have enjoyed my needing him as a big brother, taking care of me as my role model, defender, social coach, guardian angel—and, after my father's death, as the family breadwinner anxious to see that my mother didn't spoil me. He never held it against me that I became a priest, though he could have made it tougher, as the man of the house, for me to continue in the seminary. He could have pointed out, as my sister did, that it was I, not he, who worried my father the most by my decision to sign up as a Catholic.

He was not, in any outward way, remotely religious. As far as I know, he wasn't even baptized. He asked me once why I had taken up with a church that so many scholars, scientists, and other bright people regarded as nonsensical. I gave him one of the smug answers that preconciliar Catholics were famous for, then asked him if he believed in God. "I would have to be a fool not to," he said. In the time we spent together that was as close as we ever came to a discussion of religion. I have no way of telling if he was close to God, or if he said prayers, but I may find out in heaven that his prayers were the ones that kept me going all the way to ordination.

The only concern he showed for me as a priest was his worry about my getting too heavy. He asked my mother once if I had to kneel down in performing my duties in church; he was concerned that kneeling could be hard for me, since I was so greatly overweight.

He was intelligent and a keen observer, and the wilder he was on his antic days, the quicker he was to figure things out. Besides, he read a lot. I'm sure that in his own way he must have researched the question of God's concern for his world, especially after he met proselytizing preachers who offered him bibles and born-again nurses who wanted to bring him to Jesus. How could he not have tried to put God to the test, or tested the efficacy of prayer, in all the time he spent alone as he fought to survive the disaster of his life, or to help my mother and my sister carry the burdens that weighed on them like the everlasting hills. It isn't necessarily your consciousness, or the nearness or sweetness of God, that makes you a saint or a believing Christian. The mystics warn us of the long, dark night of the soul: That's when the cries go up from the heart, "Where is God? Where is he when we need him, and what is he doing to help?"

There is a secular version of this divine abandonment that could be described as the Gospel According to Hemingway. Everyone has his omega-point of pain, when everything seems lost except the struggle itself. Christ's was not in Gethsemane, when he was still able to make an act of blind faith in his father's will, but on the cross, when he cried, "My God, my God, why hast Thou forsaken me?"—when, as Chesterton noted, it seemed the Son of God had become an atheist.

The saints of Hemingway's gospel are heroes who keep a stiff upper lip and are tender in love, manly in courage, and primitive in their instincts, which bond them like brothers-in-survival to the wild things on earth. They are heirs to the kingdom in which God is our *nada*, because when the chips are down they show much grace under pressure and have obvious class as straight-shooters.

Hemingway wrote, "If people bring much courage to this world, the world has to kill them to break them, so of course it kills them. The world breaks everyone and afterward many are strong at the broken places. But those that will not break it kills. It kills the very good and the very gentle and the very brave impartially. If you are none of these you can be sure it will kill you too but there will be no special hurry."

The omega-point of Christ's passion is a mystery to me and everyone else. Though God is Christ's own *Abba*, our Lord as he was dying felt so rejected and abandoned that he had difficulty conjuring up his Father's face. How can I build a bridge between this and my brother's mood as he waited for death in a nursing home?

My brother's was the passion of the unwashed have-nots. He was not an uncrowned saint, passionately wounded by splinters from Christ's cross. If he'd found himself in Gethsemane, he'd have left by the nearest exit to drink through the night with Hemingway's sleepless old man. George wouldn't have known what I was talking about if I told him he was a victim drawn into the circle of God's pain. He would have said, "Given the choice, I'd rather be with the sunshine boys."

The heavenly Father couldn't have allowed him such a large portion of pain only to allow it to lie fallow and unredemptive. Where love is, there is God, says scripture. Where pain is, there is God's son on the cross. You can get there on the *via dolorosa* which leads to Calvary from a hundred million directions. Getting there, you bow your head and beat your breast as though you were visiting the Wailing Wall. I can believe all this as an act of faith, but it's nebulous compared to Hemingway's gospel of guts. If mercy came into my brother's life, it had no discernible shape. But I didn't see doubts there, either. Though he may have had hopes, I don't think George expected anything. He didn't die beaten or mute with fear.

I've seen my brother's face when the ghosts of old tears behind his smile were struggling to keep fresh tears from emerging. What do you do with the remembrance of things past that dates all the way back to the lost childhood, when innocence is first lost and the child is no longer conscious of himself as nature's high priest, trailing clouds of glory? Of course neither of us brothers was so Wordsworthian, nor would we have wanted to be if it meant perceiving that the shades of the prison house were beginning to close upon the growing boy.

It's only as an adult that you reach for the nearest available metaphor to describe how it felt as a child to discover that you could no longer rely on having a good time every day, that the adults who kept reminding you that you were no longer a baby usually had an axe to grind, and they could get in your way like darkness. But where were any of us when we first became aware of tears and the death of things, and understood the sadness of that time as a warning for the future—realized that the blues we were getting were an affliction that could follow us around like cold germs?

For years and years I saw the sadness in my brother's eyes as I left him behind in hospital rooms, nursing homes, and, once or twice, in a jail. Usually, I'd be heading off to have dinner at a fancy restaurant with friends who were picking up the tab. I've been to so many places where he couldn't follow me, for the shy, explorative, and easily embarrassed love that existed between us didn't mean that either of us could go trespassing into the other's world.

Carrying an empty suitcase, he once checked into a hotel where I had stayed, just to prove that the place wasn't off limits to him. After checking in, he found he was lonely and had nothing to do, so he went home without paying, leaving the empty suitcase behind. He suspected that I was embarrassed by him, ashamed of him, and he was probably right, though I was ashamed of myself for being embarrassed.

It would be selfish and unfair of me to save up graces for myself with which to grease God's palm if I felt that George would once again be left outside to cool his heels, gawking up at the marquee. I would be sick with guilt if I could even faintly foresee it would happen that way. How could I love God without bitterness if I couldn't trust Him not to give my brother the back of his hand? I love him, and am ashamed of him no longer, and am almost tempted to praise him elegiacally as "the sweetest, wisest soul of all my days and lands." But why make him greater in death than he was in life, except as an act of homage which would bring peace not to his soul but to mine?

When you say *kaddish* for my brother, please don't pull strings to get him into a pie-in-the-sky kind of heaven; don't arrange for haloed Veronicas to meet him or virgin-martyrs to fall over him. He'd take no pleasure from a Catholic heaven, lit with candles and reeking of incense, cluttered with statues from the catacombs. The crowd he runs with in heaven should be composed of simple folk: street people, eccentrics living hand-to-mouth, the invisible drifters who became visible to him after they helped him survive with their gutter-wisdom.

While I was watching him crawl toward the grave, maybe I should have encouraged the Salvation Army to approach him with fife, trumpet, and drum, offering to furnish him with midwives capable of delivering him into born-again innocence. My brother would have had a great deal of respect for a religion which makes a duty out of serving coffee and doughnuts to winos who would starve without the charity they receive from a skid-row mission. But he wouldn't have cared to live there as a captive audience. Why would I expect him to be comfortable as the everlasting houseguest of any denomination holding leases to the mansions of glory in a city with jewelled walls and gates of pearl?

Reason, in the Catholic tradition, is regarded as the handservant of faith; and faith, in St. Paul's definition, is "the substance of things hoped for, the evidence of things unseen." What substantial thing can we reasonably hope for in heaven? Oh, says St. Paul, reason doesn't come near it. Out of love for us, God created this incredibly beautiful world— which can't hold a candle, Paul says, to the one to come. God's heart has reasons that our reason cannot know. Heaven is his masterpiece, and we will dance for him there as though we were honored guests at the Stardust Ballroom at the end of the world.

I can imagine God dancing but, of course, God is more supernatural than that. I can imagine an Emerald City but, of course, heaven's more ineffable than that. I can imagine iridescent angels and archangels with aquamarine eyes the color of Yeats' unicorns but, of course, the heavenly choirs are more ethereal than that. What I can't imagine is a hereafter where the lame and crippled aren't allowed to enter first.

Rather than believe those pre–Vatican II diehards complacently assigning the soul of my unbaptized brother to a place in limbo (or worse), I'd trash theology and start over. My brother can slip through the narrow gate as an "anonymous Christian," as Karl Rahner describes those "who are justified by grace even while they remain outside the Christian community—even if they're not church members, have not been baptized, do not confess Christ, and do not believe explicitly in God." This hopeful view is a spinoff from the teaching of Vatican II in *Lumen Gentium*.

I don't want to claim my brother was a saint—even an "anonymous saint"—whom the church would be justified in "anonymously canonizing." But I'd like to think the poor, dear chap had as much chance to grab the brass ring as the rest of us. Insisting that "outside the church there is no salvation" seems to leave him doomed.

My brother's funeral service was as simple as could be. The casket couldn't have been cheaper or more modest, but it had dignity, and it was better than plain boards, and he wasn't buried by the welfare department in a potter's field. I had to borrow the money for the funeral, and dignity was all I could afford.

The casket wasn't opened. The body, zipped in a body bag, wasn't made up for viewing. I was sorry I made that arrangement: Not seeing him made saying good-bye more impersonal than it needed to be. Despite his tough life, my brother never lost his good looks, but I hadn't liked the idea of the cosmeticians practicing their arts on him, applying rouge and powder that would leave his fine face looking waxy, or fussing with that magnificent head of hair until it looked like a wig. Still, I wish I could have seen him laid out, and I realized my sister would have preferred an open casket. My mother wasn't there and couldn't have been even if I had told her of George's death, which I didn't. God love her, she was getting ready to die herself. I should have bought him a new suit for his burial. I felt I owed him one, remembering the suit of his I tried to rip off.

The Congregational minister in charge of the service kept offering to play hymns and asking if I wanted to share the prayers and readings with him, but my prayers were said privately. George didn't have any great taste for hymns, especially those on tape like Muzak. I did ask for Lord Tennyson's "Crossing the Bar," which has always been read at our family funerals.

But religion, too, can be a form of cosmetics used to change the complexion of things. I didn't want to give my "anonymously Christian" brother a sendoff as though he were a doctor of the church. I did for him in death what I knew he wanted: I saw him laid to rest in the snug harbor by the sea next to my father. It was done with love, devotion, and sorrow, but without frills.

I owe it to my brother not to turn his life into a lie, and I've had to struggle against the unctuousness that can be a part of the clergyman's style. I've been tempted to say, "He wasn't heavy—he was my brother," but it isn't true. He was a heavy cross to bear, mostly because he was a cross to himself and a cross to my family. I've wept for him again and again, and have died inside when I've seen him forced to live in some of the saddest places in all the world. I could have been a cross to him as a priestly phony, judged by his cronies to be a pompous bastard who wouldn't give them the time of day. If so, he never let me know that his pals had a poor opinion of me.

I would love to claim him for Christ, though he may have lived and died an agnostic. I want his life to have counted for something, but I have no right to try to appropriate him posthumously for the church, as though I had evidence for believing that, in his heart, he was a Catholic lad like me.

I can't rob George of the right and dignity to be who he was, even if he was only a loser who never got the breaks. If he was a victim more sinned against than sinning, maybe his life could count as a protest against man's inhumanity to man. But when you say *kaddish* for my brother, you shouldn't completely disregard the possibility that he may have been one of the unsung heroes who ran secret errands for the powers that be.

THE LOST YOUTH
OF MICKEY ASHFORD

Mickey Ashford was a very real nine-year-old whom I befriended as though he were the little prince. I spent two years being his closest grownup friend, loving him as best I could without spoiling him. Later, I would be asked if I were trying to impose myself on Mick as a father, but I knew better than that.

I've been thinking of Mick because it's the Year of the Family at Notre Dame. It would make more sense to me if it were the Year of the Child: Without children, the family is just a marriage.

I met Mick in 1963, on my way to supper on Mount Auburn Street in Cambridge, Massachusetts. I noticed a small fellow on a bike too big for him. He told me his name was Mickey Ashford and he stayed with his grandmother, who lived three houses from Sacred Heart School. The grandmother took care of him and his sisters, Lainie and Kimberly, while their mother worked.

I asked him if he ever heard of a chap his age named Mousey Cronin Junior, sidekick and blood relative of the highly-respected Hop-along Cronin of Dodge City, Iowa, who had a daughter, Cupcakes Cronin, sweetheart of the Grange. I said, "Mousey's father is the senior Mousey in the family, and so young Mousey is known as the Pocket-

Sized Mouse." In those days I practiced being the Pied Piper; well-rehearsed whimsy was my stock-in-trade.

When we arrived at my destination, Sacred Heart rectory, Mick shinnied up a lamppost to be eye-level with me as we continued to get acquainted. He gave the impression he was a loner who hated to lose sight of me. Rather than close the door in his face, I sent him home to eat, promising to call his grandmother for permission to take him and his sisters out for ice cream. Then I watched him ride down the street and into the sunset, looking like a range-partner of Hopalong Cronin, sitting high in the saddle on the trail of the Lonesome Pine.

Mickey Ashford, I soon discovered, was well known in the rectory as a born hellion, notorious for his bad temper, for getting into fights with children in the school yard, and for being imaginatively destructive. At five, he sawed off the supports of an old woman's porch. Once he got into trouble with the monsignor for pulling the fire alarm in church.

The next afternoon I rang the doorbell at Mick's grandmother's house. Lainie, his older sibling, was miserable with a toothache. Kim, the runt of the litter, was whimpering adenoidally, wearing hand-me-down dresses like an orphan of the storm. The grandmother's hands shook, rattling the cup when she served me coffee. She had the reputation of being a drinker, but nerves, not liquor, made her shaky that day. She acted as though she thought I was there to repossess the children; when we were alone, her first words were, "Are you here to take Mickey away from me?"

The words were so encrusted with heartbreak that they brought tears to my eyes and I wanted to hug her. I was quick to say, "I'm here to help you, if I can," and then I sat quietly so she could study my face to find out if I was sincere and harmless as well as stupid.

The children's mother, Jean, came tearing home from work as soon as her mother phoned to say Father Griffin was paying a visit. She said, "Why should I need help?" I started to grin as I reviewed the *curriculum vitae* of the devil's imp, and she replied, "I know Mick's pain because I share it. He's grown up rejected, and every time he feels rejection staring him in the face, he starts acting wild because the anger inside him has no place to go."

Jean's husband was not Mick's father, though the record said he was. Jean explained, "He hated the idea of raising another man's child,

The Lost Youth of Mickey Ashford   267

so he abused Mick. Once, when Mick was still a baby, he threw him across the room." Mick, as a loving child, adored his putative father and couldn't understand why he was treated so badly. Jean finally broke up the marriage to save Mick from misery.

I had too much of a messiah complex in those days to wonder if I was biting off more than I could chew. When Jean asked, "How can you help?" I thought of Lainie suffering from a mouthful of cavities. "I could take the children to see a dentist," I answered. So I started the summer taking Lainie, Kim, and Mickey to have their teeth fixed.

Mick helped me that lovely summer, saving me from the doldrums, as much as I helped him. Free of anger he was a charmer, and sometimes his insights were wonderful. He told me once after Mass why he enjoyed going to communion: "It's like if you're hungry when you eat it—well, after you eat it, you're not hungry anymore."

Mick and I tried everything at least once. We went to Cape Ann and found the rockbound coast too slippery to stand on when we cast a line. On our next excursion we went to a lake, where our host took us out in a boat so we could fish in the rain. We sailed from Boston to the amusement park at Nantasket, where Mick immediately got sick on the loop-the-loop; I had to buy him a new shirt and some pants so he wouldn't smell sour. We went to Fenway Park to see the Red Sox play.

I found it hard work to be responsible for the well-being of a child. Sometimes, coming home on the bus, he would fall asleep, and I would have to carry him piggy-back from the bus to the house, though I was dying of weariness myself. I learned from Mick the discipline of putting my own needs in second place to the needs of a child, making some of the sacrifices my own father must have made. For over two years I made sure Mick and the girls had new clothes for school, warm clothes for winter, birthday and Christmas gifts, and other good things that should come with the territory when you're very young.

The hardest thing that happened was the weekend Jean's husband came to town for a visit. I knew it was a sin to be jealous, but I *was* jealous when Mick told me how, when his father was shaving, he had smeared the lather playfully on the boy's face. I don't usually entertain children when I'm shaving.

To tell the truth, I was afraid that Jean's old man had come home to stay. That would have been the best thing that could happen, if only he would keep his abusive mitts off Mick, though I suspect Mick would have cheerfully endured even a few black and blue marks if his father would show the worshipful youngster some tender, loving care. But Jean's other half blew out of her life again quicker than a rolling stone that gathers no moss.

Throughout this time Jean warned me: "Mick needs love, but 'tough love' doesn't work with him. All his life, people have told him they love him, but when he tests them they scream at him. Rage seems to be the way love turns out in his life." Nearly a year went by before I caught him putting me to the test: Then I screamed at him, like everyone else.

One Sunday I took Mick, Lainie, and Kim to see *Mary Poppins*. Afterwards, at the entrance to the subway, Mick started showing off. I was tired of managing children and sad because the weekend was over and I had spent all my money. I blew my stack at Mick, who dashed off into the darkness of Boston Common, and for fifteen minutes I played an exasperating game of hide-and-seek with him among the trees.

I wasn't going to win that contest, so I stood still under a light and waited for him to come out when he was damned good and ready. When I told Jean later how scared I was by her son running around at night among the creeps in a city park, she said, "I warned you that he would test you. Seeing you get mad must have hurt him to the quick; and no matter how reasonable you may think 'tough love' is, it doesn't work with Mick."

The second time I was furious with myself was on our fifth day at the New York World's Fair in 1964. Mick decided he wanted to walk on the rail of a bridge spanning the Long Island Expressway. I yelled at him for being an idiot and again he ran off. When he finally let me catch him, we sat in front of the Unisphere as Mick explained in a very hurt voice that he didn't want to be friends with me anymore. We were three hundred miles from Boston; it was a helluva time for him to decide to strike out on his own.

I treated him the way any parent treats an unreasonable child: I bribed him. I bought him a $30 camera that was round like a watch; it got broken before he ever used it. I wasn't proud of bribing him or of his needing to be bribed. I think he accepted the camera as a symbol of good will and as a way for him to save face. As for me, I was buying time.

The first time I used Mick to serve my own needs was when I surprised him with a dog: It was a male German shepherd, named by Mick the Red Baron. It quickly grew into a magnificent animal too big and strong for a small boy to handle. Walking Baron on a leash, Mick got tugged this way and that as though he were riding behind a harpooned whale. He would come home worn out like an Olympic athlete about to die young, but Baron was so far from being out of steam he could have hauled a milk wagon.

One night in Jean's apartment Baron, with energy to burn because it went unused every day, showed the classic signs of having a nervous breakdown. So the Ashford family decided he should be moved out of Boston. I found him a place in the country and would pay for his board and room, and Mick could visit him on weekends if he wished.

The second folly I committed, allegedly for Mick's benefit, was buying a pony. Mick and his sisters weren't in a sweat to get a pony, but I needed Misty galloping through my life to help me get over a fantasy that began when I was four: Seriously sick with pneumonia, I was promised a Shetland pony by my grandfather as soon as I got well. When I was better, I asked where the pony was, and my grandfather broke the news: My pony had died coming over the water from the Shetland Islands.

I grew up imagining how fulfilling it would be to own a pony. I had been taking Mick and Kim to a riding academy in Weston; seeing them mounted, booted, spurred, and ready to ride, I decided it would be neat if they could show their pals on Mount Auburn Street pictures of their own snow-white Pegasus. Misty wasn't expensive, and I borrowed $175 from the bank to buy her. In the summer Misty earned her board and room, provided we would allow other children to ride her. But after Labor Day, when the schools reopened, no children except Mick and Kim went to Weston to ride. So I had to pay for Misty's upkeep during the winter months and for the shoes she kept casting off.

Later I became aware that Misty had a nasty habit of nipping the children when she nuzzled them in search of sugar. That's when I fell out of love with ponies once and for all. In January Misty went to live on the farm with the Red Baron. Since I couldn't afford to support two animals, I gave them both to the farmer's son as a gift. I don't think Mick and Kim wept to lose them.

By this time, I had reached the end of my tether in helping Jean. I was punch-drunk from monitoring my other affairs and was making too many bad mistakes. Suddenly, I was no longer in control of the direction of my life. My superior was sending me to Notre Dame for R&R, and I hated the idea of being eleven hundred miles away from my own family. I hated also to move away from the boy. The time I had spent with him had made a difference in his life.

The last summer before leaving the East, I arranged for Mick to attend a boys' camp in Maine. In the fall he and Kim were beginning their second year at a fine private school run by the Dominican nuns in Belmont, and their grandfather had promised to pay the tuition to keep them there until they finished. Jean's last words were: "For helping Mick grow up, we will always be grateful."

I've only seen Mick once since saying goodbye. He was fourteen then and no longer looked like an elf. The Mick I used to know had disappeared and was hidden from view in the lost childhood.

THE FLOWER-CHILD PRIEST
COMES HOME TO THE CROSS

Rose has written me four times in two years—four notes on blue paper, in script that reminds me of uncoiling barbed wire.

The first note was to tell me that Cyril, the ex-priest to whom Rose had been married, had AIDS and was being moved to a hospice in New Mexico to die.

The second note came two months later with the news of Cyril's death. His religious community had taken him back into the fold on his deathbed, and he'd been buried as a priest at the monastery in Saint Louis where he had been ordained. Rose, who is Jewish, added, "Joshua, whom you baptized, would enjoy hearing from you, and so would I."

`The third time, she wrote: "Do you remember that you baptized Joshua, my son, who is already seventeen? He's grown up Jewish, by his own choice, from the time Cyril and I brought him to live in Israel. Is there anything you'd like to say to him? My family doesn't even mention Cyril's name. Josh can tell from their conspiracy of silence how angry they are."

The final note, written at New Year's, said: "I'm sorry you never got the chance to write Joshua. He's very confused right now, crying out for help, and nobody's answering. He's a freshman at New York University and says he wants to quit. He was bar-mitzvah'd late, and now he's blaming his grandfather for trying to turn him into a 'pillar of the kike religion.' His grandfather claims he's revving up his engines to follow in his father's footsteps. You can imagine how well that would go over on Brooklyn Heights."

I really don't know how any decision of Josh's would go over on Brooklyn Heights because I don't know what he's "revving up his engines" to do. He could be getting ready to emerge from the closet as a recovering Roman Catholic, or as a homosexual, or as a combination of the two. Those are the footsteps his father left for him.

How can I help persuade a Jewish lad to be at peace with the ghost of his father, a Catholic priest who died of AIDS? As a disease that priests die from, AIDS seems like the outward and visible sign of an inward and spiritual loss of grace, or a sacrament of the fallen-away that hurts the Body of Christ. Cyril didn't get sick from a blood transfusion or from shooting drugs with a dirty needle. So in addition to the sadness I feel for any AIDS patient, I'm mad as hell at Cyril because no priest with AIDS is an island, if you get my drift.

For two thousand years the church has survived the scandal of clerics who lose their heads over wine and women, simony and nepotism, and ambition that makes a virtue out of vice. But even priests have doubts about where we're going when they hear of priests with AIDS. None of us is so Simon-pure that he doesn't tremble when he sees a stricken confrere and say, "There, but for the grace of God, go I."

But if the priesthood should be struck hard by AIDS, then the *Titanic* may have again rammed the iceberg. The confessionals in many churches already look like ghost towns. If Catholics start wondering if celibacy is a lie told by hypocrites, then the church, as a watering hole of faith, could become less popular than Death Valley after the wells have been poisoned. Who would trust priests to be their spiritual fathers if statistics ever seemed to unmask them as phonies who use their religion as a closet?

Not even shrinks who charge $200 an hour are as trusted with the care of souls and the secrets of the heart as priests are. If priests screw up their act with dirty little secrets that betray them in the end, then the church will have to go into business as a snakepit.

When I first met Cyril twenty years ago, he was a thirty-nine-year-old monk studying for a degree in the theology of marriage. To reach the Midwestern farm where he grew up, he told us, you had to cross the Mississippi and keep going "until you have traveled beyond the Sabbath." This was his way of mocking the Sunday piety of his small town, narrow-minded with Lutheranism, where his parents still live in a German-Catholic ghetto that shoved Cyril toward the seminary when he was twelve.

At the dinner table in the rectory in Manhattan's Hell's Kitchen he was like a flower child of the church's *aggiornamento*, making you hopeful the church was on the threshold of a second spring. In his company the other priests didn't feel so old, tired, or shabby. The vice in the neighborhood that saddened us excited Cyril because he imagined himself the apostle of the gutter.

Agnes the housekeeper often said Cyril was "too good-looking to be a priest," implying that he couldn't be trusted with all the women who loved him. Unless he was watched, she thought, he might love some of them back. The truth is, everyone loved Cyril, from the schoolchildren whom he made feel important to the widows for whom he turned the blessing of the rosary into a big production number, converting the prayer formula into a form of flirtation. And the priests enjoyed him because he brought a breath of fresh air into that moribund rectory.

On one of his nights out he met Rose, and he brought her back to the rectory for counseling. Her Jewishness was as different from his sophistication as gefilte fish is from lake trout. If you think Barbra Streisand is beautiful, then you'd think Rose was beautiful. At thirty-five she had the warmth and attentiveness of an earth mother. As a New York Jewish princess, she was royalty from Brooklyn. Listening to her, you could get the feeling that she was about to take you home and spoil you and serve you as a queen serves a king.

All the priests were half in love with Rose, so perhaps all of us were subliminally into match-making as Cyril was wooing and winning her. Maybe that's why she was flattered to catch the eye of Prince Charming, goaded on by an entourage of celibates as silly as the Seven Dwarfs. She thought she was getting a prize specimen, not knowing he had the astrological readings of a loser—a flower-child of the *aggiornamento*, "too good-looking to be a priest," and spoiled so badly by his groupies that he never had a chance to grow up. But who could have known that?

I'm not proud to admit that I was the one who advised him he could dissolve his sacramental ties with the Catholic Church if he were to leap over the wall and marry Rose. I had picked up this wee smidgin of Canon Law from a canonist experienced in bringing the New Breed back from the limb they had climbed out on. After he was Rose's husband, Cyril could ask for an indult which would allow him to receive the sacraments again and have his marriage blessed.

Anyway, 1971 was the height of the silly season in the postconciliar church, and all of us enjoyed being bit players in this version of *Abie's Irish Rose*. To those of us who had wept as seminarians over Abelard's castration because he wanted Eloise, romance among flower children seemed fated by the stars. Cyril loved Rose and Rose loved Cyril—and so, because love is an alchemist, these lovers belonged together. Vatican II had been convened for such moments of truth.

My conscience didn't bother me until the wedding. The marriage vows were received and duly registered with the state of New York by a maverick rabbi. He wasn't half as much out of place as the Catholic padre, vested in alb and stole, who stood at the rabbi's side.

The reception had too much of the air of an underground liturgy not to turn me off. Dressed in a Roman collar, I felt like a mixed metaphor in a singles' bar. Rose was the only woman in sight worth her salt, I thought: What she did, she did for love. The Catholics were there to make a political statement which they wished the pope could read. Tom Wolfe should have been there as a social reporter to describe the nuns acting radically chic, as he once described the Black Panthers being entertained by Lenny and Sylvia Bernstein in their Park Avenue apartment.

The real kick in the head, though, was Cyril's response to a question I pitched while trying to locate a matzo ball on a platter of munchies. Noticing a pair of love beads on the table with the wedding gifts, I asked, "What are those?" Cyril answered in a small boy's voice full of reverence, "They were given to me by the first woman I ever went to bed with."

I wasn't aware that Cyril had been sleeping around; it was none of my business. Yet the colossal bad taste of displaying those beads like something collected on a panty raid, well, the damned nonsense of all that caused my heart to sink like a rock, and then some. Later, when the beads were mentioned in conversation, a friend of Cyril's from the old neighborhood told me, "Cyril's forty-one, going on nineteen. Any streetwise adolescent is less confused by his sexual emotions than Cyril, despite his graduate degree in the theology of marriage."

When I visited the newlyweds at Christmas, they were living in a one-room basement pad while Cyril worked as a landscape gardener and waited for his luck to change. His teaching credentials were too Catholic for the secular schools, and his secularization made him too gamey for the Catholic ones. But he still had the joyfulness of a flower child, able to charm the heart out of an obelisk.

The following summer he was back in good stead with the church, or so he led me to believe. He arranged to have the new baby baptized, but the chrism wasn't dry on young Joshua's head before Cyril let me see the way things were. "Now he's a baptized Christian and a ritually circumcised Jew," he said. "That's a lot of initiation to wish on one little cowpoke, but he can decide which he likes better when he's old enough." Cyril should have known better than to insist on having his cake and eating it, too. Neither the church nor the synagogue feels it's appropriate to give the child of a mixed marriage the best of two worlds.

The next time I met Cyril and Rose they were pushing Josh down Sixth Avenue in a stroller. Cyril still didn't have a regular job, but wasn't that lucky? He meant they had no obligations to keep them from migrating to Israel to begin work on a kibbutz. Cyril's handsome veneer now had the patchy surface of a neglected piano; he looked as stagey as a soap-opera actor fighting off age with a sunlamp. And he was too old for his bell bottoms. The season of life when he could pass as a flower child was over.

The next time I heard of them, I was flat on my back in a hospital, suffering from congestive heart failure. I had my eyes closed, and when I opened them Father Mahoney from the cathedral gave me the news: "Cyril and Rose are back. Their marriage is over. Cyril has decided he's gay."

Now, before I tell Josh how his father died, I'd like to ask the help of a rabbi. Jewish thinkers have been turning gray under their yarmulkes longer than Christians have, trying to understand why a good God allows bad things to happen to good people, or why worse things happen to people than they really deserve. Does anyone deserve AIDS? If the victims who have AIDS deserve such a scourge, then AIDS should be understood as a punishment from God. But no rabbi worth his phylacteries would want a lad to think the new leprosy which has terminated his father's life was divine retribution. Neither Christianity nor Judaism believe the Heavenly Father could be so vindictive.

But God sometimes writes straight with crooked lines, because Cyril, after the sickness struck and before his mind was closed down by the final coma, was allowed a period of grace and reconciliation with the church, when he consented once more to be a priest. It may be that his return to the priesthood lasted for a brief time; what does it matter? The grace to be *alter Christus* was offered again and accepted. And from that time on, his sickness was that of a minister of the church. And his dying and death were those of a priest.

Catholic lads are ordained to an eternal priesthood. Their well-wishers at the ordination wish them *ad multos annos*. The Latin phrase expresses the hope that the *ordinandi* will live to become seasoned old relics who die peacefully in their sleep at their summer houses. But God may have more ambitious plans for his young servants. Could anyone have imagined that it might be a priestly service for a man to die for other men, from an illness to which a stigma is attached? Christ died on an instrument of suffering to which a stigma was attached.

All kinds of illnesses take human beings hostage. If AIDS takes a priest hostage, that only means the priest has the same weaknesses as other men—but is that a surprise? If a priest goes through that ordeal, accepting his cross in obedience to God's will, it may be a far finer hour for him than anything envisioned by the well-wishers at his ordination. Physically, Cyril may have been more the image and likeness of Christ humiliated and wounded than he was at any Mass he said in his life.

"Ripeness is all," wrote Shakespeare. If I had been in that room when the labored breathing of Cyril was ended, I trust I could have said, "Ripeness is all". . . and "Ripeness is here."

STOP THE FIGHTING

In Boston, they say, the streets follow pathways originally made by live-stock on their journeys to and from the Common where they were pas-tured. That's why even now, Boston's street plan doesn't make sense. The mind, too, can be erratic when it wanders here and there like those livestock.

In the science of God I'm a bantam-weight, so I tend, out of loyalty and habit, to rely for my moral vision on the mind of the church. I keep listening for one clear voice from mission control, but a lot of what I've heard lately is about as helpful as an earful of static.

The liberated women and theologians who serve them claim that the recent popes and their Ratzingers, by foot-dragging, have left our re-ligion looking so archaic it has lost credibility. For me, AIDS and abor-tion have become all-American tragedies about which the Holy Father can have nothing to say once he's restated the tradition.

The National Conference of Catholic Bishops has told us: "Ameri-cans cannot disagree with the immorality of abortion but can differ about the best way to fight legalized abortions. Most Catholics are quite aware that abortion is the killing of an unborn child, and most Catho-lics would say that this is not an acceptable procedure. Disagreements arise when it comes to dealing with current law in the United States. Is it better to hold out for no abortion at all, or is it better to support the efforts that are becoming more frequent to limit abortions? That's a question on which there can be honest differences of opinion."

The guidelines leave much to be explained, yet they're deceptively simple when you consider that the chaos caused by abortions is killing us. The bishops give us some of the answers we need as Catholics, but I'm concerned about the questions I should ask as an American living in a country where people rely more on their consciences, enlightened by common sense and reasoning, than they do on saving grace delivered to them by churches.

As Vietnam was ending, the abortions—as a consequence of *Roe v. Wade*—were starting. When the sign at the Golden Arches registered the number of burgers sold at thirty million, we found that statistic mind-boggling. If abortion clinics had signs outside which registered the thirty million legalized abortions since 1973, maybe the sexual revolutionaries would become ashamed. Abortion is infanticide, and once infanticide takes on the earmarks of a national industry, you wonder if the nation has a death wish and is arranging its own genocide.

As a Catholic, you worry because in the abortion crisis there seems to be no middle ground between warring camps. Pro-life or pro-choice can cost you friends.

A Notre Dame student asked me why I never speak well of Operation Rescue. I said, "The scenes I see on television scare me." Her response was, "The media are not fair to Christians who oppose abortions." I said, "Sure, but the cameras didn't invent those faces I see on the evening news."

The ghastly slaughter of the innocents is a tragedy too numbing to weep over, but nothing justifies the abuse of women when they're already in pain. God doesn't require interventionists to pounce on the unmarried schoolgirl or the abused wife, throwing themselves down as human stumbling blocks. The televised street brawls that start as sit-ins staged by pro-lifers usually turn into teach-ins staged by pro-choice women, who also have faces that show anger. *Roe v. Wade* serves as their Emancipation Proclamation, but their anger is more ancient than their memory of backroom abortions.

Women are angry when they remember the way the Pharisees acted toward the woman taken in adultery in the New Testament story, and the way the elders in Israel acted toward Susanna, whom they falsely accused of adultery, in the Old Testament. They are angry on behalf of Hester Prynne, sentenced to wear her scarlet letter, and for Anita Hill and welfare mothers and those forced to be mothers by a society that has decided it's always the women who should pay. They are angry at husbands who turn marriage into slavery, and for all I know they may be angry with God for the biology that makes them the sexual partner who bears the young.

Women grow livid when they hear of foreign popes encouraging the bishops to meddle with the freedom U.S. women have to choose abortions. Bishops, too, are on the women's enemy-list for opposing an amendment to the Bill of Rights that would guarantee a woman's inalienable right to pro-choice. These women have turned their campaign for liberation into a religion that wants to neuter God, males, and the reproductive system.

Even Catholic women felt that childbirth condemned them to go alone into the valley of the shadow of death; and if danger threatened, the baby's welfare came first. In Adam's fall, we fell all, and so became exiles in a vale of tears. But women especially, tradition said, were condemned to bear the brunt of our banishment as the poor children of Eve.

Now feminism has changed all that. Gynecology has taken the grimness out of childbirth. Pro-choice turned childbirth on its head by making it optional. If the bishops had a clue to what's going on, would they still think they could turn back *Roe v. Wade*? Would they alter their stance on AIDS?

The bishops say, "Good morals are good medicine." Magic Johnson might agree that abstinence is the safest course, but he warns kids, "If you must play the mating game, it's better to use condoms than go unprotected." The bishops' counter-warning is: "Reliance on condoms could kill you."

———

Lately, like parents and pastors everywhere, I've been concerned with the ground rules students should be following if they want to stay free and clear of the AIDS virus. AIDS could be the pestilence to come at the end of the ages, yet twelve years after the outbreak of the sickness, we can only wish the church were halfway to the launching pad with inspired guidelines. So far, the closest we can get to a canonized insight is: "To avoid being burnt, stay away from the fire."

It's not enough. Though I trust the bishops, what they've done is shrug off the problem. That's why so many of us must trust our common sense. To save kids playing Russian roulette, we must risk making mistakes, tempering compassion to the endangered lamb.

AIDS has Catholic parents trapped between a rock and a hard place. "Good morals is good medicine" has in it some of the wisdom of Solomon. But parents, relying on their sixteen-year-old's willpower to resist the tease in his nerve-ends and his body's hunger, could end up with nice guys who finish last. If that sixteen-year-old has to go home and tell his parents he is sick with sexually transmitted AIDS, I can't imagine them saying: "Son, at least you were too good a Catholic to use condoms, and we're proud of you for that."

I'm too traditional not to preach sexual abstinence, come hell or high water. And don't think I don't resent the way the Planned Parenthood crowd is trying to stampede youngsters into using condoms as though they were failsafe. That's not loving, responsible, or useful: Condoms as a life preserver is part of the big lie that has turned the sexual revolution into such a disaster. Still, I'm angered as well by the father who tells me he goes through the glove compartment of his son's car to remove any prophylactics he finds stashed there.

As much as I agree with them, the bishops sound quaint and dated and preconciliar when they direct their wrath against condoms. At this late stage of the sexual revolution, one might expect condoms to enjoy a grudging respectability. Now that eleven-year-olds are starting to show up at the school nurse's office to be diagnosed for VD, and pedophiles (some of them priests) are traumatizing children in every neighborhood, it would seem that condoms should have outlived their usefulness as a Catholic worry.

Newsweek pictures a pair of adolescents as they're leaving their school. One says, "Three months vacation. Do you know what that means?" The other answers, "Sure. No more free condoms." It's this give-away that the bishops oppose, though as shepherds they should be able to see that abstinence cannot be relied upon exclusively. Abstinence doesn't always work, even for the pure in heart. But to make condoms as available to fourth-graders as the paper napkins at a free lunch could be a signal that neither church nor state has much hope for their innocence. How wise is it to put youngsters on notice that grownups don't trust them very much?

Supplying school children with condoms isn't a decision the schools should be making. Do parents have that right? Should the bishops be advising parents, or should parents be advising the bishops? Or should teenagers be advising the parents, the priests, the bishops, *and* the schools about the wisdom of these give-away programs? A bishop should be in charge of his own conscience; could we ask him to allow us our freedom of conscience when defending the welfare of the children?

Locking horns with fundamentalists of any stripe turns nasty very soon. In any religion, fundamentalists turn into a great nuisance because of their unwillingness to think, or to allow others to think differently than they do, or to wonder and have honest doubts.

Protestant fundamentalists claim there's only one way to read the Bible. Catholic fundamentalists want all the church's teaching to be monolithic. In their view, the truth starts with God, who shares it with the infallible pope, who shares it with bishops who are semi-infallible, who share it with the pastors (many of them blockheads), who share it with the faithful who come to Mass on Sunday. The job of the faithful is to pay freight on the faith that is taught them, though it may be shopworn from all that trickling down.

Fundamentalists—bishops, pastors, Mass-goers, or anyone else who sounds more Catholic than the pope—feel obliged to keep the rest of us honest. When they talk down to us, they diminish Christ's Mystical Body to a good-ol'-boys club. The tiresome part of fundamentalists is that they want to neuter our conscience so they can be the channel through which their brand of truth can pass from God's mind into yours.

A friend and mentor of mine has warned me against seeming to adopt the pro-choice reasoning, or appearing to challenge the church's teaching on abortion, by asking questions I leave unanswered. The problem, he says, lies not in disliking Operation Rescue but in not acknowledging that the church—which is distinct from Operation Rescue—has specific answers to the questions raised: Yes, the embryonic child is a human being. No, hunger and poverty are not excuses for abortion.

When I don't give these answers, he tells me, I imply this is all open to discussion. From society's point of view that may be true, but from the church's point of view it isn't. My concern that pro-lifers not get caught up in hating and vilifying their opponents is an important one, my friend assures me. "But it is also important that, as a priest, you do not appear to be undercutting the church's teaching."

When I sort through the pro-choice arguments, it's to see if people who have a different idea of God—who are, maybe, agnostics or atheists—are unreasonable, irresponsible, or even vicious for believing that it's permissible to lay violent hands on new life burgeoning in the womb. It would be closed-minded to the point of bigotry not to take a look at pro-choice. How can deliberately ignoring the reasons why thirty million women have had abortions help anyone?

Why do I ask questions that seem at odds with the party line? Why, as my friend complained, am I apparently willing to challenge the church's teaching on abortion by asking questions I leave unanswered? Maybe it's because the abortion struggle has become the church's Vietnam, and we are not showing the least sign of winning.

As Catholics we are members of Christ's kingdom, which, as he told us, "is not of this world." If it were of this world, we would base our obedience on his new commandment of love to make us persuasive when we defend God's truth. As Americans enamored of power structures, we try to make the system work for us. We're entitled to do this, though sometimes we surely leave the Holy Ghost compromised by the way we rely on politics rather than grace to defeat the darkness around us.

The use of religion to keep the nation upward bound seems traditional; and though we believe in the separation of church and state as the American way, still the church at times has a clear duty to keep the state honest. But America is a democracy, not a theocracy. As Americans grateful for our freedom, we're obliged by our patriotism to render unto Caesar the things that are his, just as we're obliged by our piety to render unto God the things that are Christ's.

Since *Roe v. Wade*, we've been mindful that an appreciation of the holiness of life in the womb is more of a religious insight than a civic one. Shouldn't we be ever so gentle, as well as fair and sensitive, in the way we ask the state to support the will of God insofar as we have discerned his will in our religious tradition?

As Americans, we shouldn't be battling in the streets over the right to kill. We should be struggling to establish the great society where nobody at all is afraid to have children.

If this country were to face up to the scandal of children and old people in the cities going to bed hungry every night, there would be fewer abortions and fewer Catholic politicians defending a woman's right not to be heroic in welcoming a baby she thinks is born to lose. Couldn't the "friends of the children" in pro-life and pro-choice be friends with one another and draw up guidelines to protect the children from the neo-Nazis who couldn't be more contemptuous of children's rights if they were running death camps?

The great rank-and-file in pro-life are the sweethearts of our revealed religion. Catholic fundamentalists can be charming, too, but the crisis-intervention teams of Operation Rescue have the mean and hungry look of stormtroopers. They make the church top-heavy with too many mini-popes, fat with an infallibility that never came from God.

But what will you say when the shock troops of pro-life ask: "Where were the decent German people when the boxcars were loaded with Jews, gypsies, decadents, and other expendables? What will you tell God if he asks: 'Where were you when the latter-day expendables filled the world with the agony of their silent screams?'"

The Jews and the fetuses: it's not the same thing, is it? I can think of more reasons for saying it is than for saying it isn't.

This is one of the dilemmas of a Catholic conscience in the age of AIDS and pro-choice. What if the fundamentalists with all their hatefulness are right, and all the sweet-tempered, tolerant Christians are wrong in the way they condone the crimes against the underdogs which cry to heaven for vengeance?

ALTER CHRISTUS

Waiting for the Lord has been the story of my life. Even when I want his attention, I choose a corner where I will be very visible, then wait to see what he has in mind. I can tell from the payoff if I'm where he wants me to be.

In my first summer of priesting in Manhattan, I was the Catholic Father on duty at Incarnation Parish when the call came: "We have a jumper threatening suicide on the George Washington Bridge. Can a priest come over to talk to this fruitcake before he takes a belly-flop on the Hudson?"

The payoff that time was that the police, using great gentleness, talked the jumper off the bridge. My prayers may have helped.

At Holy Cross Church in Manhattan, a block from Times Square, the payoff to the priest on duty is sometimes an initiation into horror. Security at the bus terminal had found a dead baby wrapped in plastic in a coin-operated locker. "Would Father like to come over and confer his church's magic on the tiny corpse before it's taken to the morgue?"

Neither bell, book, nor candle can help the soul of a dead baby. But a priest should feel he's never off duty as God's stand-in. Besides, security at the Port Authority wanted a priest to dignify the small body with a corporal work of mercy.

I learned a lot about works of mercy when serving as a spear-carrier to Brother Eymard, C.S.C., who visited South Bend nursing homes to meet the elderly. Once a week for several years I followed him on his rounds of Wrinkle City, wearing himself out as an apostle of charity, shoring up the ruins for the senior citizens reaching their death valley days. Where, for me, was God in all this? I see in hindsight that he couldn't have been closer.

I met all kinds of people on my rounds with Eymard in the Morningside, one of South Bend's welfare hotels which I came to know as a kingdom of the lonely God. I still have a blue cardigan sweater with the Notre Dame leprechaun that I bought as a Christmas present for Leonard, a cripple confined to a wheelchair in that hotel. Leonard died before ever seeing if the sweater fit, and it was returned to me in its Christmas wrapping.

The Leonard sweater always reminded me of how wretchedly the poor man lived, never leaving his roach-infested room except to go see the doctor. On winter nights he went to bed at six o'clock because he was afraid the chill in his room would be the death of him. Every time he opened the refrigerator when I was with him, I would gag on the smell from the half-eaten cans of chunky Dinty Moore stew and of peach slices slithery with juice, that he kept there as his supper.

In a way, Leonard took his own life, though not deliberately. One Christmas Eve he sent the go-fer who shopped for him to the liquor store for a pint of Old Jameson's. After years of sobriety, he chug-a-lugged the pint as soon as he got his hands on it. His heart, amazed at the shock of firewater racing though his body, stopped beating. Suddenly Leonard was a dead man.

The last time I wore the Leonard sweater, I noticed it had a couple of buttons missing and food stains down the front of it. The shock came when I stood in front of a mirror: There, but for the grace of God, I could see Leonard—who killed himself with a last hurrah after years of living with his pilot light turned down so low it was almost out.

Brother Eymard helped me see South Bend's shadowlands in all their color. He knew where the bodies were buried, many of them prematurely. He twisted arms to procure for his clients eyeglasses, hearing-aids, rides, Meals-on-Wheels, and whatever else they needed.

One of his clients—whom I'll call Fast Eddie—was a kingpin in South Bend's sporting life. He used to play the host like Toots Shor in a downtown hot spot called the Club Lido. Eymard dickered for months with a government agency to pick up the tab for new dentures for Fast Eddie, who finally died and went toothless to his grave. The following week, Eymard got the green light on bringing Eddie to a dentist for a set of teeth.

The seniors could see that Eymard was not a smart-ass professional, careless about their welfare, treating them like children. With lips flecked with brown from the snuff he chewed, in the unbrushed black suit he wore as a Holy Cross brother, he was almost as shabby as some of his clients on the dole. And if you judged from his appearance, he could have been as down on his luck as the people he brought hope to.

A number of the sad people he introduced me to went to heaven so quickly I never saw them more than once. I would inquire about the English woman, cheerful as a sparrow, whom I met propped up on a pillow (I was shocked to discover she was entirely without legs). Eymard would answer: "Well, she died."

Then I would inquire about the frail old man so tormented by body itch that his arms were tied loosely with gauze bandages to the arms of his chair to keep him from scratching himself raw. Eymard would say, "He died too."

When I said, "Perhaps he's better off," Eymard would hand me fresh grief: "Remember the old man dying of cancer who told you about the charismatic priests who can lay hands on the sick and heal them with that touch? Well, he died that same evening." The old man had been trying to find out if I was the miracle worker he prayed to meet. I had to tell him I'm not a healer. It broke my heart to see him so disappointed.

Eymard's masterpiece in the years that I caddied for him was Stanley, who lived down the hall from Leonard at the Morningside. Until I met Stanley, I hadn't stood close enough to old age to see what a defeat it can be. Souls bound upon a wheel of fire tend to be close-lipped and guarded about their troubles, but Stanley was too tired to stay stoic. At eighty-seven, he was a little man fierce with an anger that never left him. The anger must have tempted him to rage like Lear, but because he had emphysema, caused by being gassed in World War I, his face was the stage where his suffering took on a tragic grandeur.

Eymard went through hell and high water for Stanley. He got him an apartment and services as gratis as possible. Eymard even got Stanley free lunch. And through Stanley, Brother Eymard became a light to my conscience; I was edified by his example of love in action. In caring for Stanley, Eymard assumed a cross that merits a crown.

Any road can be the way of the cross that leads home when you travel it loaded down by the needs of your brother. In the gruff, curmudgeonly way some old men have, they bonded as an odd couple. Being mutually affectionate, each contributed to the other's fulfillment. Since they enjoyed needing each other, each found the yoke easy and the burden light.

Stanley was a Christ-figure. As a sometime teacher of English, I have always enjoyed discovering Christ-figures in the books I read. Now, at the age of sixty-eight, I am as apt to look to life or literature as I am to the Bible.

In my tour through the kingdom of the lonely God, Hemingway has become my Augustine, my Aquinas, and my Cardinal Newman. His prose, by its simplicity, becomes sacramental, defined as the outward sign of an inner grace whose payoff is *nada*. "Our *nada*, who art in *nada*, *nada* be thy *nada*," he once wrote in a short story. He was a half-assed Catholic of sorts. He loved rosaries and kept one hanging from his windshield mirror next to the rubber dice. When he committed suicide, the rosary was said for him at his graveside.

I read Hemingway in high school and college because I had to. I read Hemingway as a teacher because I had to—then because I wanted to. When I stopped teaching, I kept reading Hemingway, and rereading him.

Hemingway wrote simply about love, life, and death. Still, when Father John O'Hara was Notre Dame's president, he took Hemingway's books off the library shelves, claiming Hemingway was a "bum." Was O'Hara shocked by *A Farewell to Arms*, in which Hemingway wrote: "The world breaks everyone and afterward many are strong at the broken places. But those that will not break it kills. It kills the very good and the very gentle and the very brave impartially. If you are none of these you can be sure that it will kill you too but there will be no special hurry."

In an indifferent universe, death is meaningless; all that happens is that we take our turns dying. War is especially stupid. We imagine that if armies die for the sake of the abstract words, all those deaths will be meaningful. But they are not. Governments try to make war deaths a glorious sacrifice, but the promise of glory is a lie.

Hemingway's old man of the sea, Santiago, feels a kinship stronger than death with the giant marlin he's hooked in the Gulf of Mexico. The fish is killing him, Santiago tells himself. What does it matter, since the fish is a fine fish whom he loves like a brother. Hemingway, admiring the courage and love in Jesus when he was pushed to the wall, wrote a story about Santiago, who was courageous and loving as he faced the great trial of his life. In making his old man of the sea a Christ-figure in a world where God didn't count much, Hemingway was complimenting Jesus.

But sometimes I don't think Hemingway told the whole story. So I go to the Creeds to find out the whole story, or as much as we know of it. I prefer to believe the mystics who say God has a thousand faces, and the sages who say he has nine thousand names. And I read writers like Hemingway and Dostoyevski, who tell us tales of God. Many of them are more listened to than any priest.

In my fortieth year as a priest, I've learned that human suffering isn't hard to explain. But how should I answer the complaints about the cosmic silence, God's apparent indifference? One answer that was there all along—but was a long time in coming to me—surfaced when Eymard taught me to look where Christ told us we could find him: in the lives of the people waiting to be taken down from the cross. In that kingdom of the lonely God, I learned that God is lonely because so many of us fail to find him. But he is there where he wants to be found—at our side sharing pain, as he was at the side of the good thief.

Before this can make any sense, you have to believe that every story is part of the one great story of death and transfiguration, as C. S. Lewis and Tolkien have insisted. When Christian theology takes a closer look at the interrelatedness between the one and the many, Christians may start to understand that when Christ redeemed us, he empowered us to redeem one another. I have learned that as sharers of his cross we become co-redeemers with him. Sometimes unaware of what we are doing, we offer his grace, through the example of our lives, to our peers for their redemption in Christ.

Peer redemption goes on all the time. Brother Eymard's domesticating the wild beast in Stanley was a triumph of love. The exorcism of the demon bedeviling Stanley was nearly as miraculous as the taming of the fierce wolf of Gubbio by Saint Francis of Assisi.

I have watched students dropping out of a church that some of them never really joined and calling it irrelevant. I have grieved when good ol' boy alums lapsed as Catholics. Coming to a bend in the road where the heavens look dark to them, they assume that the Friend and Helper has closed up shop. Describing Christianity as the light that failed, they decide to be God-like to one another, which is lovely of them and dead on the mark, since this is what Christ wanted them to do in the first place.

Lovers, undertaking friendships and marriages that can survive hell and high water, should expect to find holes in their hands and a cross on their backs from the strain of being unselfish. Lovers who want love without the cross find that love is more difficult for those who leave Christ out of the picture.

Love that is stronger than death has its home in a church which believes that the cross is our bridge over troubled waters. Maybe it's trite to insist on the importance of the church to the community of suffering, but wouldn't it be lovely to believe that every sufferer's bed is a rung on Jacob's ladder where Christ meets his brethren upward-bound to heaven's gate? If I were an AIDS patient, I'd like to believe that He could lead me in from the cold where I've been left hanging to twist slowly in the wind.

I don't doubt for a minute that Christ is the unseen Samaritan at every AIDS hospice, using the nurses as his bright angels. Every candy-striper in Manhattan who puts a flower on the supper tray of an HIV-positive child is doing God's work.

A New York magazine carried a story about Sister Marietta in a Chelsea hospital where young Joe is waiting to die of AIDS. Putting her arms around him she says: "Look for your parents. They'll be here to lead you to a happier playground." She prays as she waits with him. Soon he tells her: "I see them, and they're even nicer than you said they'd be." And he dies.

Joe's experience sheds light on the mystery that's lingered with me since I saw my mother dying. She was blind, seeing only with her mind's eyes, and she talked of the dead as though they were very near her. She surprised me totally when she said, "I hope the children will not bother anyone."

"What children?" I said.

"The children," she answered, not very helpfully. "They've been playing around here all morning. I hope nobody minds them being here."

On the day of her burial the undertaker told me, "I moved the babies so they'd be nearer your mother, close by her head." I was aware I had older siblings who had died in infancy. I wasn't aware that they'd been buried in the family plot. When my mother spoke of the children, was she seeing the infants she had lost as a young wife? Had they come—as Joe's parents had come—to "walk" her into God's house?

In my very first visit to a Catholic Worker house, I watched as an infinitely patient college student tried to fit shoes on the cantankerous feet of an artful dodger from off the streets. The man had the face of a river rat and was busily masturbating under his clothes. Never noticing how this representative of Christ's poor was distracting himself, the student wore a look of immense concentration on his face.

If he was this concerned over all God's children having shoes in the winter, I wondered, how would he feel meeting children who have no feet? Seeing the humility with which the lad was serving this unimpressive brother of Christ, I didn't doubt for a minute that he was a practitioner of the Gospel at its purest and simplest.

A Christian living in a world which suffers as much as ours does needs to help the other fellow pick himself up by his own bootstraps. God's distance can leave us feeling that it's been a long time between drinks. A father's attentiveness should exceed that of a doctor making an occasional house call. But isn't the long loneliness we feel when he is out of sight the very space that allows us to discover the other's worth as a brother?

I trust in the Redeemer whom I cannot see, and in the redeeming love I cannot see, though it comes trickling down in gifts of grace. But if the only way he has of being present to us visibly is in the bonding we have as brothers in the church, should I not very visibly show myself to be my brother's Christ?

I have this idea about God in my mind: An old grandmother in a nursing home waits for the night nurse to help her. She's afraid of the memories that await her in the sleepless dark. If Christ would only come and let her know with a touch on her hand that he is not far away, she'd be less afraid.

Sitting up, she notices a face, tired-looking, old, as wrinkled as her own. It is, she decides, the face of her roommate in the bed across from her. Even that face is a comfort, though; if you're religious, you see Christ in the face of your neighbor.

Then it occurs to her that the bed across from her is empty; she has no roommate. That wrinkled old face, which she prayed for the faith to see as Christ's, is her own face reflected in a mirror.

In an age of anxiety, my mind stays busy waiting for the Lord on the peripheries, where he hangs out as the lonely God. I hope that I will be able to distinguish substance from shadows. This could happen as soon as the Lord I'm waiting for lets me catch up with him. On your death bed, I think, you have those clear days on which you can see forever.

SOURCES

Notre Dame Magazine is abbreviated as *NDM*.

"Late Have I Loved Thee, O Ancient of Days," *NDM* 1, no. 1 (February 1972): 70–71.

"Somewhere, a Summer of '42," *NDM* 1, no. 3 (June 1972): 79–80.

"The Pocket-Size God," *NDM* 1, no. 5 (October 1972): 52.

"Empty Spaces, Lonely Places," *NDM* 2, no. 1 (February 1973): 30–33.

"A Letter to the Class of '73: Darby and I Never Said We Didn't Love You," *NDM* 2, no. 3 (June 1973): 24–29.

"An Everlasting Morning," *NDM* 2, no. 5 (October 1973): 17–19.

"Christmas on 42nd Street," *NDM* 2, no. 6 (December 1973): 42–45.

"About Friendship," *NDM* 4, no. 1 (February 1975): 19–21.

"I Remember the Fire," *NDM* 4, no. 1 (February 1975): 44–45.

"On Ancient Rituals and Modern Youth," *NDM* 5, no. 2 (April 1976): 15–17.

"Premarital Sex: Thou Shalt Not?" *NDM* 7, no. 2 (April 1978): 14–15.

"The Holy Fool," *NDM* 7, no. 5 (December 1978): 38–39.

"A Mass for the Littlest Christians," *NDM* 8, no. 2 (May 1979): 40–41.

"You Cannot Sing a Night Song," *NDM* 8, no. 3 (July 1979): 29–30.

"Simeon's Christmas," *NDM* 8, no. 5 (December 1979): 18–19.

"Before the Daylight Fails," *NDM* 9, no. 5 (December 1980): 24–25.

"A True Confession," *NDM* 10, no. 1 (February 1981): 68–69.

"A Storybook Marriage," *NDM* 10, no. 3 (July 1981): 24–25.

"A Brother's Requiem," *NDM* 10, no. 5 (December 1981): 68–69.

"The Bag Lady's Windfall," *NDM* 11, no. 1 (February 1982): 58–60.

"Part of the Myth," *NDM* 11, no. 2 (May 1982): 8–9.

"Life in the Boot Camp Seminary," *NDM* 11, no. 3 (July 1982): 60–61.

"Bill and Pat," *NDM* 11, no. 4 (October 1982): 68.

"A Parting Gift," *NDM* 12, no. 1 (February 1983): 61.

"'You Shall Be My Special Possession,'" *NDM* 13, no. 2 (Spring 1984): 12–13.

"You Get What You Need," *NDM* 13, no. 3 (Summer 1984): 6–7.

"A Broken-Down Holy Man," *NDM* 13, no. 4 (Autumn 1984): 10.

"How He Plays the Game," *NDM* 13, no. 5 (Winter 1984/85): 8.

"Facing Life without Father," *NDM* 14, no. 1 (Spring 1985): 11.

"'I Have Chosen You,'" *NDM* 14, no. 2 (Summer 1985): 12.

"Under the Dome, Most of It Seems True," *NDM* 14, no. 3 (Autumn 1985): 12–13.

"'We Have Met the Enemy and He Is Us,'" *NDM* 14, no. 4 (Winter 1985/86): 8–9.

"'I Prayed Like Hell Every Damn Night,'" *NDM* 15, no. 1 (Spring 1986): 14–15.

"In Defense of Those Who Care," *NDM* 15, no. 2 (Summer 1986): 13–14.

"A Rabbi Hears Confession," *NDM* 15, no. 3 (Autumn 1986): 16–17.

"As American as God, Sin, and Jimmy Swaggart," *NDM* 15, no. 4 (Winter 1986/87): 74–76.

"Confessions of a Bibliomaniac," *NDM* 16, no. 1 (Spring 1987): 77–78.

"*Apologia pro Vita Mea*," *NDM* 16, no. 2 ["vol. 15" printed on cover for vol. 16 issues 2–4], (Summer 1987): 35–38.

"One Pope at a Time," *NDM* 16, no. 3 (Autumn 1987): 8–10.

"Love on Trial," *NDM* 16, no. 4 (Winter 1987/88): 73–75.

"Mortal Friends," *NDM* 17 [vol. 16 printed on cover], no. 1 (Spring 1988): 33–35.

"The Flame Keepers," *NDM* 17, no. 4 (Winter 1988/89): 21–23.

"The American Dream as a Religious Experience," *NDM* 18, no. 1 (Spring 1989): 76–77.

"A Bridge Too Far," *NDM* 18, no. 2 (Summer 1989): 23–27.

"And One of Them Was My Brother," *NDM* 18, no. 3 (Autumn 1989): 29–32.

"The Lost Youth of Mickey Ashford," *NDM* 18, no. 4 (Winter 1989/90): 76–77.

"The Flower-Child Priest Comes Home to Holy Cross," *NDM* 19, no. 1 (Spring 1990): 76–78.

"Stop the Fighting," *NDM* 21, no. 4 (Winter 1992/93): 47–49.

"*Alter Christus*," *NDM* 23, no. 3 (Autumn 1994): 26–29.